European Human Rights

AUSTRALIA
The Law Book Company
Brisbane • Sydney • Melbourne • Perth

CANADA
Carswell
Ottawa • Toronto • Calgary • Montreal • Vancouver

Agents:
Stelmatzky's Agency Ltd., Tel Aviv;
N.M. Tripathl (Private) Ltd., Bombay;
Eastern Law House (Private) Ltd., Calcutta;
M.P.P. House, Bangalore;
Universal Book Traders, Delhi;
Aditya Books, Delhi;
MacMillan Shuppan KK, Tokyo;
Pakistan Law House, Karachi, Lahore

European Human Rights
Taking a case under the Convention

L.J. Clements, M.Sc
Solicitor

LONDON
SWEET & MAXWELL
1994

Published in 1994 by
Sweet & Maxwell Limited of
South Quay Plaza, 183 Marsh Wall, London E14 9FT
Phototypeset by LBJ Enterprises Ltd. of Aldermaston and
Chilcompton
Printed and bound in Great Britain
by Butler and Tanner Ltd., Frome
Index prepared by Patricia Baker

BRITISH LIBRARY CATALOGUING IN PUBLICATION DATA
A catalogue record for this book is available from the British Library

ISBN 0–421–48100–5

'Is citizen A. bound to submit unresistingly to arrest by citizen B. in ignorance of the charge made against him? I think, my Lords, that cannot be the law of England. Blind, unquestioning obedience is the law of tyrants and of slaves. It does not yet flourish on English soil.'

Lord Simonds
Christie v. *Leachinsky*
House of Lords, March 25, 1946

'Just consider the course of events if this action were to proceed to trial. . . . If the six men fail, it will mean that much time and money and worry will have been expended by many people for no good purpose. If the six men win, it will mean that the police were guilty of perjury, that they were guilty of violence and threats, that the confessions were involuntary and were improperly admitted in evidence and that the convictions were erroneous. That would mean that the Home Secretary would have either to recommend they be pardoned or he would have to remit the case to the Court of Appeal under s.17 of the Criminal Appeal Act 1968. This is such an appalling vista that every sensible person in the land would say: "It cannot be right that these actions should go any further."

Lord Denning
McIlkenny and others
v.
Chief Constable W. Midlands Police Force
Court of Appeal, January 17, 1980

Acknowledgments

Thanks are due in particular to lawyers, librarians and loved ones:

To the Secretariat, who have through their dedication, expertise and (above all) good humour ensured the practical success of the Convention process.

To Peter Duffy of 4 Essex Court for so unselfishly allowing me to tap his unrivalled expertise and to Timothy Jones of Arden Chambers for communicating his great enthusiasm for the subject. To Phil Thomas of Cardiff Law School and Peter Clinch of the University of Wales for use of their excellent library, and likewise to Julian Lonbay of the Institute of European Law and Mary Blake for the use of the Harding Law Library, University of Birmingham. Especial thanks are also due to Neil Spencer of the Hereford City Library for frequently arranging the transfer of significant portions of the British Library to Hereford.

To my partners and friends at Thorpes and to Marianne and Nina.

Preface

This book is intended for all those contemplating making a complaint to the European Commission of Human Rights. It is a practical handbook aimed at a British audience; it is not a substitute for the many excellent academic texts upon the Convention. The text does not deal with the procedure for state initiated complaints under Article 24.

Where I have been able to resist the temptation I have eschewed the interesting for the relevant; there being many fascinating decisions which have little or no application to the U.K.—as the principles involved were peculiar to the particular country's domestic law. In pursuit of the quest to be practical throughout, I have avoided so far as possible the differences between the English and French texts of the Convention. The different meanings of certain words and phrases are the staple diet of many academic texts and have proved important to the development of the Court's and Commission's interpretation of the Convention.

The handbook does not assume that the reader has access to a comprehensive human rights library. I have where possible restricted case references to the three most important published sources, namely:

1. Decisions and Reports (DR)

The European Commission publishes a resumé of most of its important decisions and reports in this publication; with four editions a year. Decisions and Reports can be obtained via HMSO[1]. The Commission has in addition published three volumes of 'Summaries and Indexes', which are invaluable. Each volume summarises 20 volumes (1–20; 21–40 and 41–60) and lists the key decisions and reports in those volumes according to subject matter, with an excellent index.

2. Series A Reports (Series A)

The official publication for the Court's decisions is published by Carl Heymanns Verlag KG[2], and known as the Series A Reports. Each

[1] H.M.S.O. 49 High Holborn, London, WC1V 6HB; Tel: 071 873 9090. The price per volume at time of going to print is £8.00, with the most recent volume No. 61
[2] Carl Heymanns Verlag KG, Luxemberger Strasse 449, 5000 Köln 41. Tel: 0221/46010-0. Fax: 0221/4601069

volume in general contains one Court decision. The background papers to Court cases are separately published as the Series B reports[3].

3. European Human Rights Reports (E.H.R.R.)
Published by Sweet & Maxwell, these contain the full reports of the Court decisions as well as the important decisions and reports of the Commission and Committee of Ministers. The publication also contains the text of periodical revisions to Court/Commission/Commitee Rules, etc. A signal quality of the European Human Rights Reports is that they contain the text of certain decisions which have not otherwise been published; most notably the decision in the East African Asian case[4].

These three publications can be found in most large city and university libraries. Where a particular Court or Commission decision is required it can also be obtained by making a direct request to the Commission for a copy: such material being in general supplied free of charge, albeit after a reasonably long delay.

There is no doubting the great and increasing importance of the Convention. U.K. legislation is now drafted so as to be 'Strasbourg proof' and a significant number of legislative changes have resulted from adverse Court decisions. Increasingly the Convention is quoted with approval in the higher courts and a number of our most senior judges are asserting that its principles are part of the common law of our country.

A major new human rights complex is nearing completion in Strasbourg, dwarfing the current building across the River L'Ill. At the time of writing the Council of Europe has 32 members whose total populations exceed 430 million people. There is little doubt that the Council's membership will continue to rise steeply over the next few years, ultimately reaching perhaps 40 countries; the principles of the Convention then being applied to over 800 million individuals.

It is important however not to become overawed by the institution. It is true that the Convention was drafted at an idealistic moment in World Affairs and contains many fine provisions. There is no doubting the tremendous innovation in its system of application; allowing individuals direct access to its remedies, with the Court delivering binding judgments. Nevertheless there are problems with the institution. Ultimately the Commissioners and Judges are proposed by the

---

[3] In general there is one volume per case; a typical volume might contain: the Commission's request to bring the case before the Court; the Commission's full report; the Memorials of all the parties; the correspondence between the Court and the parties; third party interventions; administrative orders, etc., by the President; a verbatim record of the public hearings; decisions of chambers relinquishing jurisdiction and references back to the chamber; equivalent papers in respect of any Article 50 proceedings
[4] 3 E.H.R.R. 76

various states and inevitably a number of them tend to be 'establish-ment-minded'; many of them are too obviously part of the older generation.

The Commission is showing signs of applying increasingly severe admissibility criteria to staunch the flow of cases to the Court and thereby many very important cases have, for purely technical reasons, not been able to proceed. There is some concern that a new wave of Eastern European complaints will result in the Convention having a reduced value to the West.

The Convention is at an important crossroads. Its jurisdiction is growing at an unimagined speed, at a time when the institution itself requires a new injection of life. This new vigour may arise by reform with a single tier complaints process, and the virtual abolition of the Commission. If, however, a new spirit does not emerge, then the rapid enlargement of the Convention's jurisdiction may result in its demise; a demise that will have been caused not by that enlargement, but by a failure to 'reaffirm its profound belief in those fundamental freedoms which are the foundation of justice and peace in the world'.

LJC. January 22, 1994. Strasbourg.

Table of Contents

Table of Cases

European Court of Human Rights

Numerical List of Cases

European Court of Human Rights

Alphabetical List of Cases

Decisions from the European Commission on Human Rights

(Not Reported in Decisions and Reports)

Decisions Reported in Decisions and Reports from the European Commission on Human Rights

Decisions from the Committee of Ministers

Other Jurisdictions

European Court of Justice

United Kingdom

Table of Legislation

International Legislation

xlv

Table of Conventions and Agreements

1 The Human Rights Machinery

HISTORY OF HUMAN RIGHTS

The growth of international respect for human rights is the history of trade and hence, the interdependence of nations. Internationally recognised human rights are of little value if states are unable to enforce compliance. The greater the benefits of belonging to a club, the greater the power to enforce club rules.

Whilst respect for human rights developed in certain countries, the concept of national sovereignty prevented nations from interfering in the home affairs of other nations. Until the nineteenth century the prevailing view was that a state had an absolute right to deal with its citizens as it chose. If, however, a state mistreated the citizen of another country, that was a different matter. Outrageous treatment—culminating in the Nazi atrocities—has led to the widespread acceptance of the concept of interference. Such a concept can only be founded on accepted international standards.

Within the U.K. the European Convention for the Protection of Human Rights and Fundamental Freedoms (together with the First Protocol thereto) has become the most accessible 'standard'. It is with the application of this Convention and Protocol that this text is primarily concerned. The Convention was itself, however, developed from an earlier human rights standard, the Universal Declaration of Human Rights.

UNIVERSAL DECLARATION OF HUMAN RIGHTS (UDHR)

The UDHR was adopted in 1948 and lists a full range of human rights. As a declaration it is only effective by example, it is free-standing and unenforceable. The rights catalogued in the UDHR can be divided into two separate categories: those which all states have power to maintain and protect (freedom from torture, fair hearings, peaceful assembly, etc.) as opposed to those which to some extent depend upon national wealth and its distribution (*i.e.* housing, education, food, etc.).

1

With a view to developing the UDHR into an enforceable set of principles, these two categories have been grouped into two separate covenants:

(i) the non-economic basic rights into the International Covenant on Civil and Political Rights (ICPR); and

(ii) the social and economic rights into the International Covenant on Economic, Social and Cultural Rights (ICES).

Both covenants were adopted by the United Nations in 1966.

Tentative steps have been taken to promote the enforcement of the ICPR, which the U.K. and most Council of Europe members have ratified. The covenant creates a 'Human Rights Committee' which can (and does) request members to submit reports to it concerning the measures that a state is taking to implement the Covenant. There is, however, no individual right of complaint to the Human Rights Committee unless the contracting States have signed an optional Protocol (which the U.K. has not). The application of the ICPR and other UN measures is considered in greater detail in Chapter 9 (p. 219).

COUNCIL OF EUROPE

The Council of Europe was created at the end of the Second World War for the purpose of promoting European unity, protecting human rights and facilitating social and economic progress. The Council is a quite separate body from the European Community; the Council was established on May 5, 1949 (with the signing of the Statute of the Council of Europe) whereas the origins of the European Community date from the formation of the European Coal and Steel Community in 1951, the European Atomic Energy Community and the European Economic Community in 1957, with their eventual merger in 1967.

From the outset it was anticipated that the Council's rôle would be political ('the promotion of European Unity') whereas the initial concept for the European Community was ostensibly economic, although it was no coincidence that the commodities that came under joint control—coal, steel and atomic power—were the raw materials of war.

The membership of the Council of Europe has increased rapidly since the fragmentation of Eastern Europe; currently there are 31 members, namely Austria, Belgium, Bulgaria, Cyprus, the Czech Republic, the Slovak Republic, Denmark, Estonia, Finland, France, Germany, Greece, Hungary, Iceland, Ireland, Italy, Liechtenstein, Lithuania, Luxembourg, Malta, Netherlands, Norway, Poland, Portugal, San Marino, Slovenia, Spain, Sweden, Switzerland, Turkey and the United Kingdom. At the time of writing there are, in addition, applications for membership pending on behalf of Romania (which is at an advanced stage), Latvia, Albania, the Russian Federation, the Ukraine, Croatia, Byelorus and Moldova.

The Council has its headquarters in Strasbourg and is composed of a Committee of Ministers and a Parliamentary Assembly. The most senior official of the Council of Europe is the Secretary-General, who is elected by the Parliamentary Assembly from a short list drawn up by the Committee of Ministers.

The Parliamentary Assembly was intended to become a Europe-wide authoritative assembly but the Ministers have consistently denied it real power. The assembly is not a parliament; its members are elected by the parliaments of individual Member States. Essentially the assembly's only power is to recommend policy to the Council of Ministers who can, in turn, pass these recommendations on to Member States. In addition the Council has established a number of specialist committees to supervise its different rôles, including the Committee of Independent Experts (who oversee the European Social Charter, *see* p. 213), the European Conference on Local Authorities and the European Committee on Crime Problems.

In so far as the Council of Europe's aim was to promote European political unity, it has proved less successful than the European Community. It has, nevertheless, sponsored a range of social and cultural policies (including over 140 international treaties) which have had widespread acceptance. Its most significant achievement has undoubtedly been the creation of the European Convention for the Protection of Human Rights and Fundamental Freedoms; referred to henceforth as the 'Convention'.

The European Convention on Human Rights

The Statute of the Council of Europe requires every member to 'accept the principles of the rule of law and of the enjoyment by all persons within its jurisdiction of the human rights and fundamental freedoms'. The protection of human rights therefore is a fundamental rôle for the Council of Europe.

The Council drafted the Convention, basing it upon those rights in the UDHR thought capable of enforcement (essentially those rights which were subsequently grouped into the ICPR).

The Convention was drafted in the aftermath of the Second World War and was completed with considerable speed, being signed in Rome on November 4, 1950 by the then 15 Member States. It came into force on September 3, 1953. It now affects directly the lives of almost 430 million people; if ratified by all the European States, this figure may rise to over 800 million.

The scope of the Convention was limited by political considerations being restricted to those rights that the individual Member States were prepared to adopt. The Convention represents therefore the 'lowest common denominator' of rights acceptable to the Committee of Ministers in 1950.

The Convention is an international treaty and as such is not directly effective within domestic U.K. law. Decisions of the European Court of Human Rights are not binding upon U.K. courts. Some states have incorporated the Convention into their domestic law by amending their constitutions. There is much debate as to whether the Convention should be part of U.K. law; this could be done by passing a statute specifically incorporating the Convention, in much the same way as the European Communities Act 1972 made Community law directly applicable. For the present at least, such a step appears unlikely. There is, however, an increasing willingness to allow reference to the Convention in domestic proceedings and this aspect is discussed in Chapter 7 p. 100.

The Convention is divided into two main parts: the first lists the substantive rights protected by the Treaty and the second deals with procedural matters, such as the creation and composition of the Commission and Court and the admissibility rules for complaints.

The first part of the Convention (the full text of which is at Appendix 1, p. 227) may be summarised as follows:

Article   **Right**
1. Guarantees that all rights are to be secured for everyone within the state's jurisdiction.
2. Protects the right to life (but permits a judicial death penalty).
3. Prohibits torture, inhuman or degrading treatment.
4. Prohibits slavery, forced or compulsory labour.
5. Protects the right to liberty and security of person.
6. Lays down minimum rules for fair civil and criminal hearings.
7. Prohibits the retrospective application of criminal law or increased sentencing.
8. Protects the right to privacy and respect for family life, home and correspondence.
9. Protects the right to freedom of thought, conscience and religion.
10. Protects the right to freedom of expression.
11. Protects the right to freedom of assembly and to freedom of association with others.
12. Protects the right to marry and found a family.
13. Requires that there be an effective domestic remedy for any Convention violation.
14. Prohibits discrimination in relation to the enjoyment of the Convention's rights and freedoms.
15. Allows certain rights to be restricted in times of 'war or other public emergency threatening the life of the nation'.

16. Allows restrictions on the political activity of aliens.
17. Specifies that activities aimed at the destruction of the Convention's rights and freedoms are not protected by the Convention.
18. Emphasises that where the Convention permits certain restrictions on a right, those restrictions will be strictly construed.

The Protocols

As stated above, the Convention represented the 'lowest common denominator' of rights acceptable to the Committee of Ministers in 1950. The development of human rights since then has been through the vehicle of Protocols. These either introduce different rights which the Member States can (if they so choose) accept by ratification or they introduce procedural amendments to the Convention. The preparation and adoption of protocols is a continuing process.

The protocols which introduce further rights are:

PROTOCOL 1

This protocol (the full text of which is at p. 234) introduces three further rights, namely:
1. The right to peaceful enjoyment of possessions.
2. The right to education.
3. The duty to hold secret ballot elections at reasonable intervals.
This protocol has been ratified by the U.K.

PROTOCOL 4

This protocol introduces the following rights:
1. The right not to be deprived of liberty merely on the ground of inability to fulfil a contractual obligation.
2. The right to free movement within a state and the right to leave any country.
3. The right not to be refused entry (or expelled from) a state of which the person is a national.
4. The prohibition of the collective expulsion of aliens.
This protocol has not been ratified by the U.K.

PROTOCOL 6

By this protocol the contracting States agree to the abolition of the death penalty, except in times of war (or the imminent threat of war). This protocol has not been ratified by the U.K.

PROTOCOL 7

This protocol introduces the following rights:
1. The right of aliens not to be expelled without lawful reason, the right of review and the right of representation.
2. The right to have reviewed by a higher tribunal criminal convictions (other than convictions of a minor nature).
3. The right to compensation in cases of wrongful criminal conviction.
4. The right not to be tried twice for the same offence.
5. The right of spouses to enjoy equal private law rights and responsibilities.

This protocol has not been ratified by the U.K.

The Convention protection machinery

By Article 1 of the Convention the contracting States undertake to secure for everyone within their jurisdiction the Convention's fundamental rights and freedoms.

To ensure observance of the Convention, Article 19 required two institutions to be created:
  (i)   The European Commission of Human Rights.
  (ii) The European Court of Human Rights.

A third supervisory/enforcement agency (although today of diminishing importance) is the Committee of Ministers. At the time the Convention was drafted the Committee was already in existence. The Committee has many functions within the Council of Europe, most of which are unrelated to the Council's human rights' rôle[1].

The European Commission of Human Rights

The Commission is the first port of call for all complaints. The Commission scrutinises all complaints. Each year only 5–15 per cent. of complaints overcome the procedural hurdles within the Commission and progress to the Court or Committee of Ministers. The Commission is based in Strasbourg.

In short, the Commission's rôle is to:
1. Investigate all complaints so far as it is necessary.
2. Filter out and reject inadmissible complaints.
3. Attempt to facilitate a friendly settlement of the complaints it declares admissible.

[1] The diagram at p. 15 illustrates the complaint procedure under the Convention

4. Prepare a report and transfer the complaints to the Court or Committee of Ministers if no friendly settlement is reached.
5. Provide delegates for hearings before the Court.

COMMISSIONERS

There is one member of the Commission for each state that has ratified the Convention. In practice that member is a national of the state concerned (although in theory this is not essential). No two members of the Commission may have the same nationality. Article 21 of the Convention requires Commissioners to be of 'high moral character and [they] must either possess the qualifications required for appointment to high judicial office or be persons of recognised competence in national or international law'.

Although the Commissioners are elected by the Committee of Ministers (from a short list provided by the relevant state), they act independently. Article 23 of the Convention stipulates that Commissioners sit in their individual capacity and that during their term of office they are precluded from holding any position that would be incompatible with their independence and impartiality. Upon taking up their duties they are required to make a solemn declaration to 'honourably and faithfully, impartially and conscientiously' exercise their powers.

The Commissioners elect from among themselves a President and two Vice-Presidents. Some Commissioners (as with judges in the Court) are considered more experienced than others and consequently their opinion carries greater weight with their colleagues. In addition to the usual liberal or conservative elements, it should be noted that on some issues the Commissioners divide into different factions on religious grounds.

Commissioners are not full-time employees of the Council of Europe. The Commission is in formal session for at least 16 weeks in each year. These tend to be eight two-week sessions more or less equally spaced throughout the year, with a longer summer break. In addition the Commissioners spend an equivalent period of time in associated duties including the investigation of complaints (in their capacity as rapporteurs, *see* p. 42). Commissioners in theory still have about 20 weeks a year to devote to non-Commission business. This enables the Commissioners to retain a practical working knowledge of national legal systems which is of considerable value to the Commission when assessing the conflicting claims of governments and complainants. The trend, however, is inexorably towards longer and longer sessions of the Commission to mirror the steady rise of cases: complaint numbers have increased by an average 15 per cent. per annum for the last 10 years.

Under Article 36 of the Convention, the Commission is required to draw up its own rules of procedure. The current rules, 'Rules of Procedure of the European Commission of Human Rights', entered into force on January 7, 1992 (the 'Commission Rules'), *see* p. 243.

THE SECRETARIAT

Article 37 of the Convention states that the Secretariat to the Commission shall be provided by the Secretary-General to the Council of Europe. It is therefore the Secretary-General who appoints the Secretary and Deputy Secretary to the Commission. In practice however, the Secretariat works under the general direction of the President of the Commission.

Correspondence with the Commission is via the Secretary to the Commission and day-to-day matters are dealt with by the Secretariat. The Secretariat, unlike the Commissioners, are full-time and consequently are often as familiar (if not more so) with the details of an individual complaint as is the Commissioner (known in this context as a 'rapporteur') assigned to investigate it. The Secretariat is nevertheless a small (though ever-increasing) unit consisting of approximately 39 lawyers, 28 administrative assistants and two translators.

The Commission Rules set out the Secretariat's duties, which are: (Rule 13)

1. To assist the Commission and its members in the fulfilment of their duties.
2. To be the channel for all communications concerning the Commission.
3. To keep the archives of the Commission.

The duties extend to publishing the Commission's decisions, keeping the minutes of the Commission when in formal session and registering the date of receipt of complaints.

European Court of Human Rights

If a complaint has been declared admissible by the Commission (and has not been settled), then it will be transferred to the Committee of Ministers from which it may be referred to the European Court of Human Rights. The Court's rôle is to make a final and binding decision as to whether a violation of the Convention has occurred and, if appropriate, to consider the question of compensation, or 'just satisfaction'. The Court is based in Strasbourg.

The Court is a separate body to the Commission, although in the course of its deliberations it considers the Commission's final report and in those deliberations is assisted by one or more Commission delegates.

The administration and work of the Court are the primary responsibility of the President, and in his absence the Vice-President; these two are elected every three years by the judges from amongst their number, the procedure for which being set out in the Court Rules.

The rules for the appointment of judges are in many respects similar to those for Commissioners. No two judges may have the same nationality; on taking up office judges are required to make a virtually identical declaration of impartiality and the qualifications required for appointment are almost indistinguishable.

Differences between the two include the manner of appointment, in that judges are appointed by the Parliamentary Assembly from a short list provided by the relevant government (whereas Commissioners are appointed by the Committee of Ministers), and the duration of office, in that judges hold office for nine years whereas Commissioners are appointed for six years, although both may be re-elected. A more significant difference relates to the composition of the Court. There is one judge for each Member State of the Council of Europe whereas the number of Commissioners is limited to the number of states who have ratified the Convention.

In addition, whilst the Commission Rules stipulate that the Commission shall be in formal session for at least 16 weeks a year, the Court Rules merely require the Court to hold at least one session a year. In practice it is in session for longer periods each year—as the number of cases grows ever greater.

Under Article 55 the Court is required to draw up its own rules of procedure. The current Rules of the Court entered into force on June 30, 1990 (the 'Court Rules'), *see* p. 265.

THE REGISTRY

The full-time officers of the Court comprise the Registry, and the details of its duties and appointments are dealt with in the Court Rules (Rules 11–14). Whilst the Secretary to the Commission is appointed by the Secretary-General to the Council of Europe, the Registrar (the senior member of the Registry) is elected by a ballot of all the judges, after the President of the Court has consulted the Secretary-General. It is the Secretary-General who then appoints the Registry Officers. The Registry fulfils very much the same rôle as the Secretariat for the Commission, *i.e.* keeping records, dealing with the press, etc. The Secretariat is effectively excluded from the Court process and inevitably the existence of the two separate offices causes certain unnecessary duplication.

Committee of Ministers

The Committee of Ministers has an important rôle in respect of non-Convention business within the Council of Europe. It also continues to have a rôle (though diminishing) within the Convention process. The Committee of Ministers predates the Convention, being a creature of the original Statute of the Council of Europe of 1949.

A complaint, once it has been held to be admissible and passed through the Commission, can be referred to the Court for decision. By Article 44, only a state or the Commission has the right to bring a case before the Court. Where a case is not referred to the Court it is dealt with by the Committee of Ministers. From an individual complainant's point of view it may seem an unsatisfactory legal backwater; although in practice only straightforward complaints are dealt with by the Committee who nowadays invariably endorse the Commission's findings.

The Committee of Ministers is made up of one Minister (the Foreign Minister) for each state member of the Council of Europe (which state need not necessarily have ratified the Convention). The Committee sits in formal session twice a year, although at other times the Ministers' deputies preside. The deputies have the authority to deal with all decisions on behalf of their respective Ministers. The deputies are their countries' foreign office permanent representatives at the Council of Europe.

Although the procedure adopted by the Committee of Ministers is in no way objectively fair, independent or open, the Committee has paradoxically proved valuable in establishing respect for the Convention. In the early days of the Convention states were reluctant to sign up to a system which bound them to judicial consideration of all issues, no matter how politically sensitive. The use of an existing Council of Europe institution (the Committee of Ministers) provided a suitable vehicle to allay these fears. On signing the Convention a state does not automatically bind itself to complaints being decided by the Court. By Article 46 states have the option to make a separate declaration recognising the jurisdiction of the Court. Prior to that, complaints (after completing their course through the Commission) are decided by the Committee of Ministers. All states that have ratified the Convention have now also recognised the jurisdiction of the Court.

On making a declaration under Article 46, the individual state still retains some control, since only states and the Commission have power to refer cases to the Court. By Protocol 9, this final restriction will in time disappear, in that it will enable the individual complainant (subject to vetting by a panel of three judges) to refer his or her case to the Court. Protocol 9 has not been ratified by the U.K.

Whilst approximately equal numbers of cases have historically been decided by the Court and the Committee, the trend is for more and more cases to be referred to the Court, especially complex or legally important cases. In practice the Commission refers most cases to the Court; in general, states not unnaturally prefer the restricted process within the Committee.

Cases that are now determined by the Committee generally fall into either one of the following categories:

1. Those without any complex, unusual or important Convention issues.
2. Those where the state concerned has implicitly acknowledged the injustice by taking steps to amend national law to ensure the injustice does not recur.

In addition to its quasi-judicial function, the Committee of Ministers also fulfils the rôle of enforcing/supervising body for its own decisions as well as those of the Court.

Under Article 18 of the Statute of the Council of Europe the Committee is required to draw up its own Rules of Procedure. The current Rules are separated into those applying to Article 32, for which the most recent amendment dates from December 19, 1991, and those applying to Article 54, which were approved in February 1976 (*see* p. 257).

Reforms

In June 1992 the Commission registered its 20,000th application. The rate of growth of complaints to the Commission has been phenomenal. In 1955 the total number of registered complaints amounted to 138; in 1965, 310 complaints were registered; in 1975 the number registered had increased to 466 and in 1985 the figure was 596. The 1991 figure was 1648. With the upheavals in Eastern Europe, the populations of Hungary, Bulgaria, Poland, the Czech and Slovak States as well as East Germany have now come under the ambit of the Convention. Inevitably the system is feeling the strain.

A decision has at last been reached concerning the reform of the Convention system[2]. At a Council of Europe Summit of Heads of State and governments meeting in Vienna on October 8 and 9, 1993 a draft Protocol was approved in principle. The Summit required the new Protocol to be open for signature by May 1994. The Protocol provides for the abolition of the existing Commission and Court and their replacement by a single Court. Under the reforms the Committee of Ministers will retain its competence under Article 54, but its powers under Article 32 will be abolished.

The Council of Europe hope for ratification within two years, although it is generally believed that five years is a more realistic estimate. The subsequent implementation of the reforms will face a

---

[2] The Council of Europe's special report and resolutions upon reform are printed in full at 15 E.H.R.R. 321; and *see* New Law Journal, October 22, 1993, p. 1488

number of practical problems, not least the transitional arrangements and the effective merger of the Secretariat and Registry.

Whether or not reform will speed up the Convention system must be questionable. Fewer than 5 per cent. of all registered complaints result in a court hearing; the reforms will probably result in a quicker disposal of these cases. It is not, however, obvious how the reforms will expedite the remaining 95 per cent., which either fail or lead to a friendly settlement or a resolution of the Committee of Ministers.

Confidentiality

Confidentiality plays an important part in the Convention process. For example:

Rule 3 of the Commission Rules requires the Commissioner's Oath to include a promise to keep secret all Commission proceedings.

Rule 17 of the Commission Rules states that all Commission deliberations shall be confidential.

Article 21 of the Statute of the Council of Europe states that the Committee of Ministers shall meet in private.

Rule 19 of the Court Rules states that Court deliberations shall be in private.

The first part of the Convention complaint process is confidential. After the Commission has decided on the admissibility of the complaint and, if appropriate, a friendly settlement has not occurred, then the Commission's report is, in general, published.

Unless the complaint is determined by the Committee of Ministers, the second phase is public.

There are practical reasons for secrecy during the first phase. The most practical of all is that the state signatories to the Convention required this procedure to be adopted. In addition the absence of publicity in the early stages of a complaint probably leads to greater openness by the state. By knowing that its replies and proposals (especially during the friendly settlement negotiation phase) are not to be published, the state is encouraged to explore possible solutions.

If the individual applicant breaches the confidentiality requirement then it is open to the Commission to reject the complaint on the grounds that it constitutes an 'abuse of the right of petition' under Article 27 of the Convention.

The justification for secrecy disappears however if no settlement is reached at the end of the first 'without prejudice' phase. Thereafter publicity is part of the enforcement process so far as a successful complainant is concerned; part of the vindication process so far as a successful state is concerned.

12

Convention case statistics

Both the Court and Commission periodically publish surveys of their activities.

In 1990 the Court published a survey for the years 1959–1989. This showed that in the 30 years since the first case came before the Court[3] a total of 191 cases were referred to the Court. Of these only one involved an interstate complaint[4]. All others originated from individual complaints (although one was from a group of persons, two were made by trade unions and seven by companies).

Of the Court cases, 13 did not agree to disclosure of their identity and two cases were heard by the Court in private.

Violation of the Convention was found in two-thirds of all cases. In the first 15 years of the Convention there were 11 cases referred to the Court; in the second 16 years there were 180. In 1989 alone the Court gave judgment in 25 cases, considerably more than all the judgments in the first 15 years of the Convention. Thirty-one cases were referred to the Court in 1989, 61 in 1990 and 93 in 1991.

Most violations involved Article 6 (relating to the requirement for fair hearings) comprising 32 per cent. of all cases (63 cases), followed by Article 5 (right to liberty/arrest provisions) involving just over 12 per cent. of all cases (23 cases) and Article 8 (right to family life) involving just under 12 per cent. of all complaints (22 cases).

Nineteen per cent. of all cases involved the U.K. (37 cases) followed by 12 per cent. in respect of Belgium (22 cases) and 10 per cent. in respect of Austria (20 cases). Bearing in mind that the U.K. did not agree to the compulsory jurisdiction of the Court until 1966, the figure is of some significance. Nevertheless a straight comparison of complaint numbers is not in itself a direct measure of a country's respect for civil liberties. There has been a recent spate of cases against Italy involving the length of domestic proceedings which may well highlight Italy as the main respondent to Court cases, although in fact only one Article of the Convention is here involved. Another recent trend has been a significant increase in the number of complaints made against Sweden and in particular against France; this may indicate nothing more than an increase in the number of lawyers in those countries able and willing to undertake Convention cases.

The Commission's survey of activities for 1992 demonstrated the continued growth in complaint numbers. During that year the Secretariat received 5875 individual communications and registered 1861 individual applications. In spite of disposing of 1725 applications during the same period, the Commission ended the year with a

---

[3] *Lawless* v. *Ireland* 1 E.H.R.R. 1; November 14, 1960, Series A, No. 1
[4] *Ireland* v. *U.K.* 2 E.H.R.R. 25; January 18, 1978, Series A, No. 25

backlog of 2465 cases of which over 1574 (57 per cent.) were still awaiting their first examination. It is anticipated that this particular problem will be remedied to some extent by the introduction of the new Commission Committee and Chamber systems (*see* p. 47).

The growth in applications to the Commission shows no sign of abating. On average there has been a steady 15 per cent. increase in complaints to the Commission since 1980, although 1991 showed the first fall in numbers (from 1657 in 1990 to 1648 in 1991). The U.K. continues to attract a large number of complainants. Of the 1725 registered applications in 1992, 186 were from U.K. nationals; only France and Italy had more (263 and 195 respectively). In all, nationals from over 88 different countries had complaints registered during 1992; by Article 1 of the Convention the rights of 'everyone within the [states'] jurisdiction' are protected.

Over the years there has been a steady rise in the number of applications that are introduced through a lawyer. The 1990 Commission Survey showed that this had peaked and is now relatively steady at about 45 per cent. of all applications.

The increasing involvement of lawyers reflects the growing awareness of the practical importance of the Convention. Initially the Convention process was the primary preserve of academics and pressure groups. Such involvement precipitated significant legislative change, including changes relating to mental health law, prisoners' rights, corporal punishment, telephone tapping, homosexual discrimination, Northern Irish interrogation procedures and access to children in care.

However, the usefulness of the Convention process is now being seen in many practical areas; for instance challenges to legal aid refusals, gagging injunctions, excessive airport noise, satellite broadcasting restrictions and access to social services' files. Increasingly practitioners are appreciating the great potential scope of Article 1 to the First Protocol which protects the right to 'peaceful enjoyment of possessions' and has been held to cover such matters as planning, licensing and compulsory purchases.

COMPLAINT FLOW CHART

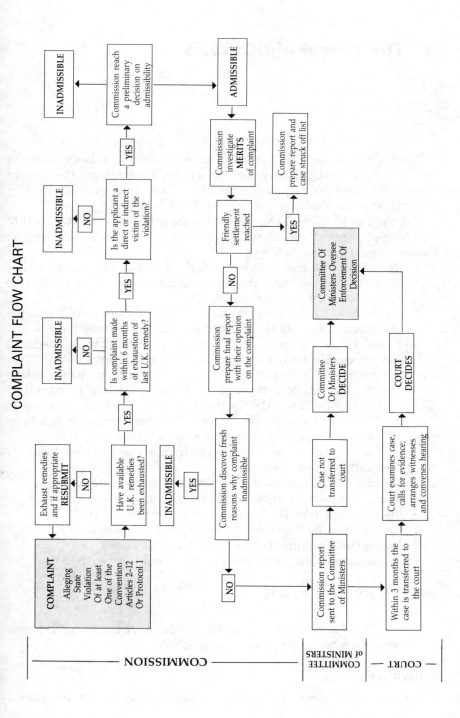

15

2 The Threshold Criteria

The individual right of complaint to an international body is one of the two most revolutionary aspects of the Convention; the second being the compulsory jurisdiction of a Court that delivers binding judgments enforceable by the Committee of Ministers.

The right of individual complaint and the jurisdiction of the Court to hear complaints do not automatically exist upon a state ratifying the Convention. They only arise, if:

1. (In relation to the individual right of complaint) the state has separately recognised the competence of the Commission to receive such complaints (Article 25).
2. (In relation to the jurisdiction of the Court) the state has separately recognised its compulsory jurisdiction (Article 46).

All states which have ratified the Convention have now also declared that they recognise both the right of individual complaint and the Court's compulsory jurisdiction. Whereas the declaration recognising these two matters has been expressed to be for an 'indefinite' period by a few states, most states make the declaration for fixed (but renewable) periods. The U.K.'s declaration is for a five-year period: it has been renewed without interruption since January 14, 1966.

There are a number of criteria which must be satisfied before a complaint can proceed. These,

1. Restrict the categories of potential complainants (*see* p. 16).
2. Require applicants to be 'a victim' of a violation (*see* p. 19).
3. Require that domestic remedies be exhausted (*see* p. 24).
4. Impose time limits for the submission of complaints (*see* p. 31).
5. Impose basic admissibility criteria (*see* p. 35).

For a diagrammatical illustration of this procedure, *see* p. 39.

WHO MAY COMPLAIN?

Article 25 stipulates that complaints may be made by *'any person, non-governmental organisation or group of individuals'*.

Individuals

Any individual (including a child[1]) may make a complaint regardless

---

[1] *See* p. 22 concerning the representation of children before the Commission

of his or her nationality. All that is required is that they be within the jurisdiction of one of the states which has ratified the Convention. This includes aliens arriving at an airport and illegal immigrants at a sea port. It does not confer a right of residence upon such persons nor an absolute right not to be deported; however, it does mean that the state must, when dealing with such persons, act in accordance with the Convention.

The periodic surveys of Commission activities show just how wide this provision really is: in 1991 for instance, complaints were made by nationals from over 72 different states (and in addition by four stateless applicants).

By Article 63 the Convention can be extended to cover a state's dependent territories. As a result of a declaration by the U.K., the Convention extends to Anguilla, Bermuda, the British Virgin Islands, the Cayman Islands, the Falklands Islands, South Georgia and the Sandwich Islands, Gibraltar, the Bailiwick of Guernsey and Jersey, the Isle of Man, Montserrat, St Helena, St Helena Dependencies, and the Turks and Caicos Islands. Articles 25 and 46 do not, however, apply to the British Virgin Islands, the Cayman Islands or the Isle of Man.

It is not contrary to the Convention for a state to grant an international institution immunity from the jurisdiction of its courts and thereby limit the application of the Convention. Such a situation arose in the Netherlands when an employee of the Iran–United States Claims Tribunal working in the Hague attempted unsuccessfully to challenge his summary dissmissal[2].

In limited circumstances a state's obligation under the Convention extends to acts outside its territory. Thus a state is responsible for the acts of persons under its actual authority even if that authority is exercised abroad[3]. In relation to Article 3 it has been held that a state has a duty not to expose anyone to an 'irremediable situation of objective danger', even outside its jurisdiction [4].

Anonymous complaints

The Commission will not accept anonymous complaints[5]. If the applicant fears for his or her safety upon the complaint being notified to the state then a request may be made to the Commission for undertakings or other protective measures to be given by the state[6].

The Commission will however respect an applicant's wish that his or her name be kept confidential, although it will have to be disclosed to

[2] DR 58/119
[3] DR 2/125; and DR 13/85
[4] DR 37/158 and *Soering* v. *U.K.* 11 E.H.R.R. 439; July 7, 1989, Series A, No. 161
[5] Article 27(1)(a)
[6] Rule 36 of the Commission Rules and *see* p. 61

the state. In such cases a request should be made for confidentiality when the application is submitted; the applicant thereafter being referred to as 'X' or by the initial letter of his or her surname.

Group complaints

The right of complaint extends to non-governmental organisations and groups of individuals. This excludes local government councils but does not exclude politicians in their personal capacity or political parties[7].

Complaints may be made by companies, or other legal entities, such as trusts, industrial provident and friendly societies. Rule 43(2) of the Commission Rules requires applications submitted by non-governmental organisations or by groups of individuals to be signed by those persons competent to represent the organisation or group. Where the group has no formal legal basis the Commission requires the complaint to be signed by all the members.

Where a professional association submits a complaint on behalf of its members (rather than as a victim in its own right) then it must identify those members and provide evidence of its authority to represent them. If it fails to identify the members, the complaint will be considered as an anonymous application and rejected [8].

If a complaint is being submitted on behalf of a group or other organisation, it is tactically sensible (if possible) to make an individual complaint as well. In the first *Sunday Times* complaint[9] for instance, complaints were made by the company (Times Newspapers Ltd.), the editor and a group of journalists. All three—the company, the individual and the group—were held to have sufficient standing[10]. The Convention does not, however, allow popular actions; the complainant must be a direct or indirect victim of the state's violation of the Convention. For this reason if the complaint is for any reason rejected on the ground that the group or organisation is not a 'victim', the complaint may still be capable of being considered if also made in a personal capacity[11].

Although there have been comparatively few complaints by organisations and companies, the potential category is wide, including trade

---

[7] *Liberal Party* v. *U.K.* DR 21/211
[8] DR 47/225
[9] 2 E.H.R.R. 245; April 26, 1979, Series A, No. 30
[10] DR 2/90
[11] DR 15/259

unions[12], churches[13], private associations for the rehabilitation of drug addicts[14] and professional associations[15].

In respect of applications by groups or organisations the Commission Rules require that those appearing before the Commission at a hearing provide evidence of their authority to act in the capacity of representatives [16].

WHO CAN CLAIM TO BE A VICTIM?

Article 25 requires that the applicant must claim 'to be the victim of a violation'.

Whilst the requirement is 'to claim' rather than 'to prove', it is nevertheless clearly necessary to satisfy the Commission and Court that there are firm grounds for the claim.

Often there will be no doubt about the applicant being the victim, for instance:

1. Anthony Tyrer[17], when sentenced by the Isle of Man Juvenile Court to be birched, was unquestionably a victim of an alleged violation of Article 3 (degrading treatment).
2. James Malone[18], whose telephone was tapped by the Metropolitan Police, was a victim of an alleged violation of Article 8 (respect for private life).
3. Alan Hamer[19], whilst a prisoner, was refused the right to marry and so was a victim of an alleged violation of Article 12 (the right to marry).

Questions arise in relation to how directly the individual must be implicated in the alleged violation to claim victim status. What, for instance is the position of someone who might be subject to corporal punishment but (unlike Anthony Tyrer) has not as yet been sentenced? Is someone (like James Malone) who is uncertain as to whether their phone is being tapped able to claim to be a victim, without having to actually prove that it has been tapped?

In the case of Campbell and Cosans[20] the Court had to consider the question of whether a child could claim to be the victim of a violation

---

[12] See for instance National Union Of Belgian Police v. Belgium 1 E.H.R.R. 578; October 27, 1975, Series A, No. 19; Swedish Engine Drivers' Union v. Sweden 1 E.H.R.R. 617; February 6, 1976, Series A, No. 20; Council of Civil Service unions (GCHQ) v. U.K. DR 50/228
[13] Church of Scientology v. Sweden DR 16/68
[14] DR 57/81
[15] DR 47/225
[16] Rule 37 of Commission Rules DR 47/225
[17] 2 E.H.R.R. 1; April 25, 1978, Series A, No. 26
[18] 7 E.H.R.R. 14; August 2, 1984, Series A, No. 82
[19] DR 24/5
[20] 4 E.H.R.R. 293; February 25, 1982, Series A, No. 48

of Article 3 (degrading treatment) if he or she ran the risk of being subjected to corporal punishment at school when they had not in fact been so punished. The facts concerned Scottish schools where it was still legal for school children to be punished by being struck with a strap. The Court decided that applicants can claim to be a victim *'if they run the risk of being directly affected'* by the alleged violation. In this case the children *were* in a school where they ran the risk of being strapped and could therefore claim to be victims.

It should, however, be clearly appreciated that merely because an applicant has been accepted as a victim it does not mean that a violation will be found in the particular case. Although Campbell and Cosans were held to be victims within the meaning of Article 25, the Court nevertheless held that the mere threat of being subjected to such corporal punishment did not in itself amount to 'degrading treatment'[21]. Thus although the applicants had crossed the admissibility hurdle of establishing themselves as victims, they fell at the hurdle of establishing that the facts amounted to a violation of Article 3.

In *Vijayanathan and Pusparajah* v. *France*[22] the applicants (of Tamil origin) were refused refugee status in France, and complained that they risked torture if returned to Sri Lanka. The Court held that the French appeal process had not been exhausted at the time the complaint was submitted and therefore the applicants were not in fact 'victims' of a violation of the Convention.

A number of guidelines have been established to deal with the question of whether an applicant is a victim. Examples of these are listed *below*:

Hypothetical breaches

Purely hypothetical breaches will not be considered. It is not sufficient to complain about the incompatibility of a national law with the Convention; the applicant must in addition show that he or she is personally affected by that law [23]. A person who cannot show that he or she is personally affected by the law to a greater extent than any other person may not claim to be a victim[24].

The fact that the applicant has suffered no tangible material loss does not in itself make a complaint merely hypothetical[25]. A person can be the victim of a violation of the Convention even in the absence of any detriment. Detriment is relevant only to the question of compensation or 'just satisfaction'[26].

---

[21] The Court did however find a violation of Article 2 of the First Protocol
[22] 15 E.H.R.R. 62; August 27, 1992, Series A, No. 241-B
[23] DR 45/211
[24] DR 42/247
[25] DR 46/214
[26] *See for instance Groppera Radio A.G.* v. *Switzerland* 12 E.H.R.R. 321; March 28, 1990, Series A, No. 173

Potential victims

This category (as in *Campbell and Cosans above*) concerns the existence of legislation or government and administrative procedures which result in the risk of Convention rights being violated. The applicant must establish a real personal risk of being affected by the alleged violation[27].

The existence of laws prohibiting homosexual acts between consenting adults in Northern Ireland made Jeffrey Dudgeon[28] a victim; as a homosexual he ran the risk of being directly affected. He did not have to have been prosecuted. The case of *Norris* v. *Ireland*[29] involved a similar complaint concerning the law in Ireland; the Court held that the same principles applied, even though Mr Norris's risk was minimal as consenting adults were not in practice prosecuted. The Court stated '*a law which remains on the Statute book, even though it is not enforced in a particular class of cases for a considerable time, may be applied again*'.

In the case of *Malone* v. *U.K.*, the fact that James Malone was unable to establish whether his telephone had been tapped was not a bar to the Commission accepting him as a victim. The relevant question was whether he was able to find out if it was occurring. Where legislation provides for the notification of surveillance to a person concerned, the person cannot generally claim to be a victim of a violation of Article 8 (right to respect for privacy) unless he or she has received such notification. On the other hand where the legislation provides that the surveillance measure may affect all users, without subsequent notification, anyone may claim to be a victim of a violation of Article 8 by virtue of being a user[30].

The issue of 'victim' has arisen in a number of cases involving abortion laws. Put simply, a man cannot bring a general complaint against abortion legislation[31], whereas a woman may[32], even though she is not pregnant. A prospective father who complains that his wife has been able legally to terminate her pregnancy without his consent may however claim to be a victim[33].

Indirect victims

A violation of the Convention may have both direct and indirect consequences. The spouse, parent or other relative of a victim may

---

[27] DR 41/123
[28] *See* note 17 *above*
[29] 13 E.H.R.R. 186; October 26, 1988, Series A, No. 142; *see* also *Modinos* v. *Cyprus*, April 22, 1993, Series A, No. 259
[30] DR 43/34
[31] DR 12/168
[32] DR 5/103
[33] DR 19/244

themselves be prejudiced by the effect the violation has had upon the principal victim. Most obviously this will arise in situations where the alleged violation results in a death. For example the parents of a person who died during an arrest by the police have been held to be indirect victims and thus able to make complaints in their own right[34].

The situation is well illustrated in certain immigration cases; for instance in *Abdulaziz, Cabales and Balkandali* v. *U.K.*[35]. Mr Abdulaziz was refused a residence permit to live permanently with his wife who was lawfully residing in the U.K. Mrs Abdulaziz was able to claim to be a victim even though she remained in the U.K. with her husband, as he remained unlawfully and under direct threat of deportation.

What is required in such cases is that the applicant show that as a direct consequence of the violation he or she has been directly affected. These cases must therefore be distinguished from those where the applicant is bringing an action in a representative capacity.

Complaints by representatives of the victim

Where the victim is incapacitated, the Commission and Court will accept complaints by suitable representatives on his or her behalf. Unless the representative is a custodial parent or legal guardian, the Commission and Court will require evidence of the person's authority to act as representative. Accordingly a parent, who after divorce had neither custody nor care and control of the children, was unable to introduce an application on their behalf, without proof of being specially empowered so to do[36].

The rules relating to representation are not strict and in no way comparable to the 'next friend' or 'guardian *ad litem*' requirements of the High or County Court. The Commission will not insist on representation even if the applicant is considered on legal grounds to lack sufficient mental capacity to manage his or her own affairs.

Death of applicant

Where the applicant dies after having made the complaint, the complaint is not automatically struck off the Commission's list. Provision exists for the complaint to be pursued by the applicant's heirs[37]. If the heirs wish to pursue the complaint then they can do so, but only

[34] DR 49/213
[35] DR 29/176; 7 E.H.R.R. 471; May 28, 1985, Series A, No. 94
[36] DR 16/105
[37] DR 14/64

if the specific nature of the complaint means that the heirs have a legal interest or for some other reason the Commission considers the complaint of general importance or wider relevance[38]. If the heirs can show no specific material interest in the complaint (or that it is of general interest), then it will be struck out[39].

Often (but not invariably) the question of whether a complaint can be continued by an heir is determined by whether, as a result of the death, the heir can to some extent be then considered as a victim[40].

In *X v. France*[41] the applicant died after the complaint had been transferred to the European Court for determination. The applicant's illness and expected death was a fundamental and relevant fact in his complaint (he suffered from AIDS and complained about the length of domestic compensation proceedings). The Court was prepared to allow the parents to continue the proceedings without looking in detail as to whether they had any other special grounds for so doing.

Adequacy of domestic redress

Someone who has received adequate redress at the domestic level for the alleged violations of the Convention cannot claim to be a victim[42]. The mere fact that a measure has been annulled does not constitute redress; it must also have been declared unlawful and, if appropriate, given rise to reparation[43]. Where an applicant has, for instance, had his or her sentence reduced specifically as a result of the domestic court finding that the judicial process has been excessively long, then that person cannot claim to be a victim of a violation of Article 6(1) (right to fair hearing within a reasonable time). If, however, the excessive length of the proceedings had not been specifically given as a reason for the reduction then the situation would be otherwise[44].

The redress must be adequate; not necessarily absolute. Thus someone who has been dismissed from employment for belonging to a union and has only obtained compensation may not claim to be a victim of a violation of Article 11 (freedom of association and right to join trade unions), provided the compensation is adequate.

Organisations or groups as victims

Whilst complaints can be made by companies, they can also, in certain instances, be made by minority shareholders. Where the

---

[38] DR 30/5
[39] DR 36/236
[40] DR 49/67 and DR 57/5
[41] 14 E.H.R.R. 483; March 23, 1991, Series A, No. 234-C
[42] DR 50/90
[43] DR 52/236
[44] DR 56/193

domestic courts accept such a shareholder as having sufficient legal standing to sue in his or her capacity as a shareholder, then that person may claim to be a victim even though the administrative act was directed at the company[45].

Where a professional association cannot itself claim to be a victim, then it is precluded from introducing a complaint concerning a measure affecting its members[46]. The same point holds true for trade unions[47] and indeed any non-governmental organisation[48].

EXHAUSTION OF DOMESTIC REMEDIES

By Article 1 the signatory States undertake to ensure that their domestic laws are in conformity with the freedoms defined by the Convention.

It follows that no complaint can be made unless it can be shown that the state has failed in this respect. In general therefore, unless all domestic judicial remedies have been exhausted, it will not be possible to establish that the state is in violation of the Convention. The state must have had an opportunity of redressing the alleged damage by domestic means.

Article 26 specifically deals with this point: *The Commission may only deal with the matter after all domestic remedies have been exhausted'*.

In general therefore, complaints should not be submitted before all effective domestic remedies have been exhausted. In fact the effective date by which the domestic remedies have been exhausted is not the date of the application, but the date on which the Commission is called upon to decide on admissibility [49]. If an application is rejected by the Commission on the ground that an effective domestic remedy has not been exhausted, then (if the remedy is still available) it should be pursued. The application can be resubmitted if the remedy turns out to have been ineffective in resolving the Convention breach.

Exhaustion

The requirement to exhaust domestic remedies only applies to effective remedies. If there is any doubt about the effectiveness of the remedy, then the remedy should be pursued. If counsel's opinion is

[45] DR 49/205; *Neves E Silva* v. *Portugal* 13 E.H.R.R. 576; April 27, 1989, Series A, No. 153
[46] DR 41/211
[47] DR 32/261
[48] DR 37/87
[49] DR 27/181

merely doubtful about the prospects of an appeal to the House of Lords, then the appeal should be attempted, even if leave to appeal has been refused by the Court of Appeal[50].

Whether the European Court of Justice in Luxembourg constitutes a domestic remedy in appropriate cases is as yet undecided, but the answer is almost certainly no. No state has as yet argued non-exhaustion on this ground[51].

(A) DEEMED EXHAUSTION

Where it is obvious that there is no prospect of an appeal or other judicial remedy being successful or effective then it need not be pursued[52]. In general the Commission will accept counsel's opinion on this point[53], provided that counsel is experienced in the relevant legal area. Unless the proceedings have been through the whole appeal process (or leave to further appeal has been refused), the U.K. Government tends to assert non-exhaustion as a matter of course. Where the Commission is provided with a junior counsel's opinion as to the futility of an appeal process, the Government will sometimes suggest that the opinion of Queen's Counsel should have been obtained. This is not usually necessary. The Commission is itself extremely astute as to the availability or otherwise of an effective domestic remedy.

The Commission will need to be shown a copy of the barrister's opinion, if such is obtained. It is important that this point is borne in mind when counsel is instructed. Counsel should be reminded that if their opinion on appeal is not favourable, then the opinion may in due course be copied to the Commission. It follows therefore that counsel should (if at all possible) be succinct and not stray into potentially detrimental areas such as premature observations on the likelihood of a European complaint succeeding, etc. Counsel should also be made aware that the opinion may well be copied by the Commission to the Government.

If an opinion is unfavourable it should explain in detail why a proposed appeal or other course of action would be ineffective. Other possible remedies or indirect benefits from an appeal should also be explored in the opinion. The Government may well criticise the opinion if it relies on first instance, rather than Court of Appeal or House of Lords' decisions. Similarly if the authority relied upon is

---

[50] DR 40/298
[51] *See* Dr. M. Mendelson; 'The impact of European Community law on the implementation of the European Convention on Human Rights', Human Rights File No. 6, Council of Europe, 1984
[52] *De Wilde, Ooms and Versyp* v. *Belgium* 1 E.H.R.R. 432; June 18, 1971, Series A, No. 12
[53] DR 33/247

relatively old, the Government may suggest that the law has progressed in the meantime and the authority is no longer safe.

Counsel should also be aware that the opinion may be published in due course. In *Warwick* v. *U.K.*[54], a case concerning corporal punishment in schools, counsel advised that a domestic appeal was hopeless because (amongst other reasons) the Court of Appeal *'like the rest of our Courts, consists almost entirely of judges whose education involved the liberal use of corporal punishment and who have no aversion to it, which makes an argument that the mere occurrence of physical injury proves an excess of force a difficult one to make attractive'*. This refreshingly honest and accurate assessment of the realities of the situation has been published in the Commission's Decisions and Reports.

Obviously if there are a long line of decided cases showing that further appeal is hopeless, or if an appeal on similar grounds has been rejected[55], then there may not be a need for the Commission to have counsel's opinion.

In general, the refusal of legal aid on merit grounds will be a very significant factor in the Commission's consideration of available remedies having been exhausted, provided the refusal has been appealed to the Area Committee. It will not, however, always be decisive, unless the applicant is illiterate or otherwise obviously incapable of conducting his or her own case. The suggestion in such cases that a renewed application for legal aid should be made before exhaustion of domestic remedies can be claimed will not find favour with the Commission unless there is clear evidence that such a renewed application would be likely to receive different treatment[56].

(B) 'NON-EXHAUSTION': THE ONUS OF PROOF

The original application to the Commission requires the applicant to set out the steps taken to exhaust the available domestic remedies. Once the applicant has claimed to have exhausted all domestic remedies, it is for the state (if it takes the point) to demonstrate that the applicant did not make use of a remedy at his or her disposal [57].

The onus therefore is upon the state to show that there was an effective remedy that the applicant failed to pursue. The state must, in addition, satisfy the Commission that the applicant had effective access to that remedy[58]. Once the state has raised the availability of an unused domestic remedy, then the burden of proving the remedy ineffective rests with the applicant.

---

[54] DR 60/5
[55] DR 14/186
[56] *Granger* v. *U.K.* 12 E.H.R.R. 469; March 28, 1990, Series A, No. 174
[57] *Deweer* v. *Belgium* 2 E.H.R.R. 39; February 27, 1980, Series A, No. 35
[58] DR 13/85

A state that fails to raise, or raise with sufficient clarity, an objection before the Commission on the grounds of non-exhaustion will be taken as having waived the right to object, or be estopped from so doing at any later stage [59].

(c) NON-EXHAUSTION DUE TO MISTAKE

A domestic remedy has not been exhausted if the appeal or other process fails because of a procedural mistake by the applicant or the applicant's lawyers. In *Cunningham* v. *U.K.*[60] the applicant sought a declaration in a High Court writ action in circumstances when judicial review was the appropriate procedure. Ultimately the applicant commenced judicial review proceedings, but by then the application was well out of time and accordingly rejected on this ground. The Commission held the application inadmissible on the ground of non-exhaustion. If, in spite of the applicant's procedural failure in the domestic proceedings, the court nevertheless examines the substance of the complaint, then non-exhaustion cannot be said to have occurred[61].

Effective remedies

(A) *EX GRATIA* OR DISCRETIONARY REMEDIES

Whilst a non-judicial remedy may be considered effective in certain situations (*see below*), there are clearly certain procedures which cannot amount to an 'effective remedy'. In this category comes the application for a Royal Pardon or for an *ex gratia* payment[62]. The fact that a remedy is in certain respects discretionary does not necessarily make it invalid. In *Reed* v. *U.K.*[63] a prisoner who had challenged his solitary confinement by complaining to the Home Office and the Board of Visitors was held by the Commission to have exhausted the available domestic remedies. In general, however, a remedy which depends on the discretionary power of a public authority cannot be considered as effective[64].

(B) TRIBUNALS AND ADMINISTRATIVE REMEDIES

The Ombudsman procedure is not an effective remedy[65]. An appeal from a tribunal, where the appeal is limited to questions of law, is not

---

[59] *Bricmont* v. *Belgium* 12 E.H.R.R. 217; July 7, 1989, Series A, No. 158; *Pine Valley Developments* v. *Ireland* 14 E.H.R.R. 319; November 29, 1991, Series A, No. 222
[60] DR 43/171
[61] DR 57/251
[62] DR 42/171
[63] DR 10/5; and *see also* W. v. *U.K.* No. 18187/91 (not yet reported in Decisions and Reports)
[64] DR 27/50
[65] DR 52/227

an effective remedy where the complaint relates to the facts or the law itself[66]. An appeal against the award of a tribunal set up to assess the amount of compensation payable following nationalisation is not an effective remedy, where the size of the award is fixed as a result of a formula laid down in a statute and the tribunal have correctly applied the formula[67].

(c) JUDICIAL REVIEW

Whether a judicial review amounts to an effective remedy depends upon the circumstances of the individual case[68]. In *M. v. U.K.*[69] an Iranian sentenced to be deported for drugs offences complained to the Commission after having appeals to the Immigration Appeal Tribunal and to the Secretary of State for asylum rejected. The Commission held that anyone who complains about a refusal of political asylum in the U.K. must seek judicial review of the Secretary of State's decision in order to exhaust domestic remedies.

The Commission reached a similar decision concerning alleged procedural irregularities in a decision of the Board of Visitors; it held that these had first to be challenged by way of judicial review.

In *G. v. U.K.*[70] judicial review was, however, held not to be an effective remedy. The case concerned the refusal of legal aid for a complex criminal appeal (in which counsel had advised against an appeal). The Commission accepted that in such cases there was no possibility of a successful judicial review challenge of the refusal of legal aid, not least because the Legal Aid Committee was not required to give reasons for its decision.

In *Soering v. U.K.*[71] the Court held that judicial review was an effective remedy in challenging extradition proceedings. This decision attracted considerable criticism and the issue was again considered in the case of *Vilvarajah v. U.K.*[72] which concerned a decision to expel five Sri Lankans from the U.K. and return them to Sri Lanka where they feared ill-treatment. The Commission held by 13 votes to one that judicial review was not in this case an effective remedy. However, the Court, by seven votes to two, felt compelled to follow its recent decision in *Soering*. Given the defects in the judicial review procedure it is questionable whether the Court can maintain this opinion indefinitely.

[66] DR 41/226
[67] *Lithgow* v. *U.K.* DR 42/33; 8 E.H.R.R. 329; July 8, 1986, Series A, No. 102
[68] *See generally* AGOSI v. *U.K.* 9 E.H.R.R. 1; October 24, 1986, Series A, No. 108
[69] DR 57/136
[70] DR 56/199
[71] 11 E.H.R.R. 439; July 7, 1989, Series A, No. 161
[72] 14 E.H.R.R. 248; October 30, 1991, Series A, No. 215

(D) EFFECTIVE IN ALL RESPECTS

To be effective, a remedy must be capable of remedying the violation directly, and not merely indirectly.

An obvious example of this principle relates to a state's expulsion of foreign nationals. It has repeatedly been held that where a person alleges that expulsion would expose him or her to serious danger, an appeal without suspensive effect cannot be regarded as an effective remedy[73]. If, however, there is no risk to the individual, then the remedy may be considered effective[74].

Other examples of remedies not considered effective in all respects include the proposal by a state to disclose personal data about the applicant in confidence to a third party (which the applicant wished to see first-hand[75]) and the remedy of suing for damages in tort where the complaint related to living conditions in a mental hospital[76].

An action for damages arising out of physical mistreatment will, in general, be a remedy that has to be exhausted before a complaint can be made, unless the allegation is that the mistreatment is part of an officially sanctioned administrative practice[77]. Where the complaint concerns an excessive period on remand, an action for damages is irrelevant to the question of exhaustion of remedies[78].

Choice of remedies

Where there is a choice of remedies open to the applicant, the Commission only expects the most obvious and sensible to be pursued. It accepts that the rule of exhaustion of domestic remedies can only be applied to reflect the practical realities of the individual's position. Where an applicant has exhausted a remedy which is apparently effective and sufficient then he or she will not be required to exhaust others which are available, but probably ineffective [79]. On the other hand, the applicant cannot ignore a remedy that is generally held to be available and effective. It also follows that where a remedy has been exhausted, the Commission will not consider the possibility of requesting the authority to reconsider the matter as constituting an effective remedy, unless significant new facts have arisen.

If a number of potentially effective remedies exist, the applicant will be required to pursue them. *Chappell* v. *U.K.*[80] concerned an Anton

---

[73] DR 41/103
[74] DR 53/210
[75] DR 45/91
[76] DR 10/5
[77] DR 20/184
[78] DR 56/62
[79] DR 34/78
[80] DR 42/137; 12 E.H.R.R. 1; March 30, 1989, Series A, No. 152

Piller search where it was alleged that documents were seized beyond the scope of the litigation in question. In such a case the Commission agreed that the following remedies existed: application for contempt of court, application for damages from the third party who obtained the order and an application to the court for return of the documents. Until these remedies had been exhausted, the application was inadmissible.

Requirement to invoke the Convention

Domestic remedies have to be exhausted before it can be alleged that the state has failed (in breach of its obligations under Article 1) to secure for the applicant one or more of his or her fundamental freedoms. It follows that the Convention rights or freedoms in issue must have been raised in the domestic proceedings. Obviously it is a more straightforward matter to raise alleged violations of the Convention in those states where it has internal effect. In the U.K. it is not possible to directly invoke the Convention (*see* p. 100). The requirement will be satisfied if the applicant has submitted the substance of the complaint to be made to the Commission in domestic proceedings, even without particular reference to the Convention [81].

The rules of exhaustion likewise do not require that the provisions of the Convention be invoked by way of defence in U.K. criminal proceedings[82].

In general it is sensible to include in the domestic proceedings specific reference to the Convention rights in issue. There will be judges who will take exception to their inclusion, but it is difficult to see what else is lost by raising them at an early stage. In judicial review proceedings, for instance, the application in Form 86A (the 'Grounds on which Relief is Sought' section) should contain a simple recital of the Convention points, in addition to the domestic law grounds. By way of example, the recital of the Convention might amount to:

> By virtue of Articles 1, 3, 8, 13, 14 and Article 1 of the First Protocol [as the case may be] to the European Convention for the Protection of Human Rights and Fundamental Freedoms, the Applicant is entitled to the following human rights and freedoms:
> 1. The right not to be subjected to degrading treatment;
> 2. Respect for her private family life and her home;
> 3. The right to an effective remedy before a national authority for any breach of her fundamental rights and freedoms notwithstanding that the violation of her rights and freedoms has been committed by persons acting in an official capacity;

---

[81] *Albert and Le Compte* v. *Belgium* DR 18/5; 5 E.H.R.R. 533; February 10, 1983, Series A, No. 58; and *see Castells* v. *Spain* 14 E.H.R.R. 445; April 23, 1992, Series A, No. 236
[82] *Arrowsmith* v. *U.K.* DR 8/123; 3 E.H.R.R. 218

4.   The securing of the enjoyment of her rights and freedoms without discrimination on any ground such as sex, race, national or social origin, association with a national minority, property, birth or other status; and
5.   Peaceful enjoyment of her possessions.

The Form 86A statement concludes:

> The Respondent's acts and omissions to date . . . violate Articles 1, 3, 8, 13, 14 and Article 1 of the First Protocol to the European Convention for the Protection of Human Rights and Fundamental Freedoms [as the case may be] and are contrary to the intentions of Parliament when passing the . . . Act and to the principles of Law reflected in those Articles.

TIME LIMITS

Article 26 stipulates that:

> The Commission may only deal with the matter . . . within a period of six months from the date upon which the final decision was taken.

The Commission applies the time limit strictly.

In *Mercier De Bettens* v. *Switzerland*[83] the Commission considered that the purpose of the rule was:

> to ensure a degree of legal certainty and to ensure that cases raising problems under the Convention are examined within a reasonable time. Furthermore, the rule is also intended to prevent authorities and other persons concerned from being in a state of uncertainty for a prolonged period. Lastly, the rule is designed to facilitate the establishment of the facts of the case which, with the passage of time, would otherwise become increasingly difficult . . .

Relevant date

THE START OF THE SIX-MONTH PERIOD

Time runs from the moment the applicant is aware of the matter of the complaint and has exhausted all (if any) effective domestic remedies. In general this will be the time when he or she is told of the outcome: either by being present when the decision is made or, if precluded from being present, by being told by his or her lawyer. If judgment is not pronounced in open court, then the six months may

---

[83] DR 54/178

run from the time it is served [84]. In certain cases time may not run until the day upon which the applicant receives the reasons for (and not merely the operative part of) the final decision [85].

When the application concerns the level of compensation after nationalisation of an industry, the six-month period does not run from the date of the Act, but from the date on which the amount of compensation for shareholders was fixed[86].

A complaint alleging that a building plan infringes the applicant's property rights must be introduced within six months of the planning approval[87].

Where an applicant is unaware of the violation, then the six-month period runs from the moment the applicant becomes aware of the act or decision in issue. In *Isabel Hilton* v. *U.K.*[88] the applicant was refused a job with the BBC. Nine years later she discovered that the refusal might have arisen from a secret MI5 vetting process. The six-month period was held to run from the time she discovered this fact.

Where a criminal case involves a number of charges, and a conviction for certain of the offences occurs before conviction for the remainder, then a complaint in respect of the first conviction must be brought within six months of its date (and not six months from the second conviction date) [89]. A similar rule applies in civil proceedings, where, for instance, the proceedings are divided into two parts; one part making a final decision on jurisdiction and the subsequent decision relating to the merits of the case. A complaint concerning the jurisdictional decision must be brought within six months of its date, and not the date of the subsequent decision[90].

CASES OF UNCERTAINTY

Time runs from the exhaustion of the last effective remedy. It does not run from the failure of a subsequent unsuccessful ineffective remedy (for instance the failure to obtain a Royal Pardon or a discretionary refusal of leave to appeal)[91]. Likewise the rejection of an application to reopen proceedings does not restart the running of the six-month period unless it is successful and actually results in a reopening.

Frequently an applicant may have to wait some time before knowing whether there is an effective appeal (or other domestic remedy) and

---

[84] DR 32/266
[85] DR 56/40
[86] *See* note 67 *above*
[87] DR 55/205
[88] DR 57/108
[89] DR 31/154
[90] DR 33/247
[91] DR 26/242

then may have to wait to see if leave is granted or the case reopened. It may be that, by the time a remedy has been shown ineffective, the six-month period has expired.

The answer to such a problem is that, if the applicant is in doubt, an application should be submitted to the Commission and the domestic appeal pursued. If the appeal is found to be an effective remedy the application will be able to be resubmitted (if then necessary). If ineffective, the application will be in time.

Where a potential complaint lies in respect of more than one breach of the Convention, it sometimes arises that the domestic remedy for one aspect is exhausted at an earlier stage than others. Here again it is sensible to submit a complaint to the Commission setting out the full claim, whilst pointing out that in respect of certain matters domestic remedies are still being pursued.

THE END OF THE SIX-MONTH PERIOD

The final date for computing whether the application is within the six-month period is the date of the first letter, telex or fax to the Commission, provided it contains basic details of the nature of the complaint. The mere submission of certain documents is not in itself sufficient; the complaints must be raised in express terms or implicitly[92].

Although Article 25 stipulates that the initial complaint should be addressed to the Secretary-General of the Council of Europe, it is usual practice simply to address the initial letter and the formal complaint to the Secretary to the Commission[93].

Continuing situations

Certain breaches of the Convention are not single events but amount to continuing violations. A statute may be enacted which violates the Convention; for instance in *Norris* v. *Ireland*[94] the applicant challenged the laws criminalising homosexual acts. Apart from being a homosexual, the applicant did not allege that he had been arrested or threatened with charge for contravening the law. The Irish Government accordingly asserted that he was not a victim within the meaning of the Convention, and that the complaint was merely a 'popular action'. The Court however held that *'the Convention entitles individuals to contend that*

---

[92] *See for instance Oberschilck* v. *Austria* May 23, 1991, Series A, No. 204
[93] This is advocated by the Commission in its explanatory leaflet *Lodging an application with the European Commission of Human Rights*
[94] *See note 29 above*

the law violates their rights by itself, in the absence of an individual measure of implementation, if they run the risk of being directly affected by it . . . either [he] accepts the law and refrains from engaging—even in private and with consenting male partners—in prohibited sexual acts to which he is disposed by reason of his homosexual tendencies, or he commits such acts and thereby becomes liable to criminal prosecution'.

Where the complaint relates to a continuing situation against which there is no domestic remedy, the six-month period runs from the end of the situation, and so long as this lasts, the six-month rule does not apply[95].

Where a statutory Order was made banning processions for a two-month period, this was deemed to be a continuing situation during the currency of the prohibition. The six-month period did not begin to run against the applicant until the date of its planned procession (and not the date of the original Order) [96].

Amended or supplemental complaints

The Commission, in undertaking an examination of a complaint, can consider and raise with the relevant state any violation the reported facts disclose. Whilst an applicant is not required (in theory) to specify the applicable Articles [97], a failure to detail the precise nature and extent of the complaint may result in all or part of the complaint being rejected on time grounds. In *B. v. U.K.*[98] the applicant complained about civil service disciplinary proceedings arising out of a press comment he had made connected with his employment at Aldermaston Atomic Weapons Research Establishment. Subsequent to his original application, in correspondence he raised complaints concerning the violation of other Articles arising out of the same incident. The Commission held that these further matters were out of time and therefore inadmissible.

Obviously it is a matter of construction as to whether subsequent clarification of the original complaint is merely clarification, or whether it amounts to a fresh complaint; if it is the latter then it risks being rejected as being out of time. The moral is that the original complaint must deal with the full breadth of the alleged violation(s); one should not assume that the Commission will pick up any omissions.

Delay after the initial letter

The Commission now gives time limits for the completion of the application form subsequent to the submission of the initial letter

[95] DR 54/52
[96] DR 21/138
[97] DR 57/108
[98] DR 45/41

outlining the complaint. The Commission has, however, shown considerable patience in the past with dilatory complainants. In *Rubinet v. Italy* the applicant contacted the Commission in 1978 and gave the substance of his case. He then endeavoured, unsuccessfully, to effect a domestic remedy. When he contacted the Commission 3 years later, it was nevertheless prepared to accept the date for the introduction of the complaint as being 1978[99]. In the absence of compelling reasons the Commission will not, however, accept such delay [100].

Mistakes by the Commission

The Commission is not infallible. If an application is rejected on grounds which show a plain mistake by the Commission or facts presented to the Commission turn out to be incorrect, then they may be prepared to reconsider the matter. In *Ewing v. U.K.*[101] the Commission ruled that part of an application was inadmissible for non-observance of the six-month rule. The Commission subsequently accepted that as a result of certain of the disclosed facts being untrue, a mistake had been made and agreed to reopen the examination of the application.

ADMISSIBILITY DECISION

One of the Commission's primary rôles is to sieve through the large number of applications and exclude the hopeless, either because they do not come within the scope of the Convention, or because at best they could never amount to a violation. Accordingly, in addition to the above detailed grounds for rejecting applications (non-exhaustion, out of time, not a victim, etc.). Article 27 sets out further grounds, namely:

1. The Commission shall not deal with any petition submitted [by an individual] which:
   (a) is anonymous, or
   (b) is substantially the same as a matter which has already been examined by the Commission or has already been submitted to another procedure of international investigation or settlement and if it contains no relevant new information.
2. The Commission shall consider inadmissible any petition . . . which it considers incompatible with the provisions of the present Convention, manifestly ill-founded, or an abuse of the right of petition.

[99] DR 28/138
[100] DR 54/178
[101] DR 45/269; and *see also* DR 47/27

Anonymity

Anonymous complaints are inadmissible. However, the application form contains provision for the complainant to request that his or her identity not be disclosed. Although the Commission's decision on this point is final, it has invariably respected the individual's wishes (p. 17).

Petitions 'substantially the same' as previous applications

This restriction is aimed at preventing successive applications by the same applicant in respect of the same facts. The Commission does not interpret the provision as restricting applications in respect of different instances even if the issues are substantially the same as previous applications. Likewise the provision does not restrict a second complaint where new facts have arisen (facts not in existence or known at the time of the first complaint). Such a situation can commonly occur either:

(a) where the first complaint is rejected on the ground that a local remedy has not been exhausted; the applicant then exhausts that remedy and submits a second complaint (the new facts being that the domestic remedies have now been exhausted and the alleged violation has not been remedied by the domestic law); or

(b) where a complaint is made about the excessive delay of legal proceedings in contravention of Article 6(1) (the right to a fair and public hearing within a reasonable time) and rejected by the Commission on the ground that the delay does not as yet amount to a violation. The continuation of the proceedings for a significant further period after rejection may subsequently be such as to constitute a new fact which allows the Commission to examine a new complaint[102].

Examination by another international body

This restriction has not arisen in practice. Potentially a U.K. complainant may have a choice of complaining either to the European Commission of Human Rights or to the United Nations Human Rights Committee. At present the U.K. has not signed the optional protocol which would enable the UN Human Rights Committee to receive individual complaints and accordingly this conflict of complaint possibilities does not yet exist. The UN Human Rights Committee is discussed at p. 224.

[102] DR 48/102

Whether the European Court of Justice at Luxembourg constitutes another international investigation has not yet been determined, although it is doubtful[103].

Incompatible with the provisions of the present Convention

Many complaints made to the Commission fall outside the scope of the Convention. Obviously these include cases where the complainant is not within the jurisdiction of a signatory State. It also includes cases where the complaint is not directed against the state at all. Complaints made against individuals or non-governmental organisations are incompatible with the Convention unless there is evidence to show that the state caused, permitted or was responsible for the alleged violation. Individuals acting in an official capacity may represent the state but this is not invariably the case. A solicitor for instance, although an officer of the court, is not deemed to be a state representative by the Commission. The European Communities is not a signatory State and therefore complaints may not be directed against it as such[104].

Many complaints are deemed incompatible because they do not concern the rights or freedoms protected by the Convention. These have included complaints relating to the right to work, the right to nature conservation, the right to compensation for injuries as a result of an accident, the right to free choice of medical assistance, the right to a driver's licence, the right to conscientious objection, the right to linguistic freedom, the right of appeal as such, the right to diplomatic protection, the right to financial assistance from the state, the right to housing and the right to hold a position in public service.

Manifestly ill founded

The term 'manifestly ill founded' is interpreted by the Commission as applying to complaints which, on a preliminary examination, do not disclose *any possible ground* upon which it could be established that the Convention has been violated. In fact, it is not so much a test of '*any possible ground*' as a '*prima facie*' test. Indeed the Commission in pursuit of its screening rôle often appears to go further than merely requiring the establishment of *prima facie* grounds; in cases of doubt it could sometimes be accused of rejecting cases which it considers weak even though on an objective analysis the *prima facie* admissibility test had been satisfied. 'Manifestly ill founded' also encompasses complaints

[103] *See* note 51 *above*
[104] DR 13/231

based upon facts which are demonstrably wrong or incapable of substantiation.

Abuse of the right of petition

The fact that an applicant's motives for complaining are impure does not in itself make the complaint an abuse of the right to petition. That a complaint is motivated primarily by the desire for publicity or propaganda or a wish to make a political point, therefore, does not constitute sufficient grounds in itself for the complaint to be rejected.

An inadmissibility ruling on this ground may arise if the complaint contains obviously untrue evidence or where the complainant is demonstrably vexatious (for instance because he has previously submitted a large number of meritless applications). The repeated failure of a complainant to respond to Commission correspondence may also result in a determination of 'abuse of right to petition'.

In some cases the use of offensive language in a complaint may be considered an abuse of the right to petition.

A flagrant breach by the applicant of the requirement of confidentiality may be deemed sufficient to require a rejection of the complaint under this provision.

An abuse of the right to petition is closely connected with the principle articulated by Article 17 (the absence of a right to undermine the rights of others). *See* p.198.

PRE-ADMISSIBILITY PROCEDURE

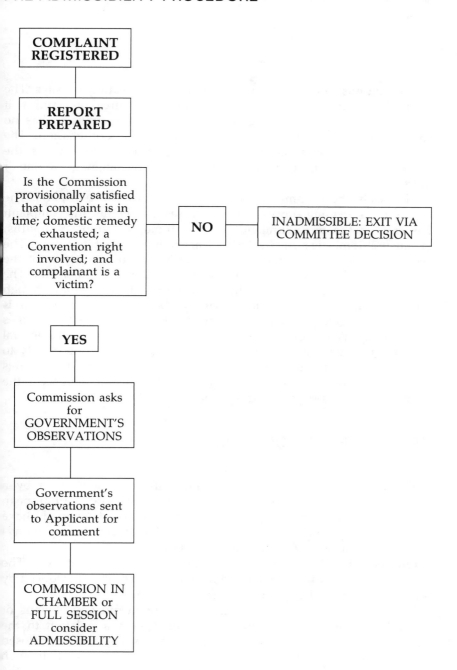

COMPLAINT REGISTERED

REPORT PREPARED

Is the Commission provisionally satisfied that complaint is in time; domestic remedy exhausted; a Convention right involved; and complainant is a victim?

NO — INADMISSIBLE: EXIT VIA COMMITTEE DECISION

YES

Commission asks for GOVERNMENT'S OBSERVATIONS

Government's observations sent to Applicant for comment

COMMISSION IN CHAMBER or FULL SESSION consider ADMISSIBILITY

3 The Commission

The Commission can deal with a complaint in a variety of ways. The method it adopts depends primarily on the degree of scrutiny it believes the complaint to require. In the main the applicant has no control over which mechanism is chosen by the Commission. The applicant's aim must be to use each opportunity to express the complaint clearly and to relate it directly, in simple language, to one or more of the Convention Articles.

Classically the Commission's investigation falls into two parts. The first is the screening process where it assesses whether the complaint has crossed the procedural hurdles (*i.e.* brought within six months, exhausted domestic remedies, etc.). This is the admissibility stage. The second phase is the Commission's investigation of the merits of the complaint and includes the possibility of a friendly settlement. The second phase only arises after the first has proved successful. Although the two parts are dealt with separately below, the Commission is increasingly looking in detail at the merits of a complaint as it examines admissibility. Where observations on admissibility are sought or an oral hearing arranged, the Commission will seek to use the opportunity to obtain comment and information on the merits at the same time. In this Chapter reference to 'Rules' is (unless otherwise stated) a reference to the Commission Rules *see* p. 8 and Appendix 3, p. 243.

RECEIPT OF THE COMPLAINT

The initial letter to the Commission will be acknowledged by a member of the Secretariat on behalf of the Secretary to the European Commission of Human Rights. Although Secretariat lawyers do have knowledge of other states' legal systems, the lawyer dealing with a U.K. complaint will generally be a U.K. lawyer.

On receipt of the letter a provisional file will be opened. The complaint will not be registered immediately unless it is introduced by a lawyer and complies with the formal requirements.

The first letter from the Secretariat may point out any obvious or potential admissibility difficulties that could exist in relation to the complaint. Copies of similar reported complaints may also be enclosed to focus the issues of difficulty perceived by the Secretariat. In such cases it is prudent to telephone the Secretariat lawyer to discuss the best way forward or whether he or she considers the admissibility obstacle to be overwhelming.

The Commission cannot refuse to register a complaint; however there is little to be gained from pursuing a complaint in the face of hard evidence from the Secretariat showing why such a complaint would be doomed to an early inadmissibility decision.

There is at this stage a high fall-out rate. In 1990 for instance, of the 4942 provisional files opened by the Commission, only 1657 complaints were actually registered. Of the two-thirds that fail to result in formal complaints, the vast bulk lapse as a result of the comments in the Secretariat's response: that the applicant is out of time, that domestic remedies have not been exhausted, that the issue raised is not a point covered by the Convention, etc. It should be realised that as anyone can write to the Commission, they inevitably receive each year quite a number of bizarre complaints. They have no choice in every case but to open a provisional file, and if the correspondent insists, on formally registering the complaint.

With the first letter from the Secretariat will be the application form and a letter of authority, if the complainant proposes to be legally represented in the proceedings. The Commission Rules[1] are quite relaxed about representation, provided the Commission is supplied with the letter of authority. The applicant can conduct his or her own case or be represented by a lawyer or any other person [2], subject to the Commission deciding otherwise. The rules of representation are considerably stricter in the Court, where the applicant is in general not permitted to act in person and required to have qualified legal representation[3].

Because of previous difficulties with dilatory complainants, the Secretariat now stipulates that the completed application form and all relevant documents should be returned within a period of six weeks. Provided the time limit is met, the date for the introduction of the complaint will normally be taken as the date of the applicant's first letter.

On receipt of the completed forms the Secretariat (in accordance with Rule 14) formally registers the complaint, the date of its deemed registration (usually the date of the complainant's first letter to the Commission) and assigns to it a file reference number.

The Secretariat's letter acknowledging receipt of the complaint stipulates the reference number (which must be quoted in all future correspondence) and the date the complaint is deemed to have been

[1] Rule 32(2) of the Commission Rules
[2] *See for instance* DR 11/221 where the applicant's representative before the Commission was a religious charity worker
[3] *See* p. 75 and Rule 30 of the Court Rules

introduced. In addition the letter specifically reminds the applicant that the contents of case files, including the observations of the parties and correspondence, are of a confidential nature and must not be made public.

Much of the Commission's correspondence is standardised. The reference on their letters will often contain not only the initials of the Secretariat lawyer dealing with the application, but also the letters 'SL' followed by a number. This stands for Standard Letter and the number refers to the particular precedent letter.

RAPPORTEUR'S INVESTIGATION

Rule 47 stipulates that once a complaint has been registered, it:

1. . . . shall be referred to a member of the Commission who, as rapporteur, shall examine the application and submit a report to the Commission on its admissibility and a proposal on the procedure to be adopted.
2. Rapporteurs, in their examination of the application:
   (a) may request relevant information on matters connected with the application, from the applicant or the [state] concerned;
   (b) shall communicate any information so obtained from the [state] to the applicant for comments;
   (c) shall decide whether to refer the application to a Committee.
3. The report of the rapporteur on the admissibility of the application shall contain:
   (a) a statement of the relevant facts, including any information or comments obtained under paragraph 2 of this Rule;
   (b) if necessary, an indication of the issues arising under the Convention in the application;
   (c) a proposal on admissibility and on any other action to be taken, as the case may require.

The President of the Commission selects the Commissioner who is to act as rapporteur for the particular complaint. The President tries to balance the case load of all the Commissioners, but the choice will, of course, be restricted to those familiar with the legal issues raised by the complaint. The rapporteur's identity is not disclosed to the applicant.

The actual degree of involvement by a rapporteur in the investigation of the complaint varies from one rapporteur to another. Some are content to leave the bulk of the investigation to the Secretariat lawyer, whereas others take on a far more active rôle. As the Secretariat is full-time and the Commissioners are not, inevitably the Secretariat fulfils a more important rôle in the handling of a complaint than a bare reading of Rule 47 would at first suggest. If the complaint is obviously defective or hopeless then the rapporteur's rôle will be minimal: merely endorsing the Secretariat's assessment and referring the case to the Committee procedure (*see below*) for early rejection. All steps however are overseen by the rapporteur and he or she is responsible for the investigation.

In theory the rapporteur's rôle at this stage is to ascertain whether the complaint is admissible. As has already been pointed out[4], a complaint can be ruled inadmissible because it is 'manifestly ill founded' or so lacking in merit as to be hopeless. In practice the merits of the complaint and the admissibility criteria are both of relevance to the rapporteur.

The Secretariat or rapporteur will at an early stage formulate a view as to whether the complaint raises issues of substance. It is vital therefore that the essence of the complaint is expressed in simple and immediate terms.

Where the complaint shows apparent merit the Secretariat will prepare a summary of the facts. This often involves further correspondence/telephone discussions with the complainant to clarify any unclear points. Rule 47 also enables requests to be made to the state for information and in such cases for this information to be referred to the applicant for his or her comments. Such a request to the state does not constitute 'communication' of the complaint to the state. Such requests are seldom made in routine, non-urgent complaints cases.

The summary of facts constitutes the first part of the rapporteur's report. The report also contains a section dealing with the 'Relevant Domestic Law and Practice' and a summary of the complaints made by the applicant. In addition, the rapporteur (or frequently the Secretariat) prepares a set of questions that he or she suggests that the state be asked; the object of which is to probe the issue(s) at the heart of the complaint. Finally the report contains the rapporteur's view on admissibility and whether the complaint should be considered by the full Commission or a Chamber (*see below*). The report is then considered by the Commission.

COMMUNICATION TO THE GOVERNMENT

Rule 48 stipulates:

1. The Commission shall consider the report of the rapporteur and may declare at once that the application is inadmissible or to be struck off its list.
2. Alternatively, the Commission may:
   (a) request relevant information on matters connected with the application from the applicant or the [state] concerned. Any information so obtained from the [state] shall be communicated to the applicant for comments;
   (b) give notice to the [state] against which it is brought and invite that party to present to the Commission written observations on the application. Any

[4] *See* p. 37

observations so obtained shall be communicated to the applicant for any written observations in reply.

Where the Commission is satisfied that the application shows merit it will decide that it should be communicated to the government. In its deliberations the Commission may amend or add to the questions to be put to the government. The government is then sent the rapporteur's report (with the exception of his or her preliminary views on admissibility), together with the set of questions it is requested to answer. At the same time the applicant is notified of this step and sent a copy of the papers. In addition the applicant will be invited to apply for legal aid, if this is relevant.

Whilst the original complaint may have ranged widely, and invoked a number of Articles, the questions asked of the government may be restricted to a few Articles and the government told that its observations are not sought in respect of the other complaints. The questions may be straightforward, for instance: 'Does the . . . constitute an interference with the applicant's right to respect for family and private life contrary to Article 8 of the Convention?'

Alternatively if the issue is complex the inquiry may be broken into a number of basic questions, for instance: 'Does the applicant's Article 8 rights oblige the state to . . .? If so, is it appropriate that . . .?'

The Commission requests at the time of communicating the complaint that the government give its observations within a specified period, usually within six weeks, although frequently the government requests an extension of this period. Typically extensions are granted for a further three weeks depending upon the complexity of the issues, etc. Not unusually the government will fax its observations to the Commission on the final day of the deadline, sending the hard copy and annexes by post to arrive later.

THE GOVERNMENT'S RESPONSE

The government's observations on the admissibility of the complaint are generally set out in a statement subdivided into four main sections together with an annexe containing copies of the texts to which the statement refers. The statement usually comprises a summary of (1) the facts; (2) the law and practice; (3) admissibility and merits; (4) conclusions.

(1) The Facts. The statement will set out the government's view as to the facts surrounding the alleged violation of the Convention.

The government will not always confine itself to the facts. Often it will stray into the arena of making value judgments based upon its outline of the facts.

The government will have access to a number of different sources of information and will not hesitate to use them, if they show that the applicant has misled the Commission in any way.

During the preparation of its response the relevant government department may write requesting that the applicant provide a letter of authority to enable background information to be obtained from a third-party source. Obviously it may be difficult to know how to deal with such a request. On the one hand there is the wish to be seen to have nothing to hide; on the other, there is the applicant's right to respect for his or her privacy. If such a request is made, its extent and purpose should be clarified. The relevant department should be asked to put in writing precisely what information it wants and why, and the letter of authority drawn accordingly.

(2) **The Law and Practice.** The government will here provide a detailed analysis of what it considers to be the domestic law relating to the complaint, and what it considers to be the relevant legal safeguards. Where necessary it may draw upon governmental or other reports or inquiries. If the safeguards include an element of ministerial action, the government will set out what present and past ministers have done. As with the statement of facts, whilst the government's legal analysis may be the truth, it may not be the whole truth. What is left out of the legal analysis is often of considerable significance.

(3) **Admissibility and Merits.** This section primarily deals with the questions communicated to the government by the Commission. Not infrequently the government will make a preliminary point by alleging that the application fails to satisfy one of the basic admissibility grounds, *i.e.* a failure to exhaust domestic remedies[5].

In general the government will argue everything; and will do so with great skill. It will reject alleged violations both in respect of the substantive right, and by analysing the qualifications permitted by the Convention to that right.

(4) **Conclusions.** The government's conclusions are generally purely formal in requesting the Commission to declare the application inadmissible.

APPLICANT'S REPLY

The government's reply is copied to the applicant for comment, with similar time limits being imposed. If the time given for the reply is inadequate then an extension will almost invariably be granted. To obtain an extension, a letter or fax should be sent to the Commission

See p. 24

explaining why the extra time is required, and suggesting the preferred new deadline for response.

Typically the extension will be of the same order as granted to the government, usually three weeks. Obviously longer extensions can be made if the reason is substantial. If for a genuine reason it becomes impossible to meet the amended deadline then the Commission will often be flexible over an extra day or so, provided it is telephoned and the difficulty explained. As with the procedure adopted by the government, the Commission does not object to the reply being sent by fax on the day of the deadline, with the hard copy and annexes (if any) following on by post.

Sometimes the government's response may raise issues which can only be replied to if information, correspondence or other material is disclosed by the government. A request for such material should be addressed to the government's agent (whose name will appear at the end of the government's observations), at the Foreign and Commonwealth Office, London, SW1A 2AH. The request should explain precisely what is required and why. The request should be as limited as possible and not appear to be a general probe for information. It should be shown to arise directly from what has been raised by the government in its observations.

CONSIDERATION BY THE COMMISSION

Ultimately the admissibility of a complaint is decided by a Commissioners' meeting. The type of meeting is determined by the nature of the complaint, and may be by committee, chamber or a full session of the Commission.

Article 20(2)–(5) provides:

2. The Commission shall sit in plenary session. It may, however, set up chambers, each composed of at least seven members. The chambers may examine petitions . . . which can be dealt with on the basis of established case law or which raise no serious question affecting the interpretation or application of the Convention. Subject to this restriction and to the provisions of paragraph 5 of this article, the chambers shall exercise all the powers conferred on the Commission by the Convention.

   The member of the Commission elected in respect of a [state] against which a petition has been lodged shall have a right to sit on a chamber to which the petition has been referred.

3. The Commission may set up committees, each composed of at least three members, with the power, exercisable by a unanimous vote, to declare inadmissible or strike from its list of cases a petition . . ., when such a decision can be taken without further examination.

4. A chamber or committee may at any time relinquish jurisdiction in favour of the plenary Commission which may also order the transfer to it of any petition referred to a chamber or committee.

5. Only the plenary Commission can exercise the following powers:
   (a) the examination of applications [made by states];
   (b) the bringing of a case before the Court [Article 48];
   (c) the drawing up of rules of procedure [Article 36].

Committee hearings

The committee system was introduced to enable the Commission to reduce its substantial backlog of complaints by providing a quicker system for rejecting cases considered to have an obvious defect; for instance, because they had failed to exhaust local remedies, were out of time or did not involve a right protected by the Convention.

The committee process is referred to as the Short Summary Procedure. The committees are composed of a minimum of three Commissioners. In 1993 there were six such committees operating from a total of 22 Commissioners. Three committees sit during each session of the Commission with the other three sitting at the next session and so on.

A committee may dispose of a relatively large number of complaints at a single sitting. During a Commission session each committee may get through 50 or 60 cases. The committee sit in private with members of the Secretariat in attendance. The rapporteur's report will set out the details of the particular complaint and recommend rejection on specified grounds. The Commissioners on the committee will often accept the recommendation with little or no discussion. Complaints referred to the committee can only be declared inadmissible if the Commissioners are unanimous. In general only hopeless complaints are referred to the committees. Sometimes a Commissioner may request additional information about a matter (in which case the file is obtained and the answer extracted) but it is rare for a case to survive the procedure. If unanimity does not exist however, the case is automatically transferred to a chamber.

If during the procedure a complaint is thought to warrant further examination, it is referred back to the Commission for separate consideration.

Chamber hearings

Whilst the majority of obviously hopeless cases are weeded out in the committees by the short summary procedure, the remainder are either examined by a chamber or at a full session of the Commission. Only those complaints which cannot be dealt with on the basis of established case law or which raise fundamental questions concerning the application or interpretation of the Convention are dealt with by a full session of the Commission. By way of example in the June/July 1992 session of the Commission, an admissibility decision was taken on 169 cases of which 119 were determined by committee, 26 by chamber and 24 by a full session of the Commission. It is expected in time that the chambers will hear a greater proportion of non-committee cases.

The Commission Rules stipulate:

Rule 49

1. An application shall be referred to a Chamber unless it has been referred to a Committee . . . or its examination by a Chamber is excluded under Article 20(2) [see above].
2. Applications shall normally be referred to the Chamber which includes the member of the Commission elected in respect of the [state] against which the application is made.
3. If there is a reasoned request from a party that the application should be referred to the Plenary Commission, that request shall be considered by the Plenary Commission.
4. The members of the Commission shall be informed of the decisions of the Chambers.

Rule 50

Before deciding upon the admissibility of the application, the Commission may invite the parties:

(a) to submit further observations in writing;
(b) to submit further observations orally at a hearing on issues of admissibility and at the same time, if the Commission so decides, on the merits of the application.

Once the rapporteur (with the assistance of the Secretariat) has obtained all the necessary information, he or she will prepare a brief for the Commission. If the issues are unusual or complex, the information gathering process may involve a number of separate questions and further questions to the state with the applicant being given an opportunity to comment in each case on the replies received.

The Commission will consider the rapporteur's brief and may decide there and then to reject the complaint, without further investigation or hearing. Failing such an inadmissibility ruling, the Commission may proceed to decide admissibility without hearing the parties, although frequently it will decide to convene an oral hearing. Before the hearing the state and the applicant will be invited to send their final arguments to the Commission so that these submissions can be translated and be available to the Commissioners at the hearing. The hearings in general take half a day (usually a morning), with the parties each allowed about 45 minutes to elaborate and clarify their case. The submissions made at the hearing need to be short, clear statements that will focus the Commissioners' minds on the key elements of the case. As ever the difficulties of translation must be appreciated and idiom avoided. Factual argument at the hearing should also be avoided if at all possible: hearings are not well equipped to deal with evidential matters.

ORAL HEARINGS

Oral hearings are very important occasions. From the Commissioners' viewpoint, a case can come alive at a hearing; it follows too that a case can also be buried by poor presentation and preparation. The U.K. Government's agents and representatives are extremely capable in presenting the Government case at such hearings.

It is important to concentrate throughout on the Convention, and at admissibility hearings to show that the issues are sufficiently substantial to warrant further examination of their merits. The chances of success at an admissibility hearing are no more than one in four, so substantial preparation is required.

Oral hearing procedures before the Commission follow the same format and are subject to the same rules. They are always in private. The notice of hearing will set out the hearing's purpose; the facts or issues which the Commission wishes to establish/investigate.

The state will normally be represented by counsel, frequently Queen's Counsel, who will appear together with one or more 'agents' from the Foreign Office's Council of Europe Unit, who in turn will be accompanied by several advisers (departmental experts and lawyers). The applicant can appear in person or with the assistance of a representative. Unlike the Court Rules[6], the Commission Rules place little restriction upon who can act as the applicant's representative. Rule 32 allows 'a lawyer or any other person, resident in a Convention country, unless the Commission at any stage decides otherwise'. The Commission can summon any witness whose attendance it considers necessary, although it has no real power to compel attendance. The summons to the applicant (and any witness) will specify the arrangements proposed to reimburse travelling and subsistence expenses [7].

At least 14 days before the hearing, the parties may file a statement setting out, in as much detail as they wish, the further submissions they propose to make to the Commission at the hearing. There are advantages and disadvantages in filing such a statement. The advantage being that it is copied (and where necessary translated) to the Commissioners prior to the hearing, ensuring that they are conversant with the principal issues raised by the complaint and ready to ask relevant questions. The disadvantage is that it is copied to the Government, forewarning its representatives of the likely line of argument; frequently the Government does not itself file further evidence. Where it is the Government that is to open the oral hearing it is therefore sometimes wise to keep one's options open by not making

[6] *See* note 4 *above*
[7] *See* p. 97

a further statement. Where further evidence is filed, it should be concise; there is a general perception among continental judges that whilst U.K. lawyers' advocacy is second to none, this is not so when it comes to their ability to file concise skeleton summaries of the key points of a case. There tends to be an excess of detail in such written material, and a loss of the principle issues of a case.

At least 10 days before the hearing the Commission must be notified of the names and functions of the persons who will appear on the applicant's behalf. The Commission has the power to limit the number of representatives or advisers present. Those present at the hearing include the parties, their witnesses (if any), the Commissioners and the Secretariat, as well as interpreters who give simultaneous interpretation. The hearings are in English or French, although permission can be given for any person to speak in another language if he or she has insufficient knowledge of French or English. The notification letter accompanying the details of the hearing advises that the parties should:

(a) bear in mind that many of those present will be listening to the proceedings in a language which is not their own;

(b) speak clearly and at a moderate speed;

(c) if speaking from a prepared text, make a copy available before the hearing for the exclusive use of the interpreters—even an outline or notes of what is to be said can be helpful—and there is no need to adhere rigidly to the text provided.

Evidence at the hearings (which is rare) is given under oath/declaration, the form of which is prescribed by the Rules. Conduct of the hearing is rather like a meeting, with all questions nominally being put through the President. Robes are not worn and the representatives remain seated whilst making their submissions. The hearings are held in the Commission's meeting room in the Human Rights Building.

On arrival at the Human Rights Building the parties are provided with a security pass and then shown to a private office/consulting room. Shortly before the hearing the representatives meet the President who outlines the proposed arrangements.

At the hearing (plenary) the Commissioners sit on the outside of a large horseshoe-shaped table, with the President and Secretary at the top. On entering, the parties are handed a seating plan identifying the individual Commissioners.

The representatives each sit at the bottom of (and perpendicular to) one of the open ends of the horseshoe, facing the Commissioners. Behind the representatives are tables for their agents, etc. All tables are equipped with headphones for simultaneous translation.

The proceedings are recorded on tape from which the Secretariat subsequently prepares a verbatim record. The hearing normally occupies the first part of the morning (9.00 am to 11.00 am with a short break in between). The state usually speaks first followed by the applicant; each speaking for about 30 minutes.

It is seldom possible to predict how the state will use its 30 minutes. In its preparation it will of course have access to substantial information about the background to the case. In its oral submissions it may choose therefore to launch a forthright and possibly unflattering broadside against the character of the applicant or highlight any misleading or contentious statements in the complaint papers[8]; alternatively the state may choose to concentrate upon an admissibility requirement upon which the Commission has not hitherto sought observations or otherwise raised with the applicant.

After the parties' opening addresses the President will indicate that he and/or other Commissioners have certain questions, and these will then be asked by the individual Commissioners. It is sensible to note the name of the Commissioner and the details of the question, as an immediate response to the questions is not required. After the various questions have been asked the session is adjourned for about 20 minutes and the parties return to their consulting rooms to consider their responses to the questions and to prepare their final submissions.

Once the hearing is reconvened the parties each have 15 minutes to deliver their responses/final submissions; the state representative again speaking first. At the conclusion the President thanks the parties and asks them to leave so that the Commissioners can deliberate in private.

Outside, the parties will be met by members of the Secretariat and asked to deal with the following:

1. A draft Press Release will have been prepared setting out the main facts of the complaint (but obviously at this stage lacking the Commissioners' decision). The Secretariat requires the draft to be approved by the parties so that it can be released as soon as the Commission's decision is announced.
2. The Secretariat will want to know the whereabouts of the parties that afternoon, so that the Commissioners' decision can be telephoned/faxed to them as soon as it is known. Alternatively a party can agree to return to the Human Rights Building later on; this can provide an opportunity to gain an informal reaction to the decision, including an initial indication as to the Commission's reasons.

---

[8] Counsel of Europe Information Sheet 28 shows how rugged oral applications can become on occasions; counsel for the government in *Kostovski* v. *Netherlands,* (12 E.H.R.R. 434; November 20, 1989, Series A, No. 166) in the course of argument stated "the proceedings at various stages of the investigations show that the defence lawyers were more interested in putting together the file to submit to the European Court than in providing an effective defence of their client's rights". This provoked a formal complaint from the applicant's lawyer, which resulted in the Court confirming that lawyers have immunity where their statements do not go beyond acceptable limits, under Article 2 of the European Agreement relating to Persons Participating in Proceedings in the European Commission and Court of Human Rights 1969

3. Where Council of Europe legal aid has been granted, a clerical member of the Secretariat will wish to finalise the claim and make arrangements for payment; payment in cash can be made, although in general the Commission prefers to make payment by direct bank transfer. Parties should therefore bring with them their air tickets/counterfoils as proof of payment, together with the bank account details. It is also wise to take a prepared claim form, detailing the total amount claimed; stipulating for instance that two days subsistence expenses are sought (in view of the early commencement times for Commission hearings, travel to Strasbourg on the preceding day is unavoidable).

Post-hearing procedure

In the late morning or early afternoon, in the absence of the parties, the Commissioners discuss the case and reach a decision on admissibility. If they are not unanimous then the decision is taken by a majority vote (Article 34).

A press release is issued by the Commission after the hearing, giving a basic outline of the case; the details of which are agreed by the representatives prior to publication.

After the hearing the Secretariat is left to complete proceedings. This consists of telephoning the state agent and applicant to advise them of the decision. The Secretariat then collates its notes with the rapporteur with a view to preparing a draft record of the decision. Their record of the applicant's submission is sent to the applicant about four weeks after the hearing, who is required within a specified time limit (usually 28 days) to approve or correct and return it. The draft report of the decision is then considered by the Commission and the final version approved. This process takes about a month.

The Commission's reasoned decision on admissibility is usually sent to the parties about six weeks after the hearing. In format it resembles any short law report. It records the facts of the case, the complaint(s), the law as applied to the Convention and the Commissioners' decision. The report will state whether it was a unanimous or majority decision. If the decision is by a majority, the decision will not say (nor will the Secretariat) what the actual majority was or which way the individual Commissioners voted. A copy of the decision is sent to the applicant.

If the Commission declares the application inadmissible, that is the end of the matter. If, however, the complaint is declared admissible, it enters the next phase of scrutiny: that of a detailed examination of its merits. Essentially the complainant, having crossed the procedural hurdles, now has to persuade the Commission that the complaint discloses a fundamental violation of one or more of the Convention Articles.

ADMISSIBILITY FLOW CHART

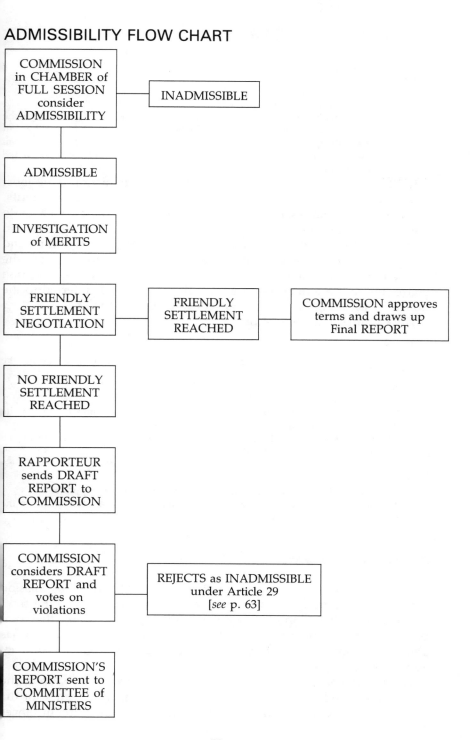

COMMISSION in CHAMBER of FULL SESSION consider ADMISSIBILITY

INADMISSIBLE

ADMISSIBLE

INVESTIGATION of MERITS

FRIENDLY SETTLEMENT NEGOTIATION

FRIENDLY SETTLEMENT REACHED

COMMISSION approves terms and draws up Final REPORT

NO FRIENDLY SETTLEMENT REACHED

RAPPORTEUR sends DRAFT REPORT to COMMISSION

COMMISSION considers DRAFT REPORT and votes on violations

REJECTS as INADMISSIBLE under Article 29 [see p. 63]

COMMISSION'S REPORT sent to COMMITTEE of MINISTERS

EXAMINATION OF MERITS

Article 28 stipulates:

1. In the event of the Commission accepting a petition referred to it:
   (a) It shall, with a view to ascertaining the facts, undertake together with the representatives of the parties an examination of the petition and, if need be, an investigation, for the effective conduct of which the states concerned shall furnish all necessary facilities, after an exchange of views with the Commission.

In its consideration of admissibility, the Commission will most probably have invited submissions from the state on its merits. Inevitably the Commission will have formed a generalised view as to the merits of the complaint. It is necessary for it to have a complete and thorough understanding of all of the legal issues (both domestic and European) in order for it to discharge its further obligations under the Convention: which may include assisting in the friendly negotiation phase, preparing a final report and, if the complaint is referred to the Court, by assisting the Court in its consideration of the case.

The Commission Rules stipulate:

Rule 53

1. After deciding to admit an application, the Commission shall decide on the procedure to be adopted:
   (a) for the examination [of the merits];
   (b) with a view to securing a friendly settlement.
2. In order to accomplish its [examination of the merits] the Commission may invite the parties to submit further evidence and observations.
3. The Commission shall decide in each case whether observations should be submitted in writing or orally at a hearing.

Rule 54

1. The Commission shall appoint one or more of its members as rapporteur.
2. The rapporteur may at any stage of the examination of an application invite the parties to submit further written evidence and observations.

Assessing the merits

Having decided that a complaint is admissible, the Commission appoints a rapporteur to carry out a detailed examination of the case. The extent of the rapporteur's investigation depends upon the complexity of the complaint and the degree to which the Commission has already examined the merits when considering the question of admissibility.

The Court has emphasised that under the Convention system the investigation and verification of the facts are primarily a matter for the Commission and that it would only be in exceptional circumstances that the Court would become involved in further fact-finding investiga-tions[9]. The Commission's findings are therefore vital and it is essential that the complainant's message is clearly communicated at this stage.

Where further evidence or observations on the merits are required from the parties then, as before, the Commission will state precisely what information is sought and will specify time limits within which the responses must be provided. Where further oral hearings are required, they will follow the same format as the admissibility hearing[10].

The Rules are drawn widely to allow the Commission considerable scope in deciding how to deal with the investigation. By Rule 34 it is empowered to take any action which it considers expedient or neces-sary for the proper performance of its duties. In particular, it may delegate one or more of its members to take any action, including examining documents and visiting any locality.

The rapporteur or other special delegates of the Commission can conduct their investigations other than in Strasbourg. This occurs very rarely and only when exceptional circumstances exist. In the interstate complaint *Ireland* v. *U.K.*[11], the Commission's delegates took evidence from 113 witnesses at seven separate hearings which occurred in London and Sola Air Base in Stavanger, Norway as well as in Strasbourg.

In general, investigations will only be conducted away from Strasbourg where serious state-sanctioned administrative malpractice is alleged, as was the case with the above interstate complaint and as occurred in Cyprus and Turkey; both of which states were visited by Commission delegates during the investigation of separate interstate complaints.

While the Commission may form its provisional view of the merits of the complaint when it determines the question of admissibility, it may, having heard further evidence on the merits, reach its provisional opinion at a later stage. This provisional view is orally and in confidence notified to the parties. The Commission's view is inevitably an influential factor in the possibility of the parties reaching a friendly settlement.

FRIENDLY SETTLEMENT PROCESS

The friendly settlement process is perhaps the centre-piece of the Convention. Politically it is advantageous for the state to resolve

[9] *Cruz Varas* v. *Sweden* 14 E.H.R.R. 1; March 20, 1991, Series A, No. 201
[10] See p. 49
[11] 2 E.H.R.R. 25; January 18, 1978, Series A, No. 25

violations, either within the domestic legal setting or, if this fails, voluntarily and without the need for censure by the Court or Committee of Ministers.

In the first 25 years of the Convention friendly settlements were rare. The fact that they now occur more frequently is largely due to the increasing case law from the decisions and reports of the Commission and the judgments of the Court. The development of an extensive case law has placed the parties in a much better position to predict the likely outcome before the Court. This in turn results in the states in particular being more willing to settle when they anticipate being condemned by the Court. That the conciliation process is in private may also encourage the state to explore a settlement if avoidance of adverse publicity is a factor. The benefits of a friendly settlement for an applicant are many; of particular relevance (especially in child care, immigration, etc., cases) is the avoidance of delay.

The friendly settlement phase runs in tandem with the Commission's investigation of the merits. The duty to promote such a settlement stems from Article 28(1)(b), which stipulates:

> [the Commission] shall at the same time [as investigating the merits], place itself at the disposal of the parties concerned with a view to securing a friendly settlement of the matter on the basis of respect for human rights as defined in this Convention.

In addition to being advised of the Commission's provisional view of the merits of the complaint, the Commission will write to the parties inviting them to put forward their views on the possibility of a friendly settlement. At this stage the Commission tends merely to act as a postbox: if the parties are interested in exploring a settlement, the Commission acts as a go-between, forwarding the respective proposals. If a settlement appears to be emerging, the Commission can be requested to provide more active assistance. It can, in such cases, act as a mediator; not unlike the rôle of ACAS in an employment dispute.

A friendly settlement which failed to address the violation at the heart of the complaint would conflict with the requirement that friendly settlements must be upon the basis of a respect for human rights, and in theory the Commission could refuse to endorse such a settlement.

Post-settlement procedure

If the Commission succeeds in effecting a friendly settlement, then it is required by Article 28(2) to draw up a brief report which, by Rule 57, contains details of the parties and their representatives, a statement of the facts and the terms of the settlement. The report is signed by the

President and the Secretary and is then sent to the state concerned, the Committee of Ministers, the applicant and the Secretary-General of the Council of Europe for publication. Subsequent to the signing of the report, the case is struck off the Commission's list in accordance with Article 30(1)(b).

The performance of friendly settlements negotiated during the Commission process are not supervised by the Committee of Ministers, unlike orders of the Court or friendly settlements negotiated during the Court procedure (which are rare). In practice, states have complied with all friendly settlements and so the issue of enforcement has not arisen.

Private settlements

A number of complaints are settled privately by the applicant and state concerned, without the involvement or sanction of the Commission. In such cases the Commission compiles a short report of what has occurred and strikes the complaint from its list. Obviously the Commission could, if it felt a serious violation had not been dealt with satisfactorily, continue its investigation and refuse to strike out the complaint. In practice this has not occurred.

McDermitt v. *U.K.*[12] is an example of a private settlement. The complaint concerned the applicant who was arrested in 1984 for breach of the peace as a result of which he spent 17 days in prison on remand. At the trial before a stipendiary magistrate he was refused legal aid despite qualifying on financial grounds. The applicant complained to the Commission who in due course convened an oral admissibility and merits hearing which did not however take place. Prior to the hearing the Government submitted to the applicant a statement admitting that the magistrate had misdirected himself and offering an *ex gratia* payment and to pay the applicant's legal costs. The offer was accepted and the applicant withdrew his complaint.

There are now many friendly settlements negotiated every year, of which the following are illustrative examples.

Examples of friendly settlements

Min v. *U.K.*[13]

A Burmese doctor working for the NHS complained that her Burmese husband and son could not remain with her in the U.K. for

[12] DR 52/244
[13] DR 48/58

more than six months. The situation was otherwise for the wives and children of foreign male doctors in the same situation.

The complaint was held admissible on March 14, 1984, shortly before the test case of *Abdulaziz, Cabales, and Balkandali*[14] came before the Court concerning a virtually identical point. The Government requested that the *Min* case be adjourned pending the Court decision, and subsequently granted the husband and son a 12-month (extendible) permit to remain. In addition the Government agreed to pay the applicant's costs amounting to £2,592.00 plus VAT.

Searle v. U.K.[15]

A prisoner complained that on at least two occasions his mother and sister went to visit him, only to be told on arrival that he had been transferred to another prison.

After the complaint was declared admissible on March 13, 1984, the applicant's solicitors and the Government exchanged correspondence, which was channelled through the Commission. A meeting was then arranged with the Secretary to the Commission in London to further the friendly settlement negotiations. At this meeting a settlement was concluded on the following terms:

(a) The Government undertook to amend the relevant Prison Circular Instruction to deal with the question of transfers at short notice.

(b) Out of pocket expenses were paid to the applicant's mother and sister incurred in respect of their abortive visits.

(c) The applicant's mother received a 'statement of regret' and the sum of £800 for the inconvenience caused.

(d) The Government agreed to pay the applicant's reasonable costs.

K. v. U.K.[16]

The applicant was the putative father of a child for whom the local authority had applied for a care order. The complaint (one of many) concerned the then law which did not recognise putative fathers as parties to such proceedings.

After the complaint was declared admissible on October 15, 1986, an exchange of correspondence took place between the parties and the Commission in which the comments by the Government upon proposed legislative changes indicated that a settlement was possible. As a result a meeting was arranged in London between the parties and the Secretary to the Commission accompanied by several members of the Secretariat. Outline agreement occurred at the meeting, which was subsequently concluded on the following terms:

[14] 7 E.H.R.R. 471; May 28, 1985, Series A, No. 94
[15] DR 50/70
[16] DR 56/138

(a) The Government confirmed that it would bring into force pending legislation that would go some way towards rectifying the problem experienced by putative fathers in such cases. This would occur 'as soon as possible'. In addition it would introduce legislation to rectify the balance of the problem 'as soon as the Parliamentary timetable allows'.

(b) The Government would make an *ex gratia* payment to the applicant, the 'amount to be negotiated between the parties, if necessary using the good offices of the Commission, in the light of the Article 50 judgments of the European Court of Human Rights in the *O.,H.,W.,B.,& R.* cases[17]. If the parties do not reach agreement within three months of these judgments, the amount will be determined, at the request of either of the parties, by the Commission'. (The sums awarded to the applicants in the *O.,H.,W.,B.,& R.*, cases varied from £5000–£12,000 for non-pecuniary losses.)

(c) The Government agreed to pay the applicant's legal costs which had been 'actually incurred, necessarily incurred and were reasonable as to *quantum*'.

Channel 4 TV v. U.K.[18]

Channel 4 and a production company agreed to produce a daily programme reporting the trial of Clive Ponting on charges under the Official Secrets Act. The programme was to be screened every evening and to consist of a studio reading of a transcript of the day's proceedings. At the opening of the case the trial judge made an order under the Contempt of Court Act banning the programme until the trial had finished. The judge refused to hear argument from Channel 4 or the production company as they had no standing in the proceedings. Channel 4, the production company and the National Union of Journalists complained to the Commission concerning the absence of a remedy against such an order. The complaints were declared admissible on March 9, 1987. The parties forwarded their views on a settlement to the Commission which then arranged for a meeting to be convened in London at which the parties attended together with the Secretary to the Commission and a member of the Secretariat. A settlement emerged on the following terms:

(a) The Government agreed to table an amendment to the Criminal Justice Bill enabling an aggrieved person to appeal (with leave) to the Court of Appeal against such an order.

(b) The Government agreed to pay 75 per cent. of the legal costs which had been 'actually incurred, necessarily incurred and were reasonable as to *quantum*'.

[17] 10 E.H.R.R. 29–95; July 8, 1978, Series A, No. 120–1; and 13 E.H.R.R. 449–588; Series A, No. 136A-E
[18] DR 56/156

COMMISSION'S FINAL REPORT

Where a friendly settlement has not occurred and the complaint has not been struck off for any other reason, (*i.e.* because the parties have reached a private agreement, or the applicant has shown no willingness to pursue the complaint) then Article 31 stipulates:

1. . . . the Commission shall draw up a report on the facts and state its opinion as to whether the facts found disclose a breach by the state concerned of its obligations under the Convention. The individual opinions of members of the Commission on this point may be stated in the report.
2. The report shall be transmitted to the Committee of Ministers. It shall also be transmitted to the states concerned, who shall not be at liberty to publish it.
3. In transmitting the report to the Committee of Ministers the Commission may make such proposals as it thinks fit.

The final stage of the Commission's scrutiny of a complaint consists of the Commission expressing its opinion on the merits of the application. When considering the question of admissibility the Commission makes a decision: it is the principal arbiter of this issue. When considering the question of the merits, the Commission expresses an opinion: the decision being made by the Committee of Ministers or Court.

The final report of the Commission is based upon a draft report drawn up by the rapporteur. This report may have formed the basis for the Commission's earlier provisional opinion on merits. The Commission considers the draft report and first of all agrees on a statement of the facts underlying the complaint. The Commissioners then deliberate and vote on whether, in their opinion, the agreed facts disclose any violation of the Convention. In many cases the Commission will vote unanimously that they do not believe that the facts disclose a violation of a particular Article of the Convention. This does not mean that the complaint is rejected, as it is the Court which is the final arbiter of what constitutes a violation. The vote is therefore taken merely to advise the Court of the Commission's view; the Commission's opinion is obviously highly influential.

Only the Commissioners involved in the deliberations are entitled to have their separate opinions expressed in the final report. The format of the final report is prescribed by Rule 60 which stipulates:

1. The Report shall contain:
   (a) a description of the parties, their representatives and advisers;
   (b) a statement of the proceedings followed before the Commission;
   (c) a statement of the facts established;
   (d) the complaints declared admissible;
   (e) the opinion of the Commission, with an indication of the number of members forming the majority, as to whether or not the facts found disclose any breach by the state concerned of its obligations under the Convention;

(f) the reasons upon which that opinion is based;

(g) any separate opinion of a member of the Commission.

2. The Report shall contain the names of the President and the members participating in the deliberations and [the] vote. It shall be signed by the President and by the Secretary.

3. It shall be sent, together with any proposal under Article 31(3) [see above] to the Committee of Ministers and to the [state] concerned.

Whilst the Rule (as with Article 31(3)) enables the Commission to communicate proposals to the Committee of Ministers with the report, the relevant procedure is in practice dealt with by the Committee of Ministers' Rules ('Article 32 Rules'). By Rule 6 of these Rules the Committee has made it clear that it does not consider the Commission entitled to make proposals when it believes that there has been no violation of the Convention; by Rule 9(2) of the same Rules, if the Committee decides that a violation has occurred, it 'may request the Commission to make proposals concerning in particular the appropriateness, nature and extent of just satisfaction for the injured party'.

The applicant does not at this stage receive a copy of the Commission's report. The report is, in general, only published when the case is referred to the Court or, if it is not so transferred, after the Committee of Ministers has made its decision.

With the transmission of its final report to the Committee of Ministers, the Commission's work is almost complete. It has however two remaining functions. The first concerns the question of whether the case should be transferred from the Committee of Ministers to the Court for final determination, see p. 65 below. The second concerns the appointment of one or more of its members to act as delegate(s) to take part in the consideration of the case before the Court if the case is transferred, see p. 74 below.

INTERIM MEASURES

Where a complaint concerns imminent risk of a danger to life, the Commission can be asked to make an interim request to the government to take steps to secure the applicant's safety pending consideration of the applicant's complaint to the Commission. Such requests usually relate to imminent extradition or deportations.

Rule 36 provides:

The Commission, or when it is not in session, the President, may indicate to the parties any interim measure the adoption of which seems desirable in the interests of the parties or the proper conduct of the proceedings before it.

In *Soering* v. *U.K.*[19] the applicant faced deportation to the U.S.A. on a murder charge where he risked a prolonged period of potentially

[19] 11 E.H.R.R. 439; July 7, 1989, Series A, No. 161

degrading treatment on 'death row'. Following a request to the Commission, the President indicated to the U.K. Government 'that it was desirable, in the interests of the parties and the proper conduct of the proceedings, not to extradite the applicant to the United States until the Commission had an opportunity to examine the application'. As a result of the request, the U.K. stayed the extradition for the duration of the Commission and subsequent Court proceedings.

In *Cruz Varas* v. *Sweden*[20] the Swedish Government upheld a decision to deport the applicants to Chile. The applicants claimed that they ran the risk of political persecution (including torture and serious ill-treatment) if deported. The complaint was lodged with the Commission on October 5, 1989. At 9.10 am on October 6 the agent for the Swedish government was informed of the Commission's request that the applicants not be deported 'until the Commission had an opportunity to examine the application further'. However the first applicant was expelled to Chile at 4.40 pm on the same day and the other applicants remained in hiding in Sweden.

The Court held (by the narrow majority of 10 votes to nine) that a Rule 36 indication did not place a binding obligation on the state concerned. It observed that states had almost always shown total compliance with such interim measure requests. Compliance, however, lay at the discretion of the state. If the state decided not to comply with a request, it 'knowingly assumes the risk of being found in breach of Article 3' and 'any such finding would have to be seen as aggravated by the failure to comply'.

In the *Cruz Varas* case the Swedish Government decided not to comply with the Commission's interim request. The deportation occurred and it transpired that the applicant did not suffer the feared ill-treatment. However at much the same time the Swedish Government also refused an interim request in relation to a Jordanian citizen. In *Mansi* v. *Sweden*[21] the applicant was expelled to Jordan where he did suffer serious ill-treatment despite the Swedish Government's belief that this would not occur. The Government rapidly agreed to a friendly settlement, allowed the applicant to permanently reside in Sweden and paid compensation and costs. In addition the settlement recorded that as 'the applicant had been expelled to Jordan after the President of the Commission had indicated to the Government that it was desirable that he should not be expelled, the Government in the context of the settlement regretted having done so'.

URGENT CASES

It is well known that the Convention complaints procedure is a slow process. In many cases the complaint will spend two or three years

---

[20] 14 E.H.R.R. 1; March 20, 1991, Series A, No. 201
[21] Application 15658/89, not yet published in Decisions and Reports

before the Commission and a further one or two years before the Court. Obviously in some cases there is a need for an expedited process. Often these will include those cases where the Commission has requested interim measures.

Rule 33 allows the Commission to depart from the usual procedure of dealing with applications in the order in which they become ready for examination, by enabling it 'to give precedence to a particular application'.

In cases of urgency, when the Commission is not in session, the President (or one of the Vice-Presidents) is empowered by Rule 34(3) to 'take any necessary action on behalf of the Commission'. In addition in cases of urgency the Secretary is authorised by Rule 46, 'without prejudice to the taking of any other procedural steps, to inform [the state concerned], by any available means, of the introduction of the application and of a summary of its objects'.

In the case of *Soering* v. *U.K.*[22] the application was lodged with the Commission on July 8, 1988 and was declared admissible on November 10, 1988. The Commission's final report was adopted on January 19, 1989 and was referred to the Court on January 25, 1989. The Court has similar rules concerning expedition of special cases and accordingly the case came before the court for final hearing on July 7, 1989 a day before the anniversary of its introduction before the Commission.

The case of *X* v. *France*[23] concerned the excessive length of French proceedings; the applicant being a hæmophiliac who was diagnosed HIV positive as a result of a blood transfusion. The complaint was lodged with the Commission on February 19, 1991 and the final Court decision was made on March 23, 1992; 50 days after the applicant had died. There are therefore procedural constraints within the present Convention system that make it virtually impossible for complaints to complete their passage from lodgment to judgment in significantly less than 12 months.

ARTICLE 29

Article 29 stipulates that:

> After it has accepted a petition . . . the Commission may nevertheless decide by a majority of two-thirds of its members to reject the petition, if in the course of its examination, it finds that the existence of one of the grounds for non-acceptance has been established.

Accordingly, even if the Commission has determined that an application is admissible, it is not precluded from changing its mind at a later

---

[22] *See* note 20 *above*
[23] 14 E.H.R.R. 483; March 23, 1992, Series A, No. 234-C

date if during the examination of its merits it discovers that one or more of the admissibility conditions have not in fact been satisfied. This late rejection of an application is rare. Such a decision may sometimes relate to only part of an application, as occurred in *Donnelly* v. *U.K.*[24] where after having held the application admissible the Commission subsequently decided that the applicants had not established 'exhaustion of domestic remedies' in respect of part of the application.

As will be seen *below* the Court is itself able to reject an application referred to it if it considers that the admissibility criteria have not been satisfied.

STRIKING OFF

Article 30 stipulates that:

1. The Commission may at any stage of the proceedings decide to strike a petition out of its list of cases where the circumstances lead to the conclusion that:
   (a) the applicant does not intend to pursue his petition, or
   (b) the matter has been resolved, or
   (c) for any other reason established by the Commission, it is no longer justified to continue the examination of the petition.
   However, the Commission shall continue the examination of a petition if respect for human rights as defined in this Convention so requires.
2. If the Commission decides to strike a petition out of its list after having decided to accept it, it shall draw up a report which shall contain a statement of the facts and the decision striking out the petition together with the reasons thereof. The report shall be transmitted to the parties, as well as to the Committee of Ministers for information. The Commission may publish it.
3. The Commission may decide to restore a petition to its list of cases if it considers that the circumstances justify such a course.

This general power of the Commission to control its list enables it to strike off cases where the applicant is not responding to the Commission's correspondence or otherwise has shown no inclination to purposefully pursue the complaint. It in theory enables the Commission to retain and investigate complaints which it considers raise serious Convention issues, even if the applicant no longer wishes to pursue them. In practice this rarely occurs although in *Tyrer* v. *U.K.*[25] the Commission decided not to accede to the applicant's request to withdraw *'since the case raised questions of a general character affecting the observance of the Convention which necessitated a further examination of the issues involved'*.

Mr Tyrer took no further part in the proceedings.

[24] DR 4/4
[25] 2 E.H.R.R. 1; April 25, 1978, Series A, No. 26

4 Committee of Ministers

An outline of the composition and duties of the Committee of Ministers is given at p. 9 *above*. In relation to human rights, the Committee has two important functions. Under Article 32 it has a decision-making function for complaints that are not referred to the Court. For reasons given *below*, this is an unsatisfactory function. Under Article 54 however, it has what has been termed its 'noble function', that of supervising the execution of Court judgments.

To reflect the Committee's two functions, it has adopted two sets of Rules. In this text they are referred to as the Article 32 Rules and the Article 54 Rules respectively. The Article 32 Rules now also contain an Appendix, which sets out the Committee's present views on a variety of ancillary points. Copies of the Rules and Appendix are at Appendix 4 to this text, p. 257.

DECISIONS ON THE MERITS

The final report of the Commission giving its opinion on the merits of the complaint is transmitted to the Committee of Ministers[1]. The Committee decide on the merits of the complaint, unless within three months of its transmission to the Committee it is referred to the Court. The three-month time period runs from the date of transmission to the Committee, and not the earlier date of the adoption by the Commission of its final report.

Article 32 stipulates:

1. If the question is not referred to the Court within a period of three months from the date of the transmission of the report to the Committee of Ministers, the Committee of Ministers shall decide by a majority of two-thirds of the members entitled to sit on the Committee whether there has been a violation of the Convention.
2. In the affirmative case the Committee of Ministers shall prescribe a period during which the [state] concerned must take the measures required by the decision of the Committee of Ministers.

---

[1] Article 31(2) and Rule 60(3) of the Commission Rules

3. If the [state] concerned has not taken satisfactory measures within the prescribed period, the Committee of Ministers shall decide [by a two-thirds majority] what effect shall be given to its original decision and shall publish the report.
4. [All state] Parties undertake to regard as binding on them any decision which the Committee of Ministers may take in application of the preceding paragraphs.

In the early days of the Convention, before all the states had recognised the compulsory jurisdiction of the Court, the Committee of Ministers was required to determine all manner of cases. Now that all the states have recognised the compulsory jurisdiction of the Court, the Committee's decision-making rôle is restricted to formally approving the Commission's reports in those cases not transferred to the Court.

The Committee now only considers cases which are without controversial or difficult Convention issues. Essentially these are in two categories, namely:

1. Those without any complex or important Convention issues (*i.e.* cases for which a Court precedent already exists: a category that is increasing as the area covered by decided Court cases increases); or
2. Those where the respondent state has implicitly acknowledged the injustice by taking steps to amend national law to ensure the injustice does not reoccur.

All other cases are referred by the Commission to the Court. This avoidance of the Committee of Ministers for non-routine cases occurs for two reasons. The first is that unlike the Court, the Committee is not a judicial body; it is considered inappropriate for controversial legal decisions to be made by a political body. The second ground relates to the Committee's past unreliability. Although the Committee has never rejected the Commission's final report, it has in five cases failed to achieve the required two-thirds majority to enable it to reach a decision (the last occasion being in 1988).

In these 'non-decision' cases the applicant is left in the worst of all situations. He or she will have navigated the difficult Convention procedures only to obtain nothing; not because the complaint lacks merit, but because a political body cannot muster a sufficient number of votes to decide. This situation is all the more unsatisfactory as not only can the respondent state vote, but also abstentions are permitted; these obviously reduce the possibility of an overall two-thirds majority being achieved. It is proposed that in due course the necessary majority be reduced to a simple majority (by Protocol 10). Nevertheless until such time as the Commission and Court system is reformed, it remains important that there is a body which can speedily 'rubber stamp' uncontroversial Commission decisions, without wasting valuable Court time.

Consideration by the Committee

Although the Article 32 Rules provide for the Committee to have all the necessary powers to reach a decision (including considering written or oral statements and hearing witnesses[2]) it would only be in the most exceptional circumstances that this would arise, as no case requiring such steps would generally be left to the Committee but transferred to the Court.

The Committee meets in private and all members are entitled to take part in the decision-taking and vote (including the respondent state's representative, although he or she is not permitted to chair the meeting)[3]. The Committee's workload of cases varies greatly although it is steadily increasing. On average the Committee meets to decide human rights cases seven or eight days a year, dealing with between one and five Article 32 cases and about the same number of Article 54 cases. The numbers obviously fluctuate. The majority of cases take about 15 months from their transfer to the Committee until a final decision, although the period ranges from a few months to almost three years.

Applicant's position

The applicant is not a party to the consideration of the complaint by the Committee, and has no standing at all. A letter explaining this is sent by the Secretary-General of the Council of Europe to the applicant when the Commission's final report of the complaint is transmitted to the Committee. By Article 31(2) the report is also sent to the respondent state. It is not at this stage published and the applicant only receives a copy at this time in exceptional circumstances: when, for instance, the Committee need a specific input from the applicant in order to resolve a particular problem (and this is rare). The applicant is unable to write to the Committee. Where he or she attempts to write directly, the Secretary-General sends an acknowledgment explaining that the correspondence will not be considered, although in appropriate cases it is pointed out that the applicant may submit a new application to the Commission if he or she wishes to invoke new information[4].

Although not obligatory, the Commission's report is published once the Committee have reached a decision, together with the Committee's decision[5].

An example of a typical final resolution of the Committee under Article 32 is given at Appendix 12.

Friendly settlements

There is no formal procedure for friendly settlements before the Committee (unlike the Commission) although such settlements do

[2] Rules 1 and 4 of Article 32 Rules
[3] Rule 7 of Article 32 Rules
[4] Paragraph 3d of the Appendix to Article 32 Rules
[5] Rule 9 *ter* Article 32 Rules

nevertheless occur[6]. The applicant is at an obvious disadvantage in such cases as, unlike the respondent state, he or she will not have seen the Commission's final report. The state will also be aware of any Commission recommendation concerning 'just satisfaction'. There are, however, advantages to a settlement at this stage; the state may wish to pre-empt an unfavourable Committee resolution and the applicant may obtain more favourable settlement terms.

Garzarolli v. *Austria*[7] illustrates such a settlement. The case concerned the excessive length of criminal proceedings, contrary to Article 6(1). The Commission's final report unanimously expressed the opinion that there had been a violation. During its examination of the case the Committee was advised by the parties that they had reached a friendly settlement, the terms of the settlement being that the applicant was granted a pardon by the Austrian President, in return for which the applicant agreed that the complaint be discontinued and that the Commission's report not be published. The Committee considered that the settlement was 'based on a respect for human rights' and therefore discontinued its examination of the case. The settlement gave the applicant a remedy which the Committee could not have ordered (a pardon) and the state avoided formal censure by the Committee and the publication of the Commission's report.

ENFORCEMENT POWERS

Committee of Ministers decisions

Article 32 stipulates that decisions of the Committee are binding upon individual states who *'must take the measures required by the decision'*. Although Article 32 states explicitly that the Committee's decisions are binding, this was not reflected in the previous Committee Rules. During the 1980s a flood of complaints arose against Italy concerning the inordinate length of civil and criminal proceedings. The cases were all similar and raised no novel Convention issues and were therefore referred to the Committee, which in each case adopted the Commission's report and in appropriate cases ordered compensation and costs. The Italian Governmental body charged with complying with Convention matters held (under Italian law) that it was not empowered to make the stipulated payments because they were not

[6] Rule 6 *bis* Article 32 Rules
[7] Resolution DH (91) 34; December 13, 1991

binding. The effect of this was that henceforth all such complaints were referred to the Court by the Commission; Court orders being unquestionably 'binding'. This undesirable situation has been resolved by the Committee bringing its Rules into line with the Convention[8]. Committee decisions are now binding and stipulate payment within three months, after which period the case is referred back to the Committee to ensure that the decision has been honoured by the respondent state.

Court decisions

Article 54 stipulates:

> The judgment of the Court shall be transmitted to the Committee of Ministers which shall supervise its execution.

The Committee is charged with ensuring that the states comply with Court decisions and the terms of any agreement resulting from a friendly settlement before the Court, but not of settlements reached during the Commission process.

The Court limits itself in its judgment to recording that a violation of the Convention has occurred, giving reasons for its finding and awarding compensation and costs where appropriate, *see* p. 82. The Court does not, however, specify what other measures are to be taken by the state to remedy the violation. This is left up to the state. The Committee supervises the enforcement of the judgment to ensure that the violation is satisfactorily remedied. Obviously in many cases the payment of compensation and costs alone may be sufficient.

APPROPRIATE MEASURES

What measures must a state take to ensure it complies with a Court decision?

A finding by the Court that a violation has occurred may require a variety of different responses from the state. The response depends upon the nature of the violation.

Material execution

Where the Court decision includes compensation and/or costs, these are directed to be paid within three months. The Committee requires

---

[8] This was effected by deleting the offending Rule 5 of Article 32 Rules

written confirmation that the payment has been made; that it has actually been received into the complainant's bank account, and not merely that the state has agreed to pay. The U.K. has always paid promptly; often within days and almost invariably within six weeks.

A difficulty can occur if the complainant owes money to the state; the question then being whether it is legitimate for the state to set the one off against the other. Such a situation arose in *Hauschildt* v. *Denmark*[9]. In this case the Court found that Mr Hauschildt had been the victim of a violation of Article 6(1) in that the impartiality of the criminal tribunals that had tried him was open to doubt. The Court held that Denmark was to pay him £20,000 for his costs and expenses. Mr Hauschildt however had been sentenced in the Danish proceedings to pay costs and compensation of three million crowns; the Danish Government therefore asserted that:

> In the particular circumstances of the present case and in view of the fact that the sum awarded by the [European] Court relates to costs and expenses and not to any pecuniary or non-pecuniary damage suffered by the applicant, it is the Government's view that the sum of £20,000 awarded by the Court should be set up against the sum still owed by the applicant to the authorities of Denmark.

The Committee of Ministers approved these measures. It is thus important to bear any potential counter-claim in mind when formulating the items to be included in the Article 50 financial claim. In such cases a specific request should be made, for instance, for reparation for the costs of the domestic court proceedings[10].

Individual measures

The circumstances of a violation may require action other than, or in addition to, a money payment. A serious irregularity in a particular domestic court hearing may necessitate a retrial or some other review proceedings instituted by the state.

In *Soering* v. *U.K.*[11] the Court held that the threatened extradition of the applicant to the U.S.A. to face a capital murder charge amounted to a violation of Article 3, because extradition would expose him to the 'death row phenomenon'. The individual measure adopted by the U.K. involved the extradition taking place upon the United States authorities confirming that Soering would not face a charge of capital murder but first degree murder which did not carry the death penalty.

---

[9] 12 E.H.R.R. 266; May 24, 1989, Series A, No. 154. Resolution DH (91) 9
[10] Including domestic court costs orders against the applicant expressed 'not to be enforced without leave', etc. *See also* p. 88 concerning the limited powers of the Court to direct that certain payments be made free of creditors' competing interests
[11] 11 E.H.R.R. 439; July 7, 1989, Series A, No. 161; DH (90) 8

General measures

In many cases individual measures alone will not be sufficient if the violation relates to a legal defect within the domestic system rather than a one-off irregularity. The defect may be a structural or a specific problem.

STRUCTURAL FAILINGS

An example of this type of situation is seen in certain complaints concerning the length of domestic proceedings. In general such complaints arise as a result of specific defects within the individual case which do not normally require legislative action by the state. If, however, a large number of similar complaints arise from a state concerning the length of similar cases, then it is clear that there is a general structural problem which requires the state to take remedial measures. This situation existed in Italy and resulted in an exceptional number of complaints under Article 6(1). As a result, Italy has decided to take fundamental action to amend its criminal code.

SPECIFIC PROBLEMS

Such cases are common and well known. Within the U.K. many domestic laws, Rules and Regulations have been amended or repealed to rectify particular violations. Obviously a state is not always able to rectify such violations immediately. The repeal of old laws or the enactment of new ones take time. In consequence the Committee has to allow a reasonable period to elapse to enable the state to take such measures.

A decision of the Court is referred to the next Committee meeting (the Committee meets most months). A given case cannot be adjourned for more than six months[12]. A state is therefore required to report at least twice a year on the steps it is taking to abide by a Court decision. Some cases have taken an inordinate amount of time for a state to rectify the defective domestic legislation. In *Marckx* v. *Belgium* [13] the Court held that Belgium intestacy laws violated the Convention by discriminating unfairly against illegitimate children. It however took the Belgium Government eight years before it changed the domestic laws to reflect the Court's decision. A motivating force for a state to take prompt remedial action is, of course, the avoidance of further similar complaints. Due to Belgium's delay inevitably further complaints arose on the same point (*see Vermeire* v. *Belgium* [14]). The Court's

---

[12] Rule 2 of Article 54 Rules
[13] 2 E.H.R.R. 330; June 13, 1979, Series A, No. 31
[14] *Vermeire* v. *Belgium* 15 E.H.R.R. 488; November 29, 1991, Series A, No. 214-C

1988 decision in *Norris* v. *Ireland*[15] that Irish legislation penalising certain homosexual acts violated the Convention required specific remedial legislation by the Irish Government. Such action has still not occurred. Every six months the Irish representative on the Committee of Ministers will have to explain why his or her Government has not taken the necessary action. Whilst such pressure may not appear particularly effective, it has eventually produced the required results.

Where, as a consequence a Court decision, a state enters a derogation (*see* p. 197), the Committee has decided that there is nothing further it can do. This has occurred most recently in relation to the derogation by the U.K. in response to the Court decision in *Brogan* v. *U.K.*[16]. The Committee takes the view that it is not its rôle to assess the validity or otherwise of the derogation.

[15] 13 E.H.R.R. 186; October 26, 1988, Series A, No. 142
[16] 13 E.H.R.R. 440; November 29, 1988, Series A, No. 142

5 The Court

An outline of the composition and duties of the Court is given at p. 8. The Court owes its existence to the Convention. Article 19 provides that the Court and Commission be set up to *'ensure the observance'* by the states of their duties under the Convention.

Although the Commission is the system's work-horse, the Court is the judicial body that makes binding decisions, that interprets and applies the Convention to practical problems. The Court decisions now cover a wide range of human rights situations; a more comprehensive body of case law than any other international human rights court has as yet produced. As will be seen, in exercising its functions the Court is assisted by the Commission, but ultimately it is the Court that decides what does and what does not amount to a violation of the Convention. There are many areas in which an interpretation adopted by the Commission has been rejected by the Court. It is for this reason that decisions of the Court carry far more weight than the Commission's reports. The reports are nevertheless of great value, not least because they are more numerous and because of the extraordinary breadth of the subject-matter to which the Commission has applied its collective mind.

In addition to making a decision as to whether the Convention has been violated, the Court's duties extend (under Article 50) to quantifying appropriate compensation and costs.

The Court is empowered to give interpretations of its judgments if, for any reason, they are unclear[1], revise its judgments if 'decisive' fresh evidence is discovered[2] and to give advisory opinions if so requested by the Committee of Ministers [3]. These miscellaneous and virtually unused powers are not dealt with in this text.

In this chapter reference to 'Rules' is (unless otherwise stated) a reference to the Court Rules, *see* p. 9 and Appendix 5, p. 265, and reference to the 'representatives' includes the agent for the respondent state, the Commission delegates and the applicant's representative.

---

[1] Rule 57 and *Ringeinsen (No. 3)* v. *Austria* 1 E.H.R.R. 513; June 23, 1973, Series A, No. 16
[2] Rule 58
[3] By virtue of Protocol 2 and Rule 59 *et seq.*

TRANSFER OF CASES TO THE COURT

Article 47 stipulates that the Court may only deal with a case if, within three months of the Commission's final report being transmitted to the Committee of Ministers, it is referred to the Court. Article 48 states that the only parties able to refer a case to the court in individual complaints are:

1. The Commission.
2. The state whose national is alleged to be a victim.
3. The respondent state.

The procedure is well illustrated by reference to the facts in *Soering* v. *U.K.*[4]. The complaint was lodged by Mr Soering, a German national who was resident within the U.K., against the U.K. Government. The Commission's final report was adopted on January 19, 1989, and immediately transferred to the Committee of Ministers. The case was referred to the Court by the Commission on January 25, 1989, by the U.K. Government on January 30, 1989 and the German Government on February 3, 1989.

In practice it is the Commission that ensures that appropriate cases are transferred to the Court. On transferring the complaint to the Court, the Commission does not pass its file to the Court, but only its report and basic details about the parties, the key dates of the Commission process and the object of the application [5]. The Commission delegates are able to provide the Court with copies of any other relevant Commission papers should the need subsequently arise[6].

COMMISSION AND COURT RELATIONS

Rule 63 of the Commission Rules stipulates that:

1. The Commission shall assist the European Court of Human Rights in any case brought before the Court. When a case is referred to the Court the Commission shall appoint, at a plenary session, one or more delegates to take part in the consideration of the case before the Court. These delegates may be assisted by any person appointed by the Commission. In discharging their functions they shall act in accordance with such directives as they may receive from the Commission.
2. Until delegates have been appointed, the President may, if consulted by the Court, express views upon the procedure to be followed before the Court.

---

[4] *Soering* v. *U.K.* 11 E.H.R.R. 439; July 7, 1989, Series A, No. 161
[5] Rule 64 of the Commission Rules and Rule 32 of the Court Rules
[6] Technically Commission papers are confidential and therefore the permission of the Commission and the observations of the representatives are required before such papers are made available

The above provisions are reflected in the Court Rules. Rule 29 stipulates:

1. The Commission shall delegate one or more of its members to take part in the consideration of a case before the Court. The Delegates may be assisted by other persons.
2. The Court shall, whether a case is referred to it by a [state] or by the Commission, take into consideration the report of the latter.

The Commission sees its main function as 'to enlighten' and assist the Court and its rôle in the Court as an impartial 'defender of the public interest'; essentially as an *amicus curiae*. Its function is to ensure that all relevant information is before the Court and to clarify and justify the opinions that formed the Commission's final report.

THE APPLICANT'S STANDING IN THE COURT

Rule 1 (the definitions clause) makes it clear that the applicant is not a party to the proceedings. The applicant's position before the Court has, however, improved substantially over the years, to the extent that he or she is now a party in every respect except name. The current Rules reflect this enhanced status.

Upon receipt of the Commission's report the Registrar of the Court is required to contact the applicant and to ascertain whether he or she wishes to take part in the Court proceedings and if so, the name and address of the applicant's representative[7]. The applicant is required to comply with this request within two weeks. A similar request is made of the respondent state (for it to provide details of its proposed agent) and of the Commission for details of its delegates.

Rule 30(1) stipulates:

1. The applicant shall be represented by an advocate authorised to practise in [the respondent state], or by any other person approved by the President. The President may, however, give leave to the applicant to present his own case, subject, if need be, to his being assisted by an advocate or other person as aforesaid.

Rule 30(2) provides that the representative or the applicant (if representing him/herself) shall have adequate knowledge of English or French subject to the President of the Court's discretion.

PRE-HEARING PROCEDURE

Once the case has been transferred to the Court, the representatives are notified of this by the Court Registrar and all are sent a copy of the

---

[7] Rule 33.3.d

Commission's final report[8]. Unless the President decides otherwise (which would only occur in exceptional circumstances) the Commission's report is published at the same time[9].

As soon as the Chamber of the Court (*see below*) has been constituted to hear the case, the representatives are notified by the Registrar of its composition. They are then consulted by the President of the Chamber as to whether they wish to make any further written submissions. The applicant is also required at this stage to file with the Court details of any compensation or costs he or she wishes to claim[10]. It is a general characteristic of a complaint that all the various aspects of its interaction with the Convention only emerge during its passage through the Commission and Court. Usually therefore, the representatives will wish to file further submissions. The applicant is, however, neither permitted to raise before the Court new complaints which were not raised before the Commission, nor to revive complaints which the Commission ruled inadmissible. Such further submissions as are filed are called 'memorials' and the Chamber President will notify the representatives as to time limits for the filing of memorials or any other documents upon which they seek to rely[11]. Typically, the time allowed for the respondent state and the applicant to file their further submissions is between two and three months. These are then copied to the Commission delegate(s) for their comments, which must normally be filed within two months.

It is at this stage that the President may allow third party interventions (*see below*) and the consolidation of similar complaints.

Memorials, together with any other documents annexed to them, must be filed in the registry; the applicant being relieved of the duty placed upon the respondent state and the Commission to file 40 copies of such submissions. Copies of all these papers are sent to the representatives as well as to the Chamber judges. Unlike submissions to the Commission, memorials are not confidential and in the absence of a direction from the President of the Chamber to the contrary, there is no restriction on their publication.

If the respondent state intends to make a preliminary objection about the admissibility or jurisdiction of the Court to hear the complaint, it must do so by no later than the expiry of the time limit laid down for the filing of its first memorial[12]. If the state fails to raise such an issue at this stage then it will be estopped from arguing the point before the Court at the final hearing[13]. The state can in any event only raise the

---

[8] Rule 33
[9] Rule 29.3
[10] *See* p. 82
[11] Rule 37.1
[12] Rule 48.1
[13] *See for instance Ciulla* v. *Italy* 13 E.H.R.R. 346; February 22, 1989, Series A, No. 148

argument of inadmissibility at this stage if it has already argued the specific point before the Commission.

Whilst the Court can review (and exceptionally reverse) the Commission's decision on certain admissibility criteria, for example that the applicant has failed to exhaust domestic remedies[14], or failed to raise the relevant Convention issues before the domestic Courts[15] or is not a victim[16], it cannot interfere with the Commission's decision to transfer a complaint to the Court, nor can it consider complaints declared inadmissible by the Commission[17].

The Court has power of its own volition or at the request of one of the representatives to undertake pre-hearing investigations by interviewing witnesses and experts and obtaining from them relevant information or opinions, etc.[18]. The Court can depute one or more of its members to conduct such enquiries, and such investigations can take place 'on the spot' or in such place or in such manner as the Chamber decides[19]. The Chamber can alternatively request any other person or institution of its choice to obtain information, or make a report upon any point[20]. The cost of obtaining such material is at the discretion of the Chamber[21]. In practice the Court's investigative rôle is even more circumscribed than that of the Commission; in *Cruz Varas* v. *Sweden*[22] the Court emphasised its opinion that the establishment and verification of the facts of a complaint are the primary responsibility of the Commission and that it will therefore only in exceptional circumstances use its powers in this area[23]. The most common mechanism adopted by the Court for obtaining an 'independent' view on a complaint is to permit third party interventions.

THIRD PARTY INTERVENTIONS

The President may, by virtue of Rule 37(2), permit any state or person to submit written comments about the complaint within such

---

[14] *Van Oosterwijck* v. *Belgium* 3 E.H.R.R. 557; November 6, 1980, Series A, No. 40
[15] *Cardot* v. *France* 13 E.H.R.R. 853; March 19, 1991, Series A, No. 200
[16] *Vijayanathan and Pusparajah* v. *France* 15 E.H.R.R. 62; August 27, 1992, Series A, No. 241-B
[17] *See for instance, Helmers* v. *Sweden* 15 E.H.R.R. 285; October 29, 1991, Series A, No. 212; and *Powell and Rayner* v. *U.K.* 12 E.H.R.R. 355; February 21, 1990, Series A, No. 172
[18] Rule 41
[19] Rule 41.4
[20] Rule 41.2
[21] Rule 41.3
[22] 14 E.H.R.R. 1; March 20, 1991, Series A, No. 201
[23] Examples of the limited investigations that the Court is prepared to undertake include ordering an opinion of a handwriting expert in *Brozicek* v. *Italy* 13 E.H.R.R. 371; December 19, 1989, Series A, No. 167 (to clarify whether it could be shown that the applicant had ever received a particular letter); and in *Müller* v. *Switzerland* 13 E.H.R.R. 212; May 24, 1988, Series A, No. 133 the Court viewed in private the allegedly obscene paintings which were at the heart of the complaint

time limits and other restrictions as the President may specify. Such interventions are known as 'amicus briefs'.

Where a state seeks permission to intervene and comment upon a particular complaint, such permission is a formality. Such an intervention occurred in *Soering* v. *U.K.*[24] where the complainant was a German national and complained about the decision of the U.K. Government to extradite him to the U.S.A. The German Government opposed the extradition and volunteered to try Soering in Germany (as German law allowed).

Where an individual or a non-governmental organisation wishes to make comment upon a pending case, the President considers the quality of the particular expertise or information that they will be able to contribute to the judicial process. The President's discretion is subject only to the requirement that the intervention should be allowed if it is in the 'interest of the proper administration of justice'. Where permission is given it will be conditional upon the submission being concise and restricted to a previously agreed aspect of the complaint; the President may also insert additional conditions upon the ambit or detail of the permissible submissions. The Court hesitates to allow such interventions as they tend to widen the issues and create delay. There is a likelihood that the Court will further tighten up the procedure with a view to restricting *amicus* briefs in the future.

Applications for leave to intervene generally occur as a result of a non-governmental organisation wishing to strengthen a complainant's case against the usually formidable resources of the state, or because they believe an important point may be missed. A typical intervention of this kind arose in the case of *Malone* v. *U.K.*[25] where the Post Office Engineering Union was given permission to file a memorial concerning the applicant's complaint that his phone had been tapped by Home Office order.

Applications can arise because a possible lacuna exists in the areas of argument; a lacuna which neither the state nor the applicant are willing to fill. Such a situation arguably arose in the case of *Young, James and Webster* v. *U.K.*[26] which concerned Article 11 and a complainant's right not to belong to a trade union (the 'closed shop'). The complaint arose during a Labour Government, which was not opposed to the principle of a closed shop. By the time the case came before the Court, there was a new government, and one which was opposed to the closed shop. The new Government was not prepared to argue that the closed shop was necessary in a democratic society; obviously the applicants did not wish to argue this aspect either. As the Court decision was inevitably

---

[24] *See* note 4 *above*
[25] 7 E.H.R.R. 14; August 2, 1984, Series A, No. 82
[26] 4 E.H.R.R. 38; June 26, 1981, Series A, No. 44

going to affect a far wider population than the U.K. alone, it was important that the Court received the best possible argument attempting to justify the arrangement. In all probability the Court welcomed the third party intervention from the Trades Union Congress, whose nominee, Lord Wedderburn of Charlton, Professor of Law at the University of London, was given permission to file a statement on the necessity of such an arrangement in a democratic society.

Tactically it is important to consider the desirability of potential interventions at an early stage. Sympathetic interventions from respected quarters can only assist a case. Co-ordinated interventions enable a state's case to be attacked from separate viewpoints; enabling those promoting the complaint to divide up the workload by each concentrating on separate aspects of the complaint. Early consideration should therefore be given to requesting such assistance from respected independent organisations who could make a valuable contribution to sustaining the complaint.

THE CONSTITUTION OF THE COURT

Chambers

By Article 43 all complaints are initially referred to a chamber of the Court consisting of nine judges, although in certain circumstances a complaint can subsequently be transferred to the full Court (*see below*). A procedure exists for consolidating similar cases; thus where a complaint concerns the same respondent state as another complaint which raises similar issues it may be referred to the same chamber[27].

Article 43 and the Court Rules[28] set out the detailed procedure by which the chamber judges are chosen. In addition to the nine judges (chosen by lot by the President) the President or Vice-President sits as an *ex-officio* member of the chamber as does the judge whose nationality corresponds with the respondent state. The Rules specify what is to occur if the *ex-officio* members are, for any reason, unavailable. In addition the Rules require the selection of a further four judges who sit on the substitutes' bench: ready to step in if any of the principal chamber judges cease to be available. Such substitutes receive all the Court papers and attend the hearing of the complaint, but, unless they replace a principal judge, do not vote.

[27] Rule 21.6
[28] Rules 21-25

Full court

Rule 51 stipulates that:

1. Where a case pending before a Chamber raises one or more serious questions affecting the interpretation of the Convention, the Chamber may, at any time during the proceedings, relinquish jurisdiction in favour of the plenary Court. The relinquishment of jurisdiction shall be obligatory where the resolution of such question or questions might have a result inconsistent with a judgment previously delivered by a Chamber or the plenary Court. Reasons need not be given for the decision to relinquish jurisdiction.
2. The plenary Court, when the case has been referred to it, may either retain jurisdiction over the whole case or may, after deciding the said question or questions, order that the case be referred back to the Chamber which shall, in regard to the remaining part of the case, recover its original jurisdiction.

Historically almost half of all Court decisions have been made as a result of a hearing before the full Court; today, as the Court's case law is extensive, only a minority of cases require a hearing of the full Court.

The Chamber can relinquish jurisdiction to the full Court at any time. This has indeed occurred in several cases after the Chamber has heard the case[29].

HEARING PROCEDURES

During the pre-hearing process the President of the Chamber liaises with the representatives in order to fix a date for the opening of the oral hearing. The representatives will also be asked to anticipate how long they will need to address the Court. The hearing date is then fixed and the representatives formally notified of this by the Registry[30]. The representatives' oral submissions will (in total) seldom last more than a day and more usually will only occupy the Court for half a day.

Save in exceptional circumstances, Court hearings are in public[31]. The hearings are in French or English, although there is provision in the Rules for a different language to be used: Dutch and German are not infrequently used in cases involving those countries. Private hearings have occurred but have been very rare indeed. In a handful of cases, however, the applicants have not agreed to the disclosure of their identity and hence are referred to as 'X' in the case titles, or in the case of children, the first letter of their surname.

---

[29] *See for instance Helmers* v. *Sweden* (note 17 *above*) and *Sunday Times* v. *U.K.* 2 E.H.R.R. 245; April 26, 1979, Series A, No. 30
[30] Rule 38
[31] Rule 18

The order in which the representatives speak at the hearing is not specified in the Rules; as with other procedural questions, it is ultimately at the discretion of the President of the Chamber[32]. In practice, all such questions are canvassed with the representatives by the Registry during the pre-hearing process. It is normal for the Commission's delegates to speak first, as the Commission's report constitutes the starting point for the whole Court process. If the Commission's report concludes that a violation of the Convention has occurred, the respondent state will in general speak next, followed by the applicant; and vice versa where the Commission considers that no violation has occurred. Obviously the particular circumstances of each case may result in this general order being displaced, *i.e.* where the respondent state is vigorously contesting a preliminary admissibility point.

The Rules enable the Chamber or its President to allow evidence at the hearing from witnesses, experts or other persons. Cross-examination by the representatives is permitted, subject to the President's control[33]. Most commonly of course, factual evidence will have been assimilated during the Commission process and during the pre-hearing procedure; either by such material being incorporated as annexes to the submissions and memorials, or as a result of pre-hearing investigations. The Court is not well equipped to adjudicate upon conflicting factual evidence, its strength lies in the more academic field of determining whether a given set of (largely agreed) circumstances amount to a violation of the Convention.

Where evidence is given at the hearing, the Rules prescribe the oath to be taken and it is at the Court's discretion as to whether the witnesses' expenses be paid by the Council of Europe or the applicant or a third party[34]. The oral evidence is to be given in French or English unless the witness, expert or other person has insufficient knowledge of either of these two languages, in which case they may use their own language, with the Registry responsible for making arrangements for translation[35].

During the hearing, any of the Chamber judges may question any representative or other person appearing before them. The Rules do not, however, contain any specific provision to enable the representatives to question each other; the hearing being directed through the President.

The Court staff at the hearing includes the registry officers who take a verbatim record of the proceedings and the translators who give

[32] Rule 39
[33] Rule 45
[34] Rule 42
[35] Rule 27

81

simultaneous translation. These officers remain during the judges' subsequent private deliberations. No other persons (including the Commission delegates) are allowed to attend the private session, except by special decision of the Court[36].

The private deliberations of the Court continue immediately after the oral hearing. Normally within about two days the Court will have reached a provisional view on the merits. Decisions are taken by simple majority voting, with the most junior judges (*i.e.* those most recently elected) casting their vote first. Where the voting is tied, the President has a second and casting vote[37]. The Court then constitutes a drafting committee consisting of three or four judges.

After the private deliberations the Registry sends to the representatives a verbatim record of their arguments, statements and evidence, in order that it can be approved as a correct account of what was said[38]. Once approved, the Registry send the record to the drafting committee, together with a draft judgment that it has prepared from its record of the private deliberations. The drafting committee may spend three or four months finalising the draft judgment, before it is returned to the original Court. The Court then scrutinises the draft paragraph by paragraph, the final votes are taken and three or four weeks later the judgment is approved, pronounced and then published. Rule 53 specifies what is to be contained within the judgment and provides that any judge who has taken part in the consideration of the case is permitted to annex to the judgment either a separate opinion, concurring with or dissenting from the judgment, or a bare statement of dissent.

SPECIFIC REDRESS

Article 50 stipulates:

> If the Court finds that a decision or measure taken by [the state] is completely or partially in conflict with the obligations arising from the present Convention, and if the internal law of the [state] allows only partial reparation to be made for the consequences of this decision or measure, the decision of the Court shall if necessary, afford just satisfaction to the injured party.

Where the Court finds that a violation of the Convention has occurred, it is required by Article 50 to consider whether the applicant is entitled to any compensation and/or costs. The Court has complete

[36] Rule 19
[37] Rule 20
[38] Rule 47

discretion as to whether or not to make an award and will only do so where the applicant has made a specific claim for such. It requires, however, that if the applicant seeks such compensation, then full details of the claim must be annexed to the memorial or if no memorial is submitted, then the details are to be filed separately at least one month before the opening date of the oral hearing (Rule 50). The details are then copied to the respondent state and the Commission for comment.

The Court cannot award anything other than compensation and costs; it cannot order the state to take, or refrain from taking, any particular action. In *Brozicek* v. *Italy*[39] for instance, the applicant requested as part of his claim for 'just satisfaction' that a domestic judgment against which he complained be declared void and be struck from his criminal record; the Court in its judgment observed that it did not have such powers under the Convention.

Where the Court has allowed compensation, the sums have varied from the purely nominal, such as the sum of 100 guilders (approx. £35) in *Engle (No. 2)* v. *Netherlands*[40] to very substantial amounts, such as the sum of IR£1,200,000 in *Pine Valley Developments Ltd. (No. 2)* v. *Ireland*[41] in respect of an interference with the applicant's property interests, and 700,000 FF (approx. £85,000) in *Tomasi* v. *France*[42] in respect of police brutality and undue delay in arranging a trial. In many cases however, the Court has held that the finding of a violation is itself 'just satisfaction' for the applicant. The object of compensation is to place the applicant, so far as is possible, in the position he or she would have been had the violation not occurred. Compensation can apply to either pecuniary or non-pecuniary loss.

Pecuniary loss

Pecuniary loss has much the same meaning as in U.K. law: including loss of earnings, out-of-pocket expenses, the lost value of an asset resulting from government action, etc. When formulating a claim under this head, compounded interest for the relevant years should not be forgotten.

The Court will allow compensation for pecuniary loss where the applicant can demonstrate that the violation has made a significant and financially quantifiable difference to his or her circumstances. The loss must relate to the breach, and must flow from and be caused by the

---

[39] *See* note 23 *above*
[40] 1 E.H.R.R. 706; November 23, 1976, Series A, No. 22
[41] 16 E.H.R.R. 379; February 9, 1993, Series A, No. 246–B
[42] 15 E.H.R.R. 1; August, 27, 1992, Series A, No. 241–A

violation found by the Court. The Court is reluctant to allow compensation when the projected loss is conjectural or hypothetical. In *Mats Jacobsson* v. *Sweden*[43] for instance, the applicant complained that he was unable to effectively challenge administrative changes which affected his building interests. The Court held that although the lack of such rights violated the Convention, it did not follow that if he had had such rights he inevitably would have been able to preserve his building interests. It therefore made no award in respect of pecuniary damage.

A similar situation arose in *Langborger* v. *Sweden*[44]. The Court found the applicant's right to an independent tribunal had been violated in respect of the composition of a Rent Review Board; but held that there was nothing to show that had the tribunal been differently constituted it would have come to a different decision. It accordingly dismissed the claim for pecuniary damages.

In *Sporrong and Lönnroth* v. *Sweden*[45] however, the Court was prepared to look at the reality of the situation. In this case a planning restriction had been placed upon the applicants' properties which had prohibited any development for over 20 years. At the time of the hearing the restrictions had been removed and there was no evidence that the current market value of the properties was any less, or that during the period of the development prohibition that there had been any diminution in the rental income. The Court accepted that during the period of the prohibition the value of the properties was substantially reduced and that this had affected the applicants' ability to raise loans by mortgage and that during that time they had been unable to develop or refurbish the buildings. The applicants had therefore sustained a loss of 'opportunity' and suffered a prolonged period of uncertainty. The Court considered possible technical formulae for quantifying these losses although in the end opted for a 'rule of thumb' assessment, awarding 1,150,000 Swedish Crowns (approx. £100,000).

Where the pecuniary damages are directly attributable to the violation then the award will generally extend to the full loss.

In *Darby* v. *Sweden*[46] the Court held that the applicant's rights under Article 14 and Protocol 1, Article 1 had been violated by a Swedish law which obliged him to pay a special church tax merely on the ground that he was not formally registered as resident in that country. The Court assessed the pecuniary damages as the amount of tax he had been required unjustly to pay plus interest.

In *Open Door Counselling Ltd. and Dublin Well Woman Clinic Ltd.* v. *Ireland*[47] the applicant companies were primarily engaged in giving

---

[43] 13 E.H.R.R. 79; June 28, 1990, Series A, No. 180-A
[44] 12 E.H.R.R. 416; June 22, 1989, Series A, No. 155
[45] 7 E.H.R.R. 256; December 18, 1984, Series A, No. 85
[46] 13 E.H.R.R. 774; October 23, 1990, Series A, No. 187
[47] 15 E.H.R.R. 244; October 29, 1982, Series A, No. 246

abortion advice. The Irish Attorney-General obtained injunctions restraining the giving of such advice, and accordingly the organisations could not function effectively. The Court, after finding a violation of Article 10, awarded pecuniary damages to the second applicant of IR £25,000 for loss of income as a result of the injunction even though it was a non-profit-making organisation.

Where possible the Court will settle the question of compensation at the same time as it decides whether the Convention has been violated. Not infrequently, however, it will have to adjourn the assessment either because it is unusually complex, or more normally because for one reason or another the question is not ready for decision. Such a situation arose in *Pine Valley Developments Ltd. v. Ireland*[48] where a complex sequence of planning permissions and revocations occurred in respect of land of great potential value, resulting in the dissolution and receivership of the applicant companies. The Court did not find violations in respect of all of the applicants' complaints and the issue of appropriate compensation was thus a highly complicated matter in its own right. Not surprisingly the Court decided unanimously that the question of compensation was not ready for decision and reserved it for a later occasion[49]. In such cases the Court will expect the applicant and respondent state to endeavour to reach an agreement. Failing this the Court may require the applicant to file a further statement quantifying and justifying, by specific reference to the adjudged violation(s), the directly attributable losses; the respondent state is then invited to respond. The procedure, including the composition of the Chamber which is to assess the compensation, is governed by Rule 54.

Non-pecuniary loss

The Court may order compensation for non-pecuniary loss; again this encompasses many of the same 'heads' as within U.K. law. Most commonly this category concerns compensation for 'prolonged anxiety', 'feelings of frustration', 'stress and anxiety', etc., occasioned by the breach of the Convention. It obviously includes damages for ill-treatment or other such pain and suffering or unlawful imprisonment.

Examples of more recent non-pecuniary awards include the following cases:

Delta v. France[50]. On December 19, 1990 the Court held that the applicant's Article 6 right to a fair trial had been violated; his conviction for robbery had been based to a decisive degree on statements by the

[48] 14 E.H.R.R. 319; November 29, 1991, Series A, No. 222
[49] Subsequently awarding the sum of IR£1,200,000, *see* note 41 *above*
[50] 16 E.H.R.R. 574; December 19, 1990, Series A, No. 191

victim and another, neither of whom gave evidence at the trial, and neither the applicant nor his counsel had the opportunity to cross-examine them. The applicant was sentenced to three years' imprisonment. The Court held that it *could not speculate as to the outcome of the trial if Mr Delta had had the benefit of all the guarantees of Article 6'*, but it did not find it unreasonable to regard him as having suffered a loss of real opportunities. On an equitable basis it awarded him compensation for non-pecuniary damage amounting to FF 100,000 (approx. £12,000).

Moustaquim v. *Belgium*[51]. On February 18, 1991 the Court held that the applicant's Article 8 rights to family life had been violated. The applicant had been born in Morocco, but had lived in Belgium with his family and close relatives since the age of two. When 21 years old he had served an 18-month sentence for 22 offences, none of which were gravely serious, after which he was ordered to be deported from Belgium. The Court held that the deportation order was excessive. Whilst dismissing the claim for pecuniary damages 'as it perceived no causal link between the breach of Article 8 and the alleged loss of earnings' it awarded the applicant non-pecuniary compensation amounting to BEF 100.000 (approx. £2,000). The applicant had suffered five years of exile during which time he had been deported to Spain, asked to leave that country, deported to Greece and then to Sweden.

Bock v. *Germany*[52]. On March 29, 1989 the Court held that the applicant's Article 6 rights to the determination of his divorce proceedings within a reasonable time had been violated. The applicant had filed a petition for divorce in March 1974 but the divorce was not finalised until May 1983, nine years later. The Court considered that the excessive length of the proceedings was highly detrimental to the applicant and 'on an equitable basis' awarded him DM 10,000 (approx. £4,000).

Eriksson v. *Sweden*[53]. On June 22, 1989 the Court held that the Article 8 rights of the applicant and her daughter had been violated. An order had been made in Sweden in 1983 prohibiting the applicant from removing her five-year-old daughter from a foster home and restricting the contact between the applicant and her daughter. No domestic court remedy then existed for the applicant to challenge the decision. The Court held that the applicants' lack of access to a court to challenge the restrictions violated the Convention. Although there was no certainty that the applicant would have succeeded had a remedy been available, an award of 200,000 Swedish Crowns was made to the applicant and 100,000 to the daughter (approx. £18,000 and £9,000 respectively).

Gaskin v. *U.K.*[54]. On July 7, 1989 the Court held that the applicant's rights under Article 8 had been violated in that he was refused access

[51] 13 E.H.R.R. 802; February 18, 1991, Series A, No. 193
[52] 12 E.H.R.R. 247; March 29, 1989, Series A, No. 150
[53] 12 E.H.R.R. 183; June 22, 1989, Series A, No. 156
[54] 12 E.H.R.R. 36; July 7, 1989, Series A, No. 160

to some of his social services file because the consent of the contributors was not forthcoming. The Court held that there should have been an independent review procedure, and that as a result of the absence of such a mechanism '*Mr Gaskin may have suffered some emotional distress and anxiety*'; accordingly the Court assessed non-pecuniary damages amounting to £5,000.

S. v. Switzerland[55]. On November 28, 1991 the Court held that there had been a violation of Article 6, in that the applicant, while in pre-trial detention on charges of arson and the use of explosives, had not been allowed to communicate freely with his lawyer for over seven months. Non-pecuniary damages were assessed by the Court in the sum of 2,500 Swiss francs (approx. £1,000).

Philis v. Greece[56]: On August 27, 1991 the Court held that the applicant's Article 6 rights had been violated. The applicant was an engineer, who as such was by virtue of a Greek decree prohibited from suing for his professional fees personally but had to rely upon a 'Technical Chamber' suing for them on his behalf. The Court held that the right to sue personally for such debts was essential in such cases. It held that the '*feeling of frustration generated by the impossibility of assuming control of the defence of his own interests, as well as prolonged anxiety as to the outcome of his disputes with his debtors, must have caused Mr Philis some non-pecuniary damage*', which the Court assessed at 1,000,000 drachmas (approx. £3,000).

X v. France[57]. On March 23, 1991 the Court held that there had been a violation of Article 6(1). The applicant had complained of unreasonable delay in domestic proceedings in determining his claim for compensation for having become HIV positive as a result of a blood transfusion. He claimed 150.000 FF (approx. £18,000) compensation before the Court, but by the time of judgment he had died. The Court nevertheless considered this reasonable, bearing in mind the psychological conditions in which the applicant had lived the remaining period of his life, and awarded the sum to the applicant's parents who had assumed conduct of the complaint on their son's death.

In many instances the Court decides that the finding that a violation has occurred is in itself sufficient 'just satisfaction' for the applicant. This most commonly occurs where the breach is technical and objectively the applicant has suffered no more than 'hurt feelings'. In *Kamasinski v. Austria*[58] the applicant, an American, was arrested for, and subsequently convicted of, aggravated fraud. His complaint to the Court alleged a large number of Convention violations, of which only

[55] 14 E.H.R.R. 670; November 28, 1991, Series A, No. 220
[56] 13 E.H.R.R. 741; August 27, 1991, Series A, No. 209
[57] 14 E.H.R.R. 483; March 23, 1991, Series A, No. 234-C
[58] 13 E.H.R.R. 36; December 19, 1989, Series A, No. 168

87

one was upheld. He asked the Court to award him $1000 dollars for each day of his imprisonment totalling $435,000. The Court held that it had only found one (and in its opinion minor) violation and therefore made no order of compensation, holding that the judgment constituted in itself adequate satisfaction for the purposes of Article 50.

COSTS

Where the claim for 'just satisfaction' includes a claim for costs, a detailed breakdown of how these are computed must be provided. There is no formal 'taxation' procedure and the Court has wide discretion as to what it allows. The award can only relate to those costs 'actually incurred, necessarily incurred' and which are 'reasonable as to *quantum*'. The respondent state and the Commission are sent a copy of the claim and invited to comment. The assessment of costs is also considered at p. 98 *post*.

In *Castells* v. *Spain*[59] the applicant claimed approximately £27,000 for his costs before the Commission and Court. He had appeared before the Court with four lawyers representing him; a number the Court held to be excessive. An award of approximately £11,000 was considered equitable by the Court.

DOMESTIC COURT COSTS

The applicant's claim for costs can include those of the domestic proceedings taken to exhaust the national judicial remedies prior to submitting the application to the Commission. Such costs would only be awarded if the applicant was responsible for their payment in full or in part. This would in general preclude an award where the applicant had domestic legal aid; although the claim should include the full amount of any domestic legal aid contribution, or any other costs in respect of work done for which the legal aid certificate did not extend.

COSTS AND DOMESTIC CREDITORS

Where costs are awarded the question arises (as with any compensation for pecuniary or non-pecuniary damages) as to whether the respondent state can set off the sum against a domestic liability, or whether it is capable of being seized by a domestic creditor. In *Hauschildt* v. *Denmark*[60] the Court awarded the applicant costs and

---

[59] 14 E.H.R.R. 445; April 23, 1992, Series A, No. 236
[60] 12 E.H.R.R. 266; May 24, 1989, Series A, No. 154

expenses amounting to £20,000. The Danish Government were allowed (by the Committee of Ministers) to set this against a debt the applicant owed to the state of almost £300,000, and thus no payment was made.

In *Philis* v. *Greece*[61] the applicant requested that the Court, when awarding costs, make an additional order that they be exempt from attachment. The Court in the circumstances of this case refused. In *Ringeisen (No. 3)* v. *Austria*[62], however, the Court specified that the award was to be paid to the applicant personally and exempt from any third party claim upon it, including the appplicant's trustee in bankruptcy. In *Ringeisen* the award related to compensation for the applicant's remand in custody, whereas in *Philis* the award consisted only of costs in respect of a violation of the applicant's civil rights. Whilst the Court will consider each case on its merits it is clearly important to anticipate such a problem when formulating a compensation claim, and, if necessary, asking the Court to make an appropriate rider to its order.

THE LEGALLY AIDED APPLICANT

Whilst the Court has stated that there is a need for human rights lawyers to be moderate in the fees that they charge applicants[63], it nevertheless accepts that the Strasbourg legal aid rates are not the correct measure for assessing the appropriate rate. In *Young, James and Webster* v. *U.K.*[64] (a case concerning the trade union 'closed shop'), the applicants were offered £65,000 by the Government to settle their costs, but rejected this, additionally claiming 342,349 FF fees for their French lawyers. In considering what was reasonable the Court held:

> . . . the high costs of litigation may themselves constitute a serious impediment to the effective protection of human rights. It would be wrong for the Court to give encouragement to such a situation in its decisions awarding costs under Article 50. It is important that applicants should not encounter undue financial difficulties in bringing complaints under the Convention and the Court considers that it may expect that lawyers in Contracting States will co-operate to this end in the fixing of their fees.
>
> Each of the applicants had the benefit of free legal aid before the Commission and then, after reference of the case to the Court . . . the applicants also had assistance from the Freedom Association, which organisation either paid or underwrote the legal costs referable to the proceedings . . .
>
> Neither the Government nor the Commission suggested that the applicants had incurred no liability whatsoever for costs additional to those covered by their legal aid . . .
>
> It is at least debatable whether, bearing in mind that the applicants had the services of counsel, they also required the services of both a firm of solicitors in London and a law firm in Paris.

---

[61] *See* note 56 *above*
[62] *See* note 1 *above*
[63] *Young, James and Webster* v. *U.K.* 5 E.H.R.R. 201; October 18, 1992, Series A, No. 55
[64] *Ibid*

> During the settlement negotiations, the Government offered to have the costs in question independently assessed or 'taxed' by a Taxing Master. In the opinion of the Court, this would have been a reasonable method of assessment . . .
> In these circumstances, the Court accepts the figure of £65,000 offered by the Government in respect of all legal costs and expenses.

The Court is prepared to order costs even where the applicant was clearly not in a position to make such a payment to his or her lawyers (had the complaint been unsuccessful). In *Pakelli* v. *Germany*[65] the applicant claimed reimbursement of his counsel's fees for domestic proceedings in 1978. The application to the Commission was made in 1978, but counsel did not in fact lodge his fee note until 1982, when he also stated that it would be in order for the applicant to defer payment having regard to the applicant's financial difficulties. No further request was made by counsel for payment because he 'knew his client to be without means'. The Government objected to paying counsel's fees, arguing that they had either been waived or that they were Statute barred. The Court held that it was not surprising that counsel, knowing his client's financial circumstances, decided not to send his fee note earlier and in any event, this being a human rights case '*a lawyer will be acting in the general interest if he agrees to represent or assist a litigant even if the latter is not in a position to pay him immediately*'. The Court rejected the statutory limitation argument on grounds of public policy and in any event it was a point that could only be relied upon by Mr Pakelli himself[66].

Where the applicant receives Council of Europe legal aid, any costs award is expressed as being subject to a deduction in respect of the legal aid already paid. There is therefore no 'legal aid charge'; the respondent state only having to pay the net difference. Thus in *Thynne, Wilson and Gunnell* v. *U.K.*[67] a case concerning the inadequacies of the parole review system for discretionary life sentences, the Court awarded Mr Thynne the amount of costs and expenses he had claimed, £4,500, less 7,845 FF already paid by way of legal aid in respect of fees. Mr Wilson and Mr Gunnell were awarded jointly £18,000, less 24,849 FF already paid to Mr Gunnell by way of legal aid in respect of fees and travel and subsistence expenses. Both these figures were to be increased by any VAT chargeable.

[65] 6 E.H.R.R. 1; April 25, 1983, Series A, No. 64
[66] *See also Eckle (No. 2)* v. *Germany* June 21, 1983, Series A, No. 65, where a similar argument concerning late fee notes was raised; here the Court noted that the government 'expressed surprise that [counsel] should have waited . . . more than five years . . . before drawing up the particular fee note in question as well as, moreover nearly all the other fee notes he has produced to the Court'. The Court however stated that it had 'no cause to believe that it is confronted with a bogus document drafted solely for the purpose of the proceedings pending before it.'
[67] 13 E.H.R.R. 666; October 25, 1990, Series A, No. 190

COSTS AND THE PARTIALLY SUCCESSFUL COMPLAINT

Where a complaint only partially succeeds before the Court the costs awarded may be reduced to reflect the level of success. In *Mats Jacobsson* v. *Sweden*[68] for instance, the judgment recorded as follows:

> The applicant sought 393,874 Skr. in respect of costs and expenses. Of this sum, 150,960 Skr. constituted [his lawyers] fees for 251 hours' work and 239,888 Skr. his expenses for outside legal advice, for the translation of various documents and for travel. The remaining 3,026 Skr. related to a number of miscellaneous items. The Court notes that a large part of the costs and expenses in question were incurred in respect of the complaint under Article 1 of Protocol 1, which complaint was declared inadmissible by the Commission. Considering this and other relevant circumstances, including the legal aid payments from the Council of Europe, and making an assessment on an equitable basis, as is required by Article 50 of the Convention, the Court considers the applicant to be entitled to be reimbursed the sum of 80,000 Skr.

The fact that the applicant's complaint is partially unsuccessful either before the Commission or the Court does not necessarily mean that the costs will be reduced *pro rata*. In *Eckle* v. *Germany*[69] the Court rejected the Government's argument to this effect, holding that the applicant's unsuccessful claims were not substantial matters (and by implication would have involved a relatively small amount of lawyer time compared to the time spent on the successful claims) and in any event these matters had failed, not because they were without merit, but because it was held that domestic remedies had not been exhausted. In *Sunday Times* v. *U.K. (No. 2)*[70] in response to the same argument, the Court stated:

> Whilst it is in the interests of a proper and expeditious administration of justice that the Convention institutions be not burdened with pleas unrelated or extraneous to the case in hand, the submissions now in question cannot be so described. They all bore on the situation created for the applicants by the injunction ordered by the House of Lords and the kernel of each of them was Article 10. [*See* Appendix 11 where the costs assessment is quoted in full.]

Enforcement of court orders

Court orders are transmitted to the Committee of Ministers, which then supervise their enforcement, *see* p. 69.

INTERIM MEASURES

Where the Commission has made an interim request to the respondent state to take steps to secure the applicant's safety (*see* p. 61), the

[68] 13 E.H.R.R. 79; June 28, 1990, Series A, No. 180-A
[69] June 21, 1983, Series A, No. 65
[70] 2 E.H.R.R. 317; November 6, 1980, Series A, No. 38

request remains effective during the Court phase of the complaint unless and until the President or the Chamber decide otherwise[71]. The Court also has powers of its own volition or at the behest of any of the representatives to request such interim measures itself, regardless of whether these have been recommended in the Commission proceedings[72].

FRIENDLY SETTLEMENTS

Whilst most friendly settlements occur during the Commission phase, the applicant and respondent state do sometimes reach an agreement to settle the complaint during the Court phase. In such cases the procedure is specified by Rule 49. The Court has a discretion as to whether to proceed with the consideration of the case, notwithstanding the parties' agreement. The Court has refused to approve a small number of settlements on the ground that they did not fully redress (and/or provide 'just satisfaction' for) the perceived violation. If, however, the Court approves the settlement, it gives judgment reciting the terms of the settlement and the case is then struck off the Court's list and the judgment forwarded to the Committee of Ministers which has responsibility for supervising the execution of the agreement, essentially of ensuring that the respondent state complies with any undertakings it has given to the applicant.

Where the Court has found a violation of the Convention, but adjourned the applicant's claim for compensation and/or costs, it not infrequently occurs that the parties settle this aspect. Rule 54.4 nevertheless requires that the Court verify the equitable nature of such agreements.

[71] Rule 36.2
[72] Rule 36.1

6 Legal Aid and Costs

U.K. LEGAL AID

There is no U.K. legal aid available for any aspect of proceedings before the European Commission or Court. The exclusion includes the Legal Advice and Assistance scheme. This does not mean that a U.K. legal aid certificate cannot cover work spent considering the Convention. In two particular situations a consideration of Convention law is a necessary part of preparing a U.K. domestic law case.

Statutory interpretation

In *R. v. Secretary of State for the Home Department, ex p. Brind*[1] the House of Lords reaffirmed the importance of the Convention as an aid to domestic statutory interpretation, stating:

> in construing any provision in domestic legislation which was ambiguous in that it was capable of a meaning which either conformed to or conflicted with the European Convention on Human Rights the courts would presume that Parliament intended to legislate in conformity with the convention . . .

Accordingly in any case requiring interpretation of a statute, it will be necessary within the U.K. proceedings to consider what the Convention has to say on the subject, as well as any relevant European Court of Human Rights cases. Time spent in the consideration of such matters will be a legitimate claim on the U.K. civil legal aid certificate.

Common law clarification

In *Derbyshire County Council v. Times Newspapers*[2] it was stated by the Court of Appeal that where the common law is unclear or ambiguous

---

[1] [1991] 1 A.C. 696, which is discussed in detail at p. 100 *post*
[2] [1992] 1 Q.B. 770 C.A., which is discussed in detail at p. 102 *post*

(in relation to an issue involving human rights) one is 'obliged to consider' the implications of the Convention. In this respect, 'ambiguous' can merely mean that there is no relevant binding Court of Appeal or House of Lords decision.

In any appeal or judicial review proceedings, consideration must be given to possible Convention issues. As emphasised at p. 30 complaints to the Commission are not admissible if the Convention points are not raised in the domestic proceedings. Consideration of the Convention at an early stage is therefore essential: in many cases such consideration will, for the reasons set out *above*, be claimable time under the domestic legal aid certificate if done at the appropriate point. In general this means early on in the appeal or review.

COUNCIL OF EUROPE LEGAL AID

Separate though very similar Legal Aid Rules apply in the Commission and the Court. The Legal Aid Rules applying before the Commission are set out in an Addendum to the Commission's Rules of Procedure and in this section will be referred to as the 'Commission Legal Aid Rules', the text of which is set out at Appendix 8, p. 300. The Court Legal Aid Rules are likewise contained in an Addendum, in this case, to the Court Rules and are referred to in this section as the 'Court Legal Aid Rules'; the text of which is set out in Appendix 9, p. 302.

Legal aid before the Commission

Although legal aid is available to help with legal expenses both before the Commission and Court, it is not available in the initial stages of the complaint process. Legal aid can only be obtained once the complaint has been communicated to the government and the government has either submitted its written observations, or the initial time limit set for the return of the government's written observations has expired[3].

Legal aid before the Commission is payable to cover the cost of a barrister, solicitor or professor of law or professionally qualified person of similar status. The legal aid will cover, where appropriate, the fees of more than one such lawyer[4].

If the Commission considers the complaint sufficient to warrant requesting the government's observations, it will (either when the observations are received or when the time limit for their provision has

---

[3] Rule 1a of the Commission Legal Aid Rules
[4] Rule 4 of the Commission Legal Aid Rules

expired) automatically write inviting an application for legal aid. The complainant can in any event apply for legal aid, should the Commission fail to invite such an application.

Legal aid is subject to a means test and is only granted where it is considered essential for the discharge of the Commission's duties [5].

The application for legal aid consists of completing the 'Declaration of Applicant's Means' form. It is sensible to complete this form with the complainant at the time the complaint is first submitted, and then to keep it on file. When the appropriate moment comes for it to be submitted, it can be signed and dispatched. This procedure enables any necessary documentation or accounts to be obtained in advance. With the exception of Scottish cases, the form has to be certified by the assessment office at the Benefits Agency, Legal Aid Assessment Office, Albert Edward House, No. 3 The Pavillions, Ashton-on-Ribble, Preston, PR2 2PA; telephone (0772) 562940. The assessment office in Scotland is The Scottish Legal Aid Board, 44 Drumsheugh Gardens, Edinburgh, EH3 75W.

The starting point for the Commission's Means Test is the same as that applied in the U.K.; thus if the complainant's financial circumstances are sufficient to obtain legal aid in the U.K., the situation will be likewise before the Commission. The Commission is not bound by the U.K.'s eligibility criteria, and may make a grant where it decides that the applicant has not sufficient means to meet all or part of the costs involved [6].

The Commission frequently grants free legal aid even where the U.K. Legal Aid Board assessment states that for domestic legal aid purposes a financial contribution would be required. Before making a grant of free legal aid, the Commission sends the legal aid application details to the government inviting its comments within a specified time [7]. Thereafter the Commission decides whether to grant legal aid or not. It normally does this during one of its sessions. It may happen that the legal aid is not granted until after the work has been done, which is invariably the case for the preparation of the original application. The legal aid is, in this respect, retrospective. In cases of urgency, legal aid can be granted by the President or one of the Vice-Presidents of the Commission when it is not in session [8].

In addition to the set allowances for specified work (*see below*), the offer of legal aid will also specify a fixed figure for expenses to cover such items as telephone calls, postage, copying or translations. The 1993 figure for this is 400 FF (approx. £50). If the legal aid covers

---

[5] Rule 2a of the Commission Legal Aid Rules
[6] Rule 2b of the Commission Legal Aid Rules
[7] Rule 3 of the Commission Legal Aid Rules
[8] Rule 7 of the Commission Legal Aid Rules

representation at Strasbourg, then the cost of an economy class return air fare from London to Strasbourg and a fixed allowance for subsistence is payable (*see below*).

Contrary to what is stated in the letter accompanying the offer of legal aid, the Commission does not normally require documentary proof of miscellaneous (postage, etc.) expenses.

At the completion of the allotted stage it is open for the applicant to request payment, although in general if there are two closely connected items (for instance preparation and comments on the government's observations), then the Commission will ask that the applicant wait until the second step has been completed before a claim is made, thereby avoiding unnecessary administration. The Commission sends out the claim form automatically. Payments take a reasonably long time to be processed, often 10–12 weeks from claim to payment. They are made by direct transfer to the applicant's bank; the claim form sets out the details the Commission requires to process the transfer.

Legal aid can be paid to cover the cost of not only barristers and solicitors but also a 'professor of law or professionally qualified person of similar status'. The cost, where appropriate (provided approved in advance), of more than one lawyer may also be covered.

Witness expenses are dealt with by Rule 42 of the Commission's Rules, rather than under the legal aid provisions. Rule 42 states that such expenses may be paid out of Council of Europe funds at the Commission's discretion. This only applies to the expenses of witnesses attending a Commission hearing. Where the Commission decides to bear the witnesses' costs the amount is fixed by the President of the Commission.

An alternative procedure is to get the Commission itself either to call the witness or request from him or her a written opinion, as in such cases it automatically bears the agreed costs[9].

Legal aid before the Court

Where the applicant has been granted legal aid before the Commission, the grant will continue in force before the Court, subject to the President's power to instruct the Registrar to reassess the applicant's circumstances[10].

Where the applicant did not receive legal aid before the Commission (or it had been revoked), the Court has the same power to grant legal aid as the Commission[11] as the Rules are virtually identical. Court legal

[9] Rule 42.2 and 42.3 of the Commission Rules
[10] Rule 3 of the Court Legal Aid Rules
[11] Rule 4 of the Court Legal Aid Rules

aid can, however, only be paid to cover the costs of a solicitor and/or a barrister while Commission legal aid can cover the cost of a 'professor of law or professionally qualified person of similar status'[12].

Witness expenses are dealt with in the Court as in the Commission. These costs are not covered by legal aid and are at the discretion of the Court, see Rule 42.1 of the Court Rules.

Legal aid rates

The legal aid monies are paid out of the Council of Europe's budget. It is little more than a nominal payment. The main benefit is that it can, subject to prior approval, cover travelling, subsistence and other necessary out-of-pocket expenses incurred by the applicant or his or her lawyer.

Legal aid is not paid on a time-costed basis, but by fixed sums to cover specified work. There is provision for the rates to be varied in exceptional circumstances but only as a result of prior consultation with the Secretary to the Commission. The scale rates are updated annually, with the exception of the daily allowance which is reviewed every six months. The scale of fees applicable as from January 1, 1993 is:

BEFORE THE EUROPEAN COMMISSION

A.

1,950 FF	(approx. £235)	Preparation of case
1,695 FF	(approx. £205)	Written observations
770 FF	(approx. £90)	Supplementary observations
1,950 FF	(approx. £235)	Commission hearings (per day)
770 FF	(approx. £90)	Friendly settlement (written proposals)
925 FF	(approx. £110)	Attending settlement negotiations (per day)
400 FF	(approx. £50)	Out-of-pocket expenses

B.

Hearing before the Commission
Daily allowance at January 1, 1994
(Revisable every six months)

975 FF	(approx. £120)	Lawyer (per day)
800 FF	(approx. £95)	Applicant (per day)

[12] Rule 6.1. of the Court Legal Aid Rules

1,850 FF (approx. £225) Memorials
  975 FF (approx. £120) Observations on Article 50
1,950 FF (approx. £235) Court hearings (per day)

As with U.K. legal aid, if the applicant's means change, the legal aid may be revoked in whole or in part (Rule 6 of the Commission Legal Aid Rules and Rule 5 of the Court Legal Aid Rules). Unlike U.K. legal aid however, there is no statutory charge. If ultimately the complaint succeeds and the government is directed to meet the complainant's legal fees, the legal aid monies already paid are merely deducted from the overall total, see p. 89.

The actual sums paid out by the Council of Europe in legal aid are relatively modest. In 1992 72 applicants received legal aid in Commission proceedings at a total cost of 332,000 FF; in 1991 54 applicants received a total of 324,000 FF.

LEGAL COSTS IF COMPLAINT UPHELD

At the conclusion of the Court proceedings, the Court can order that the respondent state pay all or a part of the applicant's costs. The Court assesses the appropriate amount to be paid; this is dealt with in detail at p. 89. Where such an order is made in favour of an applicant who has received Council of Europe legal aid, the respondent state is required to pay the balance of the sum assessed. It follows that detailed time records should be kept to enable a full costs claim to be prepared for the Court. The records must also show the precise nature of the work involved.

Where the complaint is only partially successful, the Court sometimes reduces the costs award to reflect the portion of the work carried out on the unsuccessful part of the complaint. A detailed time costing record may enable the representative to establish the precise amount of time spent upon the portion of the complaint that failed, and thereby minimise the amount of the proposed reduction.

The Court has stated that there is a need for human rights lawyers to be moderate in the fees that they charge. Where therefore the Court is making an award of costs against the respondent state, it is inclined to be conservative in what it considers to be a reasonable figure. However if unreasonably low awards are made, this would itself constitute a significant impediment to the bringing of complaints.

Before assessing the appropriate costs award the Court requires the applicant to submit a detailed claim, which is then copied to the

Commission delegates and the government for comment. In practice the government passes the claim to the Treasury Solicitor for scrutiny. In *Young, James and Webster* v. *U.K.*[13] the Court approved of the principal costs being taxed by a Taxing Master in the absence of agreement between the applicant and the Government. The Treasury Solicitor therefore prefers that the claim for costs is set out in the same format as domestic civil costs claims[14]. Full details of any Legal Aid assistance received under the Council of Europe's Legal Aid scheme should also be provided.

In *The Sunday Times* v. *U.K. (No. 2)*[15] the Court scrutinised the applicant's bill in great detail as a result of the Government's sustained objection to a number of specific items. A copy of the relevant part of the judgment is at Appendix 11. It is of importance in showing the Court's approach to such matters and in particular its assertion that it does not consider itself bound by domestic scales or standards.

CONDITIONAL FEE AGREEMENTS

The Lord Chancellor has, pursuant to s.58 of the Courts and Legal Services Act 1990, approved draft Regulations[16], which would enable parties to proceedings before the Commission and/or Court to enter into a conditional fee agreement. The maximum permitted percentage by which the fees may be increased (for the purposes of s.58(5) of the Act) is 100 per cent.

---

[13] 5 E.H.R.R. 201; October 18, 1982, Series A, No. 55
[14] Appendix 2, Part II, R.S.C., Ord. 62; containing a brief narrative of the issues involved in relation to the application; and thereafter in chronological order the various items as set out in Ord. 62. In relation to the main Preparation, Item 4, full details of attendances, letters written, telephone attendances, etc., consideration and preparation time and any necessary and reasonable travelling time should be provided. Where disbursements have been incurred, relevant copies of supporting invoices, counsel's fee notes, etc., should be submitted with the claim
[15] 2 E.H.R.R. 317; November 11, 1980, Series A, No. 38
[16] The Conditional Fees Order 1993 and the Conditional Fees Regulations 1993

7 The Convention and U.K. and EEC Law

THE CONVENTION AND DOMESTIC U.K. LAW

The European Convention for the Protection of Human Rights and Fundamental Freedoms is an international treaty to which the U.K. is a party. It has not, however, been incorporated into English domestic law unlike, for instance, the Treaty of Rome, by the European Communities Act 1972. The effect of this was spelt out by Lord Ackner in R. v. *Secretary of State for the Home Department, ex p. Brind*[1]:

> it is a constitutional principle that if Parliament has legislated and the words of the statute are clear, the statute must be applied even if its application is in breach of international law.

Statutory interpretation

Set against the *above* rule of domestic law is the principle enunciated by Lord Diplock in *Garland* v. *British Rail Engineering*[2]:

> that the words of a statute passed after the treaty has been signed and dealing with the subject matter of the international obligation of the United Kingdom, are to be construed, if they are reasonably capable of bearing such a meaning, as intended to carry out the obligation, and not to be inconsistent with it.

Brind concerned a directive issued by the Home Secretary prohibiting broadcasting authorities from broadcasting direct statements made by representatives of proscribed Northern Ireland organisations. Although the House of Lords held that the Secretary of State had not exceeded his powers in this particular case, it confirmed that it was prepared to consider (as one factor in its assessment) whether his actions had violated the Convention. Lord Bridge, who gave the leading judgment, reiterated the constitutional position, thus:

---

[1] [1991] 1 A.C. 696 at p. 733
[2] [1982] 1 Q.B. 770, C.A.

> if domestic legislation conflicts with the Convention, the courts must nevertheless enforce [the domestic legislation]. But it is already well settled that, in construing any provision in domestic legislation which is ambiguous . . . the courts will presume that Parliament intended to legislate in conformity with the Convention.

Lord Bridge went on to say that the test for whether domestic legislation is to be considered 'ambiguous' is whether *'it is capable of a meaning which conforms to or conflicts with the Convention'*.

This would seem to mean that if the legislation conforms with the Convention, then it is not ambiguous; but if it conflicts with the Convention, then it is ambiguous. Such an interpretation has to a certain extent been endorsed by subsequent decisions, most particularly in the case of *Derbyshire County Council* v. *Times Newspapers*[3] (referred to *below*).

Lord Templeman in the *Brind* decision sought not only to confirm the applicability of the Convention in such cases, but also specifically endorsed the possibility of 'proportionality' being a legitimate judicial concept within domestic review proceedings, holding:

> It seems to me that the courts cannot escape from asking themselves only whether a reasonable Secretary of State, on the material before him, could reasonably conclude that the interference with freedom of expression which he determined to impose was justifiable. In terms of the Convention, as construed by the European Court of Human Rights, the interference with freedom of expression must be necessary and proportionate to the damage which the restriction is designed to prevent.

Common law clarification

The relevance of the Convention to domestic common law was explored by the House of Lords in the Spycatcher case, *A.-G.* v. *Guardian Newspapers (No. 2)*[4] where the judgment of the Master of the Rolls in the Court of Appeal was approved. Lord Donaldson asserted *'for my part I can detect no inconsistency between our domestic law and the Convention'*.

In *Brind* the Master of the Rolls had stated in a similar vein[5]:

> you have to look long and hard before you can detect any difference between the English common law and the principles set out in the Convention, at least if the Convention is viewed through English judicial eyes.

In the Spycatcher case the House of Lords was prepared to consider the validity of the Government's claim by, *inter alia*, testing it against the criteria adopted by the Convention. Lord Goff held that:

---

[3] [1992] 2 A.C. 751; [1993] 1 All E.R. 1011
[4] [1990] 1 A.C. 109
[5] [1990] 1 A.C. 696

> In any event I conceive it to be my duty, when I am free to do so, to interpret the law in accordance with the obligations of the Crown under this treaty.

There is, therefore, an increasing trend by senior judges to 'discover' that the Convention is in fact part of common law, or at least the principles of the Convention are inseparable from the principles of common law.

In *Rantzen* v. *Mirror Group Newspapers*[6] Lord Justice Neil stated in his judgment that it was now *'established by recent authorities that the common law is consistent with Article 10 of the European Convention'*. The case concerned the appropriate *quantum* of defamation damages and the almost limitless discretion of juries in this regard. This discretion was held to conflict with the requirements of Article 10; which conflict was deemed sufficient justification for the Court to radically amend the domestic law, and thereby significantly reduce the *quantum* of defamation awards[7].

The Court of Appeal conducted a thorough and sympathetic review of the place occupied by the Convention in domestic law in *Derbyshire County Council* v. *Times Newspapers*[8]. Here the Court had to decide whether a local authority had a right to sue for libel in respect of its administrative reputation, where no financial loss was alleged. A principal reason for finding that no such right existed was that it would otherwise enable a local authority:

> to stifle legitimate public criticism of its activities and thereby interfere with the right to freedom of expression enshrined in Art. 10 of the Convention for the Protection of Human Rights and Fundamental Freedoms.

At first instance the judge had refused to consider the Convention, because in his view there was no *'uncertainty or ambiguity in relation to the ambit of English law in relation to the extent to which local authorities may sue for libel'*. The Court of Appeal disagreed, holding that ambiguity existed; in a large measure merely because there was no Court of Appeal or House of Lords' authority on the point.

Whilst inevitably in this case the Court was concerned with Article 10 of the Convention, the Court's findings could apply in appropriate cases to the other Convention rights.

---

[6] (1993) 143 N.L.J. 507

[7] *See also W (A Minor) (Wardship: Restrictions on Application), Re* [1992] 1 W.L.R. 100 where the Court of Appeal was prepared to look at the Convention for guidance when deciding whether or not to grant an injunction prohibiting the publication of an article relating to an adolescent ward of court

[8] *See note 3 above.* The Court of Appeal judgment was affirmed by the House of Lords; Lord Keith giving the leading judgment concluded, 'I have reached my conclusion upon the Common Law of England without finding any need to rely upon the European Convention . . . and can only add that I find it satisfactory to be able to conclude that the Common Law of England is consistent with the obligations assumed by the Crown under the treaty in this particular field'

Balcombe L.J. listed situations where it was valid to invoke the Convention in domestic law, namely:

1. For the purpose of the resolution of an ambiguity in English primary or subordinate legislation (*i.e.* *Brind*).
2. When considering principles upon which the court should act in exercising a discretion, *e.g.* whether or not to grant an interlocutory injunction (*i.e. W. (A Minor), Re*[9]).
3. When the common law (including the doctrines of equity) is uncertain.

He added to this list a fourth category, which he explained thus:

4. Even if the common law is certain, the courts will still, when appropriate, consider whether the United Kingdom is in breach of Art. 10. Thus, in R. v. *Bow Street Magistrates' Court, ex p. Choudry*[10], where the issue was whether the common law offence of blasphemy is restricted to Christianity, Watkins L.J. delivering the judgment of a strong Divisional Court said:
   [counsel for the respondent publishers] accepted that obligations imposed on the United Kingdom by the Convention are relevant sources of public policy where the common law is uncertain. But, he maintained, the common law of blasphemy is, without doubt, certain. Accordingly it is not necessary to pay any regard to the Convention. Nevertheless, he thought it necessary, and we agree, in the context of this case, to attempt to satisfy us that the United Kingdom is not in any event in breach of the Convention.

Lord Justice Balcombe's fourth category has the sound of a creaking door: creaking open. Why after all should one use valuable court time considering the conformity of U.K. law with the Convention, if the court is powerless to intervene if conformity is not found? Lord Bridge's definition of 'ambiguous' in *Brind* (*see* p. 101 *above*) may possibly provide an answer to this question. If, after having considered the conformity of U.K. law with the Convention, conformity is not found, then it is arguable (applying his definition) that ambiguity must exist.

In his judgment Balcombe L.J. also adopted the fiction of assessing the resilience of domestic law by comparing it to the Convention to see if it was found wanting; thus he states:

> So Art. 10 does not establish any novel proposition under English law. Nevertheless, since it states the right to freedom of expression and the qualifications to that right in precise terms, it will be convenient to consider the question by reference to Art. 10 alone.

Lord Justice Butler-Sloss's speech took Balcombe L.J.'s second category a stage further:

> where there is an ambiguity, or the law is otherwise unclear or so far undeclared by an appellate court, the English court is not only entitled but, in my judgment, obliged to consider the implications of Art. 10.

[9] *See* note 7 *above*
[10] [1991] 1 Q.B. 429

She also agreed with Balcombe L.J.'s fourth category, namely that even if the law were clear and devoid of ambiguity it would still be appropriate (in this particular case) to review the Convention to establish that domestic law was in conformity with it. The decision was approved by the House of Lords on appeal, Lord Keith finding to his satisfaction *'that the common law of England was consistent with the obligations assumed by the Crown under the [Convention]'*[11].

Domestic U.K. law and E.C. law

Unlike the Convention, E.C. law has been incorporated into domestic U.K. law. Where there is a conflict with domestic law, E.C. law takes precedence[12]. In most cases E.C. law has direct effect and can be invoked in U.K. courts and tribunals[13].

As will be seen *below*, the European Court of Justice considers itself bound to interpret E.C. law so as to conform with the Convention. The obligation to consider conformity with the Convention applies therefore not only to the Court of Justice in Luxembourg but also to any domestic court or tribunal applying E.C. law or examining whether domestic law conflicts with E.C. law. In this respect at least the Convention could be seen as entering the U.K. legal system riding on the back of our membership of the European Community.

THE CONVENTION AND E.C. LAW

All the Member States of the European Community have ratified the Convention. The European Community itself, however, is not a signatory to the Convention; indeed on its present wording the Convention is not open to signature by the E.C. The Commission has explored the possibility of the Community acceding to the Convention, concluding that *'the Community should now subscribe to the fundamental rights enshrined in the ECHR and should do so all the more in that these rights, especially those in the additional Protocols, are clearly related to Community activities'*[14]. The issue of human rights within the European Community has also been the subject of a Joint Declaration by the European Parliament, the Council and the Commission on April 5, 1977[15].

---

[11] *See* note 3 *above*
[12] European Communities Act 1972, s.2(1)
[13] For an overview of the effect of Community law *see* Mathijesen *A Guide to European Community Law*, Sweet & Maxwell, p. 304 *et seq.*
[14] Bull. E.C. 4-1979
[15] Bull. E.C. 3-1978

The E.C. Treaty, 'The Single European Act', which entered into force on July 1, 1987, recites in its preamble the resolution of the Member States to:

> implement this European union on the basis, firstly, of the communities operating in accordance with their own rules and, secondly, of European co-operation among the signatory states in the sphere of foreign policy and to invest this union with the necessary means of action, determined to work together to promote democracy on the basis of the fundamental rights recognised in the constitutions and laws of Member States, in the Convention for the Protection of Human Rights and Fundamental Freedoms and the European Social Charter, notably freedom, equality and social justice.

The Court of Justice has frequently referred to the Convention in its decisions and reiterated its view that E.C. law does not differ in any way in its respect for fundamental rights and freedoms.

In *Nold* v. *E.C. Commission* [16] the Court of Justice asserted that fundamental rights as enshrined in the Convention *'form an integral part of the general principles of law, the observance of which'* the Court ensures.

In *Housing of Migrant Workers: E.C. Commission* v. *Germany*[17] the Court of Justice had to consider the interpretation of an E.C. regulation concerning equal treatment for the families of migrant workers. The Court held that the regulation:

> must be interpreted in the light of the requirement of respect for family life set out in Article 8 of the Convention for the Protection of Human Rights and Fundamental Freedoms. That requirement is one of the fundamental rights which, according to the Single European Act, are recognised by Community Law.

In *Hoechst A.G.* v. *E.C. Commission (Nos. 46/87 and 227/88)*[18] the Court of Justice had to consider the legality of an E.C. regulation which empowered E.C. Commission officials to search company premises, copy documents and question company employees. The applicant companies challenged the legality of the regulation, claiming that it was incompatible with the fundamental freedoms recognised in the Community legal order, and therefore void. The fundamental right which the companies alleged to have been breached was the inviolability of the home. The Court of Justice considered Article 8 of the Convention (the right to respect for a person's private and family life, home and correspondence). The Court of Justice, having noted that there was no case law of the European Court of Human Rights on the issue in question[19], held that this right did not extend to business premises. It however reaffirmed that:

---

[16] (1974) E.C.R. 491
[17] [1990] 3 C.M.L.R. 540
[18] [1991] 4 C.M.L.R. 410
[19] The question has now been considered by the European Court of Human Rights in *Niemietz* v. *Germany* 16 E.H.R.R. 97; December 16, 1992, Series A, No. 251-B

The Court has consistently held that fundamental rights are an integral part of the general principles of law the observance of which the Court ensures, in accordance with constitutional traditions common to the Member States, and the international treaties on which the Member States have collaborated or of which they are signatories. The European Convention for the Protection of Human Rights and Fundamental Freedoms . . . is of particular significance in that regard.

There is no doubt that the European Community is providing a substantial impetus to the incorporation into U.K. law of the principles enshrined by the Convention. This impetus occurs at a time when domestic courts are themselves showing a remarkable (and hitherto unseen) willingness to allow direct reference to the Convention. Whilst there remains uncertainty as to how its eventual incorporation will occur, there can be few lawyers who now seriously doubt that by the year 2000 the Convention will be a central pillar of the human rights law directly applicable within the U.K.

8 The Convention and Protocols

PROTECTION OF LIFE: ARTICLE 2

Article 2

1. *Everyone's right to life shall be protected by law. No one shall be deprived of his life intentionally save in the execution of a sentence of a court following his conviction of a crime for which this penalty is provided by law.*
2. *Deprivation of life shall not be regarded as inflicted in contravention of this Article when it results from the use of force which is no more than absolutely necessary:*
   (a) in defence of any person from unlawful violence;
   (b) in order to effect a lawful arrest or to prevent the escape of a person lawfully detained;
   (c) in action lawfully taken for the purpose of quelling a riot or insurrection.

Article 2 places on the state a positive duty to protect life as well as providing an exhaustive list of situations where killing may be permitted[1]. Article 2 is one of the non-derogable rights under Article 15 (*see* p. 197). Protocol 6, which has not been signed by the U.K., abolishes the death penalty, except in times of war or the imminent threat of war.

Article 2(1), whilst not itself prohibiting a judicial death penalty, requires that the domestic law protect 'everyone's' right to life: it constitutes one of the most important rights in the Convention. The requirement is that the state must 'not only refrain from taking life "intentionally" but, further, take appropriate steps to safeguard life'[2].

In this respect the Commission has considered a number of complaints including the adequacy of steps taken by the U.K. to reduce the

[1] DR 39/162
[2] DR 14/31

risks of a vaccination programme[3], the need to provide bodyguard protection for terrorist targets[4] and whether the state should refrain from taking action which would provoke a suicide[5]. In all these cases the steps taken by the state have, on examination, been found adequate; nevertheless the requirements of the Article are interpreted strictly by the Commission.

Article 2(2) lists the permitted situations where the right to life is not protected; all are concerned with the suppression of violence and/or the maintenance of the rule of law.

In *Stewart* v. *U.K.* [6] the Commission considered a complaint concerning the death of the applicant's 13-year-old son, Brian, who was killed as a result of being struck in the head by a plastic bullet fired by the army in Northern Ireland. The Commission accepted the Government's evidence that the soldiers were confronted with a hostile and violent crowd of 150 persons who were attacking them with stones and other missiles. The Commission accepted that this constituted 'by any standard' a riot.

In investigating whether the unintentional killing of Brian Stewart amounted to a violation of Article 2, the Commission stated that it had to:

> examine whether the force used . . . was 'absolutely necessary' within the meaning of paragraph 2. [The Commission] must consider the proportionality of the use of the plastic bullet round to the aim pursued, having regard to the situation confronting the soldiers, the degree of force employed in response and the risk that the use of force would result in the deprivation of life.

The Commission thus emphasised that from the phrase 'absolutely necessary' there stems a requirement that any interference with the right to life be justified as being 'proportionate to the legitimate aim pursued' and that from the word 'absolutely' it was clear that 'a stricter and more compelling test of necessity must be applied'[7].

Abortion

The Court and Commission have yet to finally pronounce upon whether 'everyone' includes an unborn child. There can be little doubt that this stems from the highly controversial nature of the issue, one

[3] *Ibid*.
[4] DR 32/190. 'Article 2 cannot be interpreted as imposing a duty on a state to give protection of this nature [several years of police protection], at least not for an indefinite period of time'
[5] DR 50/259
[6] 39/162
[7] *Ibid*. at p. 170/1

upon which there are inevitably strongly differing views within the Commission and Court. In the recent case of *Open Door Counselling Ltd. and Dublin Well Woman Centre Ltd.* v. *Ireland*[8] the case concerned an injunction obtained by the Irish Attorney-General restraining the applicant companies from giving abortion advice. By a 15:8 majority, the Court held that the injunction violated the Convention. Although primarily concerned with Article 10 (the right to impart information), the Court was also required to consider Article 2 as a result of the Irish Government's submission that the information ban was justified to protect the rights of others, *i.e.* the unborn child.

So controversial is the issue that the the Court avoided the question, holding that it was not necessary in the context of the Article 10 complaint to decide whether a right to an abortion was guaranteed by the Convention, or whether 'everyone' in Article 2 included a foetus.

Reference has already been made to the Commission's rejection of a number of complaints concerning abortion rights on separate admissibility grounds (*see* p. 21). The Commission decision in the 1979 complaint of *X* v. *U.K.*[9] probably still represents the prevailing view of the Court and Commission on the subject. The Commission's view was that abortion did not violate the Convention where it was for the protection of the life or health of the mother. The Commission doubted that the word 'everyone' included the foetus but neither came to a final decision on this point, nor on whether there could be a stage in the pregnancy at which different considerations might apply[10].

Extra-judicial killing

A primary aim of Article 2 is to prohibit execution of persons by the state outside the judicial process. In *Cyprus* v. *Turkey*[11], the Committee of Ministers upheld complaints made by Cyprus concerning such killings during the Turkish invasion. Such complaints in general face almost insurmountable difficulties, even if made by a state; sufficient evidence has first to be obtained to convince the Commission and Court that the deaths did not result from one of the permitted exceptions (self defence, etc.) and then it has to be established that the violations were, at the minimum, condoned by the respondent state. The Irish Government failed in this respect before the Commission in the *Ireland* v. *U.K.*[12] An alternative route for such complaints lies via

15 E.H.R.R. 244; October 29, 1992, Series A, No. 246

DR 19/24

[10] *See also* DR 10/100 which concerns the issues raised by such complaints in relation to Article 8

[11] 4 E.H.R.R. 482

[12] 2 E.H.R.R. 25; January 18, 1978, Series A, No. 25. On September 6, 1993 the Commission however ruled admissible a complaint arising out of the shooting of three alleged Members of the IRA in Gibraltar by members of the SAS in July 1988

the United Nations' Special Rapporteur on Arbitrary Executions, and this procedure was adopted in relation to complaints arising out of the shooting of three alleged members of the IRA in Gibraltar by members of the SAS on July 28, 1988 (*see* p. 222)[12a].

[12a] The shooting was subsequently considered by the Commission, *see* note 12 *above*

INHUMAN AND DEGRADING TREATMENT: ARTICLE 3

Article 3

No one shall be subjected to torture or to inhuman or degrading treatment or punishment.

Article 3 is one of the non-derogable rights under Article 15 (*see* p. 197). The duty placed upon the state is to ensure that within its jurisdiction[13] no one is subjected to such ill-treatment. The obligation exists even if the victim's behaviour has been unhelpful or obstructive[14]. Whilst torture and inhuman treatment connote unnecessary assaults within the tortious meaning of the word, degrading treatment is concerned with behaviour that is designed to distress and humiliate the victim.

It is somewhat academic whether the extreme behaviour involved amounts to torture or inhuman treatment. Sadly the Commission, Court and Committee of Ministers have had a number of interstate cases to consider which contain some of the most reprehensible forms of treatment[15].

In *Ireland* v. *U.K.*[16] the Court held that ill-treatment must:

> attain a minimum level of severity if it is to fall within the scope of Article 3. The assessment of this minimum is, in the nature of things, relative; it depends on all the circumstances of the case, such as the duration of the treatment, its physical or mental effects and, in some cases, the sex, age and state of health of the victim.

The Court further defined the three categories of ill-treatment, thus:

---

[13] This duty may extend beyond the state jurisdiction, where the protection of the victim is within the state's power, see *Kirkwood* v. *U.K.* DR 37/158; and *Soering* v. *U.K.* 11 E.H.R.R. 439; July 7, 1989, Series A, No. 94

[14] DR 28/5; where the obstruction itself is the principle cause of the violation the situation may be otherwise, DR 36/200

[15] These include *Denmark, Norway, Sweden and the Netherlands* v. *Greece* (1967 complaint concerning conditions following the military coup in Greece); *Denmark, Norway, Sweden* v. *Greece* (1970 complaint); *Cyprus* v. *Turkey* (1974/5/7 complaints following the Turkish invasion of Cyprus); *Ireland* v. *U.K.* (1971/2 complaints relating to interrogation techniques and detention conditions in Northern Ireland); *France, Norway, Denmark, Sweden and the Netherlands* v. *Turkey* (1982 complaint arising out of the military coup in 1980) DR 35/143; *see also* Sieghart *The International Law of Human Rights*, para. 14.3.5, for a résumé of the different forms of torture and inhuman treatment involved in these cases

[16] 2 E.H.R.R. 25; January 25, 1978, Series A, No. 25

TORTURE:
Deliberate inhuman treatment causing very serious and cruel suffering.
INHUMAN TREATMENT:
Treatment that causes intense physical and mental suffering.
DEGRADING TREATMENT:
Treatment that arouses in the victim a feeling of fear, anguish and inferiority capable of humiliating and debasing the victim and possibly breaking his or her physical or moral resistance.

Where the complaint concerns extreme state-sanctioned behaviour in violation of Article 3, the complainant inevitably faces 'inherent difficulties in the proof' of such allegations; a point recognised by the Commission when investigating the complaints made by the Scandinavian countries against Greece. In such cases an alternative route may be via the European Convention for the Prevention of Torture and Inhuman or Degrading Treatment or Punishment, *see* p. 217.

The examination in this text is confined to what minimum criteria are required for the behaviour to violate Article 3; primarily therefore, to behaviour which attains the status of degrading treatment or punishment. There has been a wide variety of complaints alleging degrading treatment[17], but in large measure they have concerned the issues set out below.

Corporal punishment

The Court has ruled that birching as part of a criminal sentence amounts to degrading punishment, thereby violating Article 3. In *Tyrer* v. *U.K.*[18] the applicant had been birched as a result of a sentence imposed by a juvenile court in the Isle of Man. The Court held that: *'although the applicant did not suffer any severe or long-lasting physical effects, his punishment—whereby he was treated as an object in the power of the authorities—constituted an assault on precisely that which it is one of the main purposes of Article 3 to protect, namely a person's dignity and physical integrity'.*

The question of corporal punishment in schools has come before the Court and Commission on a number of occasions. In *Campbell and Cosans* v. *U.K.*[19] the complaint concerned corporal punishment in

---

[17] These include the compelling of a professional to give evidence, DR 57/81; the change of practice to deny a prisoner parole, DR 46/231; the obligation to submit to a court-ordered psychiatric examination; the legal prohibition on a mentally incapacitated victim of a sexual assault from lodging a criminal complaint

[18] 2 E.H.R.R. 1; April 25, 1978, Series A, No. 26

[19] 4 E.H.R.R. 293; February 25, 1982, Series A, No. 48

Scottish schools where the children were liable to be struck with a strap, known as a tawse. Whilst the applicants' sons ran the risk of such punishment, neither had in fact been so punished. The Court held that there had been no violation of Article 3 as the children had not, 'solely by reason of the risk of being subjected thereto, [been] humiliated or debased in the eyes of others to the requisite degree at all'.

The case of *Warwick v. U.K.*[20] concerned the striking of a 16-year-old girl's hand with a cane by her headmaster, in the presence of another master. The caning caused two large bruises on the palm of her hand, which were still visible when she was examined by a GP eight days later. The Commission held the complaint admissible under Article 3 as well as under Article 2 of the First Protocol, and the complaint was ultimately settled before the Committee of Ministers upon the Government confirming its decision to abolish corporal punishment in state schools (via ss.47 and 48 of the Education (No. 2) Act 1986) and its agreement to pay the applicant's costs.

In *Costello-Roberts v. U.K.*[21] a seven-year-old boy was hit three times on the bottom, through his shorts, with a rubber-soled shoe. No bruising was caused and no evidence was adduced of any lasting psychological effects. The punishment occurred because the boy had accumulated five demerit points (for talking in a corridor, being late for bed, etc.); in such cases corporal punishment was automatic and was administered three days after the boy was told he would be so punished. By a minimum majority of 5:4 the Court held that there had been no violation of Article 3. In order to be violated the punishment must be degrading; the humiliation or debasement must attain a particular level of severity; and must in any event be other than the usual element of humiliation inherent in any punishment. The Court also rejected, unanimously, the complaint under Article 8, but did not exclude the possibility of this Article affording a protection in such cases that went beyond Article 3. The four dissenting judges considered that such an action might be justified on the spur of the moment, but that the formalised beating of a lonely and insecure little boy in a new school after a wait of three days was degrading within the meaning of Article 3.

Discrimination

Within the Convention, as it is presently interpreted, there is no fundamental prohibition of discrimination. Article 14 prohibits discrimination in the sense that there is unequal enjoyment of the fundamen-

[20] DR 60/5 and *see also* DR 49/44
[21] *The Times*, March 26, 1993

tal rights set out in Articles 2–12, rather than discrimination *per se*, p. 193. The legality of discrimination is also covered by the UN International Convention on the Elimination of All Forms of Racial Discrimination (see p. 224).

In *Patel* v. *U.K.* (East African Asians case)[22] the Commission considered that degrading treatment was not restricted to actual assaults but included acts of a serious nature designed to interfere with the dignity of a person. The case concerned the mass expulsion of Asians from East Africa some of whom, even though they held a valid British passport, were refused residence in the U.K. The Commission considered that the immigration laws discriminated on grounds of race and colour to a degree that the complainants were the victims of degrading treatment:

> the legislation applied in the present cases discriminated against the applicants on the grounds of their colour or race. . . . discrimination based on race could, in certain circumstances, of itself amount to degrading treatment within the meaning of Article 3 of the Convention.

> . . . a special importance should be attached to discrimination based on race; that publicly to single out a group of persons for differential treatment on the basis of race might, in certain circumstances, constitute a special form of affront to human dignity; and that differential treatment of a group of persons on the basis of race might therefore be capable of constituting degrading treatment when differential treatment on some other ground would raise no such question.

> The Commission considers that the racial discrimination, to which the applicants have been publicly subjected by the application of the above immigration legislation, constitutes an interference with the human dignity which, in the special circumstances described above, amounted to 'degrading treatment' in the sense of Article 3 of the Convention.

In the subsequent complaint of *Abdulaziz, Cabales, and Balkandali* v. *U.K.*[23], (which concerned the U.K. immigration policy of refusing to allow husbands from certain countries to join their wives in the U.K.) the Court held that:

> the difference in treatment complained of did not denote any contempt or lack of respect for the personality of the applicants and that it was not designed to, and did not, humiliate or debase but was intended solely to achieve the aims [of primary immigration control]. It cannot therefore be regarded as 'degrading'.

The relevance of the these cases is not limited to the issue of racial discrimination; the Commission in its report to the Court did not

---

[22] 3 E.H.R.R. 76; because of the political sensitivity of the Commission's Report it was to be kept confidential and has not been published by the Council of Europe; it thankfully has been published by the European Human Rights Reports

[23] 7 E.H.R.R. 471; May 28, 1985, Series A, No. 94

exclude the possibility that 'degrading aspects of sexual and other forms of discrimination' could violate Article 3 although it considered it unnecessary to investigate this aspect in relation to the particular complaint.

In extreme cases, therefore, this could potentially extend to publicly humiliating and personally distressing treatment solely on the grounds of disability, illness, religion, personal beliefs or habit of life.

Detention conditions

Article 3 places a far greater obligation upon the state in respect of prisoners than merely to refrain from inflicting physical punishment. Even where the prisoners are in revolt or in total non-co-operation, the state is not absolved from its obligations under Article 3 and must continuously review the detention arrangements to ensure the health and well-being of the prisoners *'with due regard to the ordinary and reasonable requirements of imprisonment'*[24].

The Court has shown itself capable of forthright condemnation of domestic police behaviour where ill-treatment is alleged by detainees. In *Tomasi* v. *France* [25] the Court had no doubt that the applicant, who had been arrested upon suspicion of having committed terrorist offences, had been beaten up in police custody. It found that medical reports attested:

> to the large number of blows inflicted on Mr Tomasi and their intensity; these are two elements which are sufficiently serious to render such treatment inhuman and degrading. The requirements of the investigation and the undeniable difficulties inherent in the fight against crime, particularly with regard to terrorism, cannot result in limits being placed on the protection to be afforded in respect of the physical integrity of individuals.

In cases involving the possible violation of Article 3 by unsatisfactory prison conditions, reference should be made to the European Prison Rules[26]. The Commission has nevertheless held that where a short detention occurred in conditions of detention that did not come up to these standards, this alone did not conclusively amount to a violation of Article 3.[27]

---

[24] DR 20/44; 3 E.H.R.R. 161
[25] 15 E.H.R.R. 1; August 27, 1992, Series A, No. 241–A; in his concurring opinion Judge Meyer emphasised that any unnecessary use of force upon a suspect in custody violates Article 3, and the question of its intensity or severity is only relevant to determine whether there has been torture
[26] Recommendation No. R (87)3 adopted by the Committee of Ministers on February 12, 1987, which lays down minimum rules for the treatment of prisoners; *see* p. 164
[27] DR 6/170; and *see* DR 10/221

The Commission has considered a large number of complaints concerning prison conditions, and has formulated general principles on the more common situations.

SOLITARY CONFINEMENT

The Commission has held that the segregation of a prisoner from the prison community does not in itself constitute a form of inhuman treatment[28].

In *R. v. Denmark*[29] the Commission reiterated that prolonged solitary confinement is undesirable, especially where the person is detained on remand. In this case the victim (charged with drug offences and murder) had been segregated from other prisoners for 17 months. The Commission considered that a balance had to be struck between the requirements of the investigation and the effect which the isolation will have on the detained person. There was a need to ensure that the duration did not become excessive. Although the Commission felt 17 months to be excessive in the case, it held that the *'measure was not of such severity as to fall within Article 3'*.

In assessing whether such a measure may fall within the ambit of Article 3 in a given case, regard must be had to all the relevant factors, both objective (*i.e.* the duration, the reason for the measure or its severity) and subjective (*i.e.* the actual effect the measure has had upon the complainant). *'Complete sensory isolation coupled with complete social isolation can no doubt ultimately destroy the personality, and may therefore, in certain circumstances, constitute a form of inhuman treatment'*[30].

In *Hilton v. U.K.*[31] the applicant was separated from other prisoners under Rule 43 of the Prison Rules and spent 23 hours a day in solitary confinement. The majority of the Commission held that no violation had occurred despite *'the conditions of overcrowding and understaffing . . . the rigorous, impersonal application of disciplinary measures, on occasions to the point of absurdity'*. The minority of Commissioners considered Article 3 violated, stating *'we find it inadmissible that a prison system should reduce a prisoner to an "animal-like state", to use the phrase frequently mentioned in this case, whatever his difficulties'*. Given the dissension within the Commission and that this was a 1978 case, it might be that the Commission's finding would be otherwise today.

UNWELL PRISONERS

It is inevitable that the detention of prisoners suffering from serious medical disorders requires special action by the state to protect the

---

[28] DR 14/64
[29] DR 41/149
[30] *Ibid.* at p. 153. *See also* DR 49/89; and DR 2/58 concerning the conditions of detention of the Baader Meinhof group which were held to violate Article 3
[31] 3 E.H.R.R. 104

prisoners' well-being [32]. The detention of a person who is unwell may raise issues under Article 3, to the extent that this may convert the detention from being reasonable into inhuman or degrading punishment [33]. In assesssing whether the state has discharged its responsibilities in such cases, consideration will be given to whether it has followed expert medical advice, for instance, in transferring the prisoner to hospital for examination[34].

The Commission and Court have considered a number of complaints concerning the detention of prisoners in mental hospitals, the prevailing conditions in these institutions and the question of the compulsory administration of drugs [35]. It has stressed that in each case the question is one of fact and degree, assessing the threat posed by the prisoner, 'the particular conditions, the stringency of the measure, its duration, the objective pursued and its effects on the person concerned' [36].

Expulsion

Cases challenging expulsion will frequently raise issues concerning Article 8 as well as requests for interim relief (see p. 61).

The Convention does not guarantee the right of an alien to enter or to reside in a particular country, nor a right not to be expelled from a particular country [37]. Where, however, there is a serious reason to believe that the person to be expelled (or extradited, see below) will be subjected to ill-treatment contrary to Article 3, then in 'exceptional circumstances' the expulsion may itself violate Article 3 [38]. It is not necessary to establish that the feared ill-treatment will be at the hands of the receiving state; in Y.H. v. Germany[39], the complainant, a Shiite, challenged her expulsion to Lebanon, stating that she would be in serious risk of ill-treatment from the competing militia in the country though not from the state. The Commission indicated that it would be prepared to consider such a threat. It may not be necessary to establish that the ill-treatment will be deliberate. In Taspinar v. Netherlands[40], the applicant, a Turkish citizen, had been living in the Netherlands for nine years and then brought his seven-year-old son from Turkey to live with him. The Netherlands refused the boy a residence permit, although there was no one able to care for him were he to return to

[2] DR 46/182; and see DR 27/200
[3] DR 33/158; and see DR 55/27
[4] Ibid.
[5] See Herczegfalvy v. Austria 15 E.H.R.R. 437; September 24, 1992, Series A, No. 242–B
[6] DR 55/5 at p. 21
[7] DR 24/239
[8] DR 29/48; and see A., B., and C. v. France 15 E.H.R.R. CD 39
[9] DR 51/258; and DR 60/284
[0] DR 44/262

Turkey. The Commission was prepared to consider that this could amount to degrading treatment.

Where the complainant alleges that expulsion to a particular country could result in ill-treatment, the onus is upon him or her to produce the evidence that there is a serious and concrete threat; it is not sufficient merely to express a fear of danger or the possibility of persecution[41]. In two recent cases the Court has emphasised that once substantial evidence is produced, it primarily relies upon the Commission to investigate and verify the facts [42] and that the examination of the facts must be rigorous in view of the absolute nature of Article 3, in that it 'enshrines one of the fundamental values of the democratic societies making up the Council of Europe'[43].

In *Vilvarajah* v. *U.K.*[44] the applicants were Tamils who sought to challenge their expulsion to Sri Lanka on the ground that they feared ill-treatment from the Sri Lankan army. The Court examined the allegations in great detail, but eventually held that the expulsions did not violate the Convention. Whilst not denying that some of the applicants were at risk of ill-treatment, the Court did not believe that their position was any worse than the generality of other Tamils who were returning to the country. By the time of the Court hearing, some of the applicants had already been returned to Sri Lanka and had suffered actual ill-treatment. The Court, however, held that the risk had to be assessed primarily with reference to those facts which were known or ought to have been known to the state at the time of the expulsion, although it accepted that subsequent information may be of value in confirming or refuting the state's assessment.

The Commission has accepted that the repeated expulsion of an individual whose identity is impossible to establish to a country where his admission is not guaranteed may raise an issue under Article 3, especially if this occurs over a long period of time from one country to another, without any country taking measures to regularise his situation [45]. A violation can only occur however if the applicant is fully co-operative in assisting the state in resolving the problem [46].

Extradition

In *Soering* v. *U.K.*[47] the Court held that the decision by a state to extradite a fugitive may give rise to an issue under Article 3 if the state

[41] DR 53/254; and see DR 51/258
[42] *Cruz Varas* v. *Sweden* 14 E.H.R.R. 1; March 20, 1991, Series A, No. 201
[43] *Vilvarajah* v. *U.K.* 14 E.H.R.R. 248; October 30, 1991, Series A, No. 248
[44] *Ibid.*
[45] DR 21/73; and see DR 46/112
[46] DR 38/145
[47] 11 E.H.R.R. 439; July 7, 1989, Series A, No. 161

had substantial grounds for believing that the person concerned, if extradited, would be subjected to torture, inhuman or degrading treatment or punishment in the requesting country.

Extradition, therefore, raises many of the same issues as expulsion, and many of the same principles apply, although the Court has emphasised that the beneficial purpose of extradition in preventing fugitive offenders from evading justice cannot be ignored. *Soering* was unusual in that it concerned extradition to the U.S.A. and the ill-treatment complained of amounted to the possibility of the applicant having to endure many years on 'death row' whilst he pursued appeals against the death penalty.

Where human rights might be grossly violated or entirely suppressed in the receiving country, then extradition to that country may be contrary to Article 3[48]. In general there is a presumption against this being the case in a country which has ratified the Convention, although it is understood that the Commission does not necessarily apply this presumption in the case of Turkey. When considering such complaints, the Commission will consider carefully assurances given by the requesting state [49].

[48] DR 51/272; and *see* DR 36/209
[49] *Ibid*.

FORCED OR COMPULSORY LABOUR: ARTICLE 4

Article 4

1. *No one shall be held in slavery or servitude.*
2. *No one shall be required to perform forced or compulsory labour.*
3. *For the purpose of this Article the term 'forced or compulsory labour' shall not include:*
   (a) any work required to be done in the ordinary course of detention imposed according to the provisions of Article 5 of this Convention or during conditional release from such detention;
   (b) any service of a military character or, in case of conscientious objectors in countries where they are recognised, service extracted instead of compulsory military service;
   (c) any service extracted in case of an emergency or calamity threatening the life or well-being of the community;
   (d) any work or service which forms part of normal civic obligations.

The absolute prohibition of slavery and servitude under Article 4(1) is a non-derogable right under Article 15 (*see* p. 197). As yet the Court and Commission have considered relatively few complaints under Article 4 and found no violations.

Slavery and servitude

Both slavery and servitude involve the victim in working without consent for an indeterminate, substantial or potentially unlimited duration. By their decisions both the Court and Commission have indicated that for slavery or servitude to be established a degree of severity of treatment needs to be attained that realistically one would not expect to find in a Council of Europe country except in time of military upheaval. Complaints alleging violation of Article 4(1) have tended to come from prisoners or soldiers; for whom, if the complaint were under Article 4(2) (alleging forced or compulsory labour), there is the additional hurdle to be crossed of the permitted exceptions for those in detention or military service.

In *Van Droogenbroek* v. *Belgium*[50] the applicant, a persistent criminal of no fixed abode, was sentenced to two years' imprisonment and

[50] 4 E.H.R.R. 443; June 24, 1982, Series A, No. 50

thereafter to a period of 10 years 'at the Government's disposal'. After the two-year sentence he was transferred to a prison reserved for recidivists, and was advised that he would not be released until he had saved 12,000BF, through prison work. The Court held that this did not violate Article 4; the work did *'not go beyond what is "ordinary" in this context since it was calculated to assist him in reintegrating himself into society'*.

Forced or compulsory labour

The Commission and Court have confirmed that 'forced or compulsory labour' are to be interpreted in line with the definitions of the International Labour Organisation (ILO)[51].

Article 2(1) of the ILO Convention Concerning Forced or Compulsory Labour 1930 (Convention No. 29) reads:

> For the purpose of this Convention the term 'forced or compulsory labour' shall mean all work or service which is exacted from any person under the menace of any penalty and for which the said person has not offered himself voluntarily'[52].

Article 1 of the ILO Convention Concerning the Abolition of Forced Labour 1957 (Convention No. 105) states:

> Each member of the ILO which ratifies this Convention undertakes to suppress and not to make use of any form of forced or compulsory labour
> (a) as a means of political coercion or education or as a punishment for holding or expressing political views or views ideologically opposed to the established political, social or economic system;
> (b) as a method of mobilising and using labour for purposes of economic development;
> (c) as a means of labour discipline;
> (d) as a punishment for having participated in strikes;
> (e) as a means of racial, social, national or religious discrimination[53].

For violation of Article 4(2) the work must, therefore, be involuntary and done to avoid the menace of the penalty. The Commission has held that the obligation to work must be unjust or oppressive and the work itself must cause the victim unavoidable hardship[54].

---

[51] The ILO was established in 1919 and is now a UN agency; it has adopted over 170 Conventions on the human rights of working people, the implementation of which it monitors; *see Hurst Hannum* Guide to International Human Rights Practice p. 99

[52] For the full text of the Convention *see* I. Brownlie *Basic Documents on Human Rights* (third edition), Clarendon Press, 1987, p. 246

[53] *Ibid.* at p. 257

[54] DR 18/216

In a series of complaints, consideration has been given to onerous conditions attached to membership of professional bodies. Thus the fact that as a condition of being a notary, one is required to accept lower fees from non-profit-making organisations, does not itself violate Article 4, as the complainant must have been aware of this condition before voluntarily becoming a notary[55]. A similar response was made by the Commission to a professional footballer's complaint, alleging that the transfer system forced him to work for a club against his will, when the bidding club for which he wished to play was unable to pay a sufficient sum for his transfer. Whilst the Commission considered the 'prior consent' aspect to be decisive, it held that even if this had not been the case, there would have been no violation, stating *'even if [the system] can produce certain inconveniences . . . it cannot be considered oppressive or constituting unavoidable hardship'*.

The Commission's view on Article 4 was perhaps taken to its extreme in *Iversen* v. *Norway*[56]. Iversen complained that he had been compelled (on penalty of fine and/or imprisonment) to work as a dentist in Northern Norway for one year against his will, as a result of legislation passed whilst he was undergoing his dentistry training. In a much criticised decision a majority of the Commission found the complaint inadmissible, on the ground that the work was not unjust, oppressive or involving unavoidable hardship and/or that the work was required because of public emergency (Article 4.3c).

In *Van Der Mussele* v. *Belgium*[57] the applicant barrister complained that during his pupilage he was required to do free legal representation work, which amounted to about a fifth of his total work. The court, whilst regarding the situation as most unsatisfactory, did not consider the amount so disproportionate as to come within Article 4. It also noted and relied upon the fact that he had voluntarily entered the profession with knowledge of the practice about which he complained.

Permitted exceptions to forced or compulsory labour

Article 4(3) lists circumstances where forced or compulsory labour is permitted. These circumstances, with the exception of public emergencies, include situations which occur frequently within most Convention countries, such as ordinary prison work or work as part of military conscription.

---

[55] *Ibid*.

[56] Complaint 1468/62, not published in Decisions and Reports. For comment and criticism of this decision *see* J.E.S. Fawcett *The Application of the European Convention on Human Rights* (second edition), Clarendon Press, 1987, p. 58 and P. van Dilk and G.H.J. van Hoof *Theory and Practice of the European Convention on Human Rights* (second edition), Kluwer, 1990, p. 244

[57] 6 E.H.R.R. 163; November 23, 1983, Series A. No. 70

WORK AS PART OF DETENTION OR CONDITIONAL RELEASE

Article 4 only permits forced or compulsory labour where it is in the ordinary course of detention which complies with Article 5. The Court has held that the work is to be proportionate and directed towards rehabilitation. In *De Wilde, Ooms and Versyp* v. *Belgium*[58] the applicants were sent to a vagrancy centre for two years by virtue of a statute for the suppression of vagrancy and begging. At the centre they were required to do menial prison work for a very low hourly pay. The court held that as the deprivation was legal within Article 5(1e) the work was permissible within Article 4(3a) as it had *'not exceeded the "ordinary" limits . . . as it was aimed at their rehabilitation and based upon a general [legally defined] standard'*.

The work must not in any event be disproportionate or oppressive[59].

The concept of 'conditional release' from detention will include such situations as release on licence, but not extend to sentences of community service; it is for this reason if no other that the defendant is required to confirm his or her consent to such community work orders.

SERVICE OF A MILITARY CHARACTER OR REQUIRED OF CONSCIENTIOUS OBJECTORS IN LIEU

Article 4.3b does not give conscientious objectors the right to exemption from military service, but leaves each state to decide whether or not to grant such a right[60]. The exemption covers the situation where a soldier signs on for a tour of duty for several years and then changes his mind before the expiry of that period; even if he was a minor at the time of the initial signing [61].

PUBLIC EMERGENCY AND NORMAL CIVIC OBLIGATIONS

Few cases have arisen concerning these exceptions to the prohibition of forced or compulsory labour. A minority of the Commissioners in *Iverson* v. *Norway* [62] considered that the circumstances constituted an emergency threatening the well-being of the community. Cases have also concerned an obligation on the holder of shooting rights to participate in a public programme erradicating foxes during an outbreak of rabies[63] and the obligation on employers to collect PAYE and other employee contributions[64].

---

[58] 1 E.H.R.R. 373; June 18, 1971, Series A, No. 12
[59] DR 18/235
[60] DR 38/213; and *see* DR 44/155; a denial of alternative service for conscientious objectors may involve a violation of Article 9
[61] Complaint 3435–8/67, not published in Decisions and Reports.
[62] *Supra* note 56
[63] DR 39/90
[64] DR 7/148

RIGHT TO LIBERTY AND SECURITY: ARTICLE 5

Article 5

1. *Everyone has the right to liberty and security of person. No one shall be deprived of his liberty save in the following cases and in accordance with a procedure prescribed by law:*
   (a) *the lawful detention of a person after conviction by a competent court;*
   (b) *the lawful arrest or detention of a person for non-compliance with the lawful order of a court or in order to secure the fulfilment of any obligation prescribed by law;*
   (c) *the lawful arrest or detention of a person effected for the purpose of bringing him before the competent legal authority on reasonable suspicion of having committed an offence or when it is reasonably considered necessary to prevent his committing an offence or fleeing after having done so;*
   (d) *the detention of a minor by lawful order for the purpose of educational supervision or his lawful detention for the purpose of bringing him before the competent legal authority;*
   (e) *the lawful detention of persons for the prevention of the spreading of infectious diseases, of persons of unsound mind, alcoholics or drug addicts or vagrants;*
   (f) *the lawful arrest or detention of a person to prevent his effecting an unauthorised entry into the country or of a person against whom action is being taken with a view to deportation or extradition.*
2. *Everyone who is arrested shall be informed promptly, in a language which he understands, of the reasons for his arrest and of any charge against him.*
3. *Everyone arrested or detained in accordance with the provisions of paragraph 1.c of this article shall be brought promptly before a judge or other officer authorised by law to exercise judicial power and shall be entitled to trial within a reasonable time or to release pending trial. Release may be conditioned by guarantees to appear for trial.*
4. *Everyone who is deprived of his liberty by arrest or detention shall be entitled to take proceedings by which the lawfulness of his detention shall be decided speedily by a court and his release ordered if the detention is not lawful.*
5. *Everyone who has been the victim of arrest or detention in contravention of the provisions of this article shall have an enforceable right to compensation.*

125

More than half of all complaints to the Commission invoke Articles 5 and/or 6. Article 5 is arguably at the heart of the Convention, applying as it does at the end of the twentieth century in a geographical area where there is basic respect for the right to life; where inhuman treatment and forced labour, within the meaning of the Convention, are virtually alien concepts. Article 5 places a total prohibition upon a state's power to deprive an individual of his or her liberty except in six clearly defined instances. Its exhaustive list details the situations in which detention is allowed and underpins the right to habeas corpus, the right to bail and the procedures detailed in the Police and Criminal Evidence Act 1984 and the Mental Health Act 1983.

The Convention permits derogation from Article 5 under Article 15 (*see* p. 197). It is perhaps an indication of the vigour of Article 5, that as a result of the Court decision that the Prevention of Terrorism (Temporary Provisions) Act 1984 violated Article 5[65], the U.K. opted for derogation rather than compliance[66]. In justification it asserted that a public emergency threatening the life of the nation existed.

Deprivation of liberty

Not every restriction upon a person's liberty amounts to 'detention': the Commission recognises the difference between 'helping the police with their enquiries' and arrest; thus being questioned for two hours at a police station in an unlocked room was held not to constitute detention[67]. Each case however has to be considered on its own facts, and to a degree the question is a subjective one. Whilst the personal circumstances of the victim are relevant, this does not mean that there can be no deprivation of liberty unless the victim objects[68].

In *Engel* v. *Netherlands*[69] the Court considered the different types of restriction that were placed upon a soldier's liberty, to ascertain when the degree of confinement amounted to detention within the meaning of Article 5. Thus it considered that four days' 'light' arrest (being confined to barracks, but otherwise allowed to move freely, use the

---

[65] *Brogan* v. *U.K.* 11 E.H.R.R. 117; November 29, 1988, Series A, No. 145-B

[66] On March 23, 1989 the U.K. notified the Secretary-General that in relation to terrorism in Northern Ireland it was necessary to retain detention without charge for periods of up to five days and to the extent that this was inconsistent with the *Brogan* decision the Government availed itself of the right to derogate under Article 15(1) and *see Brannigan and McBride* v. *U.K., The Times*, May 28, 1993

[67] DR 24/158

[68] *De Wilde, Ooms and Versyp* v. *Belgium* 1 E.H.R.R. 373; June 18, 1971, Series A, December No. 19

[69] 1 E.H.R.R. 647; June 8, 1976, Series A, No. 22. *See also Guzzardi* v. *Italy* 3 E.H.R.R. 333; November 6, 1980, Series A, No. 39 where the victim's confinement on an island was held to constitute detention

telephone or visit the camp cinema) did not amount in this context to detention, whereas two days 'strict' arrest, locked in a cell did. *'A disciplinary penalty or measure which on analysis would unquestionably be deemed a deprivation of liberty were it applied to a civilian may not possess this characteristic when imposed upon a serviceman. Nevertheless, such a penalty or measure does not escape the terms of Article 5 when it takes the form of restrictions that clearly deviate from the normal conditions of life within the armed forces'.*

Prescribed by law

Article 5 is violated where the detention takes place in breach of domestic law. The question of whether the detention is contrary to domestic law is primarily a question for the national courts, but is subject to scrutiny by the Commission and Court[70]. If the detention is contrary to domestic law then by Article 5(5) a duty to compensate the victim arises. Violations of the 'prescribed by law' requirement have been found by the Court, including two psychiatric cases in both of which the detention took place despite it being contrary to the domestic (Netherlands) law. In the first the victim was not given an opportunity to be heard[71], and in the second the hearing occurred in the absence of a registrar[72].

Post-conviction detention

The exception to the right of liberty only applies in this case where the conviction results from a court decision. In a military setting therefore, an officer's decision is not sufficient, the conviction must stem from an independent judicial body[73].

Detention after conviction, but pending an appeal, is permitted where the time served in custody during the appeal process can count towards the final sentence[74]. Where, however, the detention is extended beyond the original sentence as a result of the prisoner committing an offence whilst in custody, then this is permitted only if the further detention results from a further court conviction[75].

Where the prisoner is released on licence, then further detention under this provision pursuant to the original sentence is permitted provided grounds exist for the decision[76].

---

[70] DR 37/225; and *see* DR 40/42

[71] *Van Der Leer* v. *Netherlands* 12 E.H.R.R. 567; February 21, 1990, Series A, No. 170

[72] *Wassink* v. *Netherlands* September 27, 1990, Series A. No. 185-A

[73] *c.f.* a remand by an officer under Article 5(1)(c) *below*

[74] *Wemhoff* v. *Germany* 1 E.H.R.R. 55; June 27, 1968, Series A, No. 19

[75] *Van Droogenbroeck* v. *Belgium* 4 E.H.R.R. 443; June 24, 1982, Series A, No. 50

[76] *Weeks* v. *U.K.* 10 E.H.R.R. 293; March 2, 1987, Series A, No. 114. *c.f* DR 59/235, DR 17/35; and *see also* the question of discretionary life sentences under Article 5(4)

Detention for breach of lawful order or to fulfil legal obligation

The Convention is here concerned with detention for primarily civil issues: breach of maintenance or other matrimonial orders, injunctions or witness attendance orders. Cases have concerned detention for a psychiatric examination after non-compliance with a court order to this effect[77], a court order to attend for a blood test[78], failure to pay a fine[79], detention to establish identity[80], to obtain disclosure of car ownership details[81] or to satisfy a terrorist security check[82].

Where detention occurs to secure the fulfilment of an obligation, the Commission has laid down stringent qualifications to the use of detention[83], including:

1. The detention cannot normally occur until the person has had an opportunity to comply with the obligation; detention must not therefore be the first option unless, for instance, the person has a history of obstruction and non-compliance.
2. At the time detention occurs, the obligation must remain unfulfilled.
3. The obligation must be 'specific and concrete'[84]. The detainee must be in no doubt about the specific obligation he or she has broken, and precisely why he or she has failed to satisfy it.
4. Detention must be the only reasonably practicable way of securing fulfilment.
5. The object of the detention must be to contribute towards the obligation being fulfilled, rather than punishing for failure to comply.

Arrest on reasonable suspicion and preventative arrest

For the arrest or detention of a person to be valid, it must be 'lawful'. In this context, lawful applies to the domestic legal system. If the arrest or detention are contrary to domestic law, then the deprivation of liberty violates Article 5 and gives rise to a right to claim compensation by virtue of Article 5(5). Therefore where the detention on remand exceeds the maximum period authorised by domestic law, a violation may result[85].

---

[77] DR 3/92
[78] DR 18/15
[79] DR 8/42
[80] DR 52/111
[81] DR 42/127
[82] DR 48/237
[83] See DR 15/35 and DR 25/12
[84] Guzzardi v. Italy 3 E.H.R.R. 333; November 6, 1980, Series A, No. 39
[85] See DR 42/63 and c.f. DR 57/47

REASONABLE SUSPICION

The arrest or detention must be as a result of a reasonable suspicion that the person has committed an offence. In *Fox, Campbell and Hartley v. U.K.*[86] the complainants were arrested under the Northern Ireland (Emergency Provisions) Act 1978, which requires that the arresting officer genuinely and honestly suspects the person of being a terrorist. The Court accepted that at the time of the arrests, the police had a *bona fide* belief that Fox, Campbell and Hartley were terrorists. On the evidence before it, however, the Court found itself unable to support the conclusion that this amounted to 'reasonable suspicion' as required by the Article, and therefore the Court found it to have been violated.

If the 'reasonable suspicion' that precipitated the arrest or detention ceases to exist, any further detention will be contrary to the Convention, unless other grounds then exist[87].

PREVENTATIVE DETENTION

The arrest or detention in order to prevent the commission of an offence must be *'effected for the purpose of bringing him before the competent legal authority'*. The arrest must therefore be part of an anticipated chain of events leading to the defendant being brought promptly before a judge or other law officer in compliance with Article 5(3). Internment without trial is not permitted by the Convention [88].

Where arrest occurs to prevent an offence, the anticipated offence must be a specific act, rather than, for instance, a generalised belief that the arrested person is a recidivist[89].

Detention of a minor

In view of the potentially wide scope of this provision it is perhaps surprising that it has been invoked in so few complaints, although the difficulty children have in getting direct access to legal representation may well be the explanation. The Court has also shown a propensity to treat children as objects of concern rather than individuals in their own right. In *Nielsen v. Denmark*[90] the Court held that a child's detention in a psychiatric hospital against his will (to stop him living with his father) was not *'deprivation of liberty within the meaning of Article 5 but was a*

---

[86] 13 E.H.R.R. 157; August 30, 1990, Series A, No. 182
[87] *Stögmüllerr v. Austria* 1 E.H.R.R. 155; November 10, 1969, Series A, No. 9
[88] *Lawless v. Ireland* 1 E.H.R.R. 15; July 1, 1961, Series A, No. 3
[89] *See Guzzardi v. Italy* 3 E.H.R.R. 333; November 6, 1980, Series A, No. 39; and *Ciulla v. Italy* 13 E.H.R.R. 346; February 22, 1989, Series A, No. 148
[90] 11 E.H.R.R. 175; November 28, 1988, Series A, No. 144

responsible exercise by his mother of her custodial rights in the interests of the child'.

In *Bouamar* v. *Belgium*[91] the applicant, when aged 16, had been detained on nine different occasions for periods of 7–14 days, totalling 119 days in all. The Government alleged that the detentions furthered an educational aim and were therefore valid within Article 5(1)(d). The Court, however, found a violation of Article 5, in that *'the detention of a young man in a remand prison in conditions of virtual isolation and without the assistance of staff with educational training cannot be regarded as furthering any educational aim'.*

Whether a secure accommodation order within s.25 of the Children Act 1989 comes within the requirements of Article 5(1)(d) will depend upon the facts in each particular case.

Detention of persons of unsound mind, alcoholics, drug addicts, vagrants, or to prevent the spread of infectious diseases

The majority of complaints that have arisen under this provision have related to detention on psychiatric grounds. In *Winterwerp* v. *Netherlands*[92] and a series of subsequent cases[93], the Court and Commission have laid down a number of factors which must be satisfied before the detention of a person of unsound mind is lawful within the meaning of the Convention, including:

1. The medical disorder must be reliably established by objective medical expertise.
2. The nature or degree of the disorder must be sufficiently extreme to justify the detention.
3. The detention should only last as long as the medical disorder (and its required severity) persists.
4. If the detention is potentially indefinite then there must be a system of periodic reviews by a tribunal that has power to discharge.
5. The Convention does not however require that the detained person be receiving some form of medication or treatment whilst detained.

---

[91] 11 E.H.R.R. 1; February 29, 1988, Series A, No. 129
[92] 2 E.H.R.R. 387; October 24, 1979, Series A, No. 33
[93] *See for instance, X* v. *U.K.* 4 E.H.R.R. 188; October 24, 1981, Series A, No. 46, and *Ashingdane* v. *U.K.* 7 E.H.R.R. 528; May 28, 1985, Series A, No. 93

The Mental Health Act 1983 is a piece of legislation shaped in part by the requirements of the Convention and particularly to accommodate shortcomings in the 1959 Act, highlighted by *X* v. *U.K.*[94].

Whilst there have been very few complaints concerning detention to prevent the spread of infectious diseases, or of alcoholics or drug addicts, it is implicit in the decisions of the Court and Commission that a similar approach would be adopted to assess the validity of detention under these grounds as to that under the criteria of 'unsound mind'.

In relation to vagrancy however, there is the added complication that the word is capable of being defined very widely. The Court has in one case been invited (and declined) to include within its ambit members of the mafia; the Italian Government submitting that it was absurd that vagrants could be legally detained but that somehow the mafiosi were accorded greater protection[95].

In *De Wilde, Ooms and Versyp* v. *Belgium* [96] the Court accepted that the Convention does not contain a definition of the term, but approved the Belgian Criminal Code's definition, namely *'vagrants are persons who have no fixed abode, no means of subsistence and no regular trade or profession'*.

Anyone doubting the potential for misuse of the vagrancy detention provisions need look no further than the Vagrancy Act 1824, which astonishingly remains on the U.K.'s statute book.

Detention of illegal immigrants or of a person with a view to deportation or extradition

The Convention does not grant the right of an alien to enter or reside in a particular country. Article 5(1)(f) does, however, ensure that the right to liberty of aliens and others threatened with deportation or extradition are protected within the rule of law; that such persons do not slip through the Convention's human rights safety net.

Detention under this provision must contain the following key elements:

1. The detention must be lawful. It must conform with the domestic laws and regulations. The rules must be sufficiently certain so that it must have been reasonably foreseeable in advance that the entry in question would be unauthorised[97]. The Commission and Court are prepared to investigate in detail the legality of the detention where the circumstances indicate that it has been

---

[94] *Ibid.*
[95] *See* note 84 *above*
[96] 1 E.H.R.R. 373; June 18, 1971, Series A, No. 12
[97] *Zamir* v. *U.K.* DR 40/42; and *see* DR 53/128

arbitrary; as occurred in *Bozano* v. *France*[98] where the Court found that the applicant had been taken out of France by the French police and into Italy via Switzerland in a premeditated *'disguised form of extradition designed to circumvent a negative ruling'* of the French Court staying the extradition to Switzerland.

2. The detention can only be justified as being *'with a view to deportation or extradition'*. Whilst this does not require the existence of a deportation or extradition order, it does require the existence of proceedings to this end. If no such proceedings are in being, the detention cannot be justified under this provision[99].

3. The detention ceases to be justified within Article 5(1)(f) if the extradition or deportation proceedings are not being conducted with necessary diligence, or amount in themselves to an abuse of authority[100].

4. A person awaiting extradition or deportation may only be so detained in order to ensure that the deportation/extradition takes place[101]. From this it can be submitted that the detention must be necessary; for instance, it needs to be established that there are grounds why the detained person should not be released on bail conditions.

Duty promptly to give reasons for detention

The duty to give prompt intelligible reasons for detention applies in all situations where liberty is restricted under Article 5(1) *above*. 'Intelligible' means in words and a language that the detained person can understand. The purpose of the obligation is to enable the arrested person to challenge the lawfulness of the detention if he or she so chooses[102]. Section 28 of the Police and Criminal Evidence Act 1984 closely parallels the requirements of Article 5(2), although the provision applies to both civil and criminal detentions (*see for instance* s.132 of the Mental Health Act 1983).

The state is allowed some leeway in the application of Article 5(2), thus there is no absolute requirement that the reasons be given in writing or that they be framed with the precision of an indictment; what is required is that the accused is aware of the grounds for the detention. Indeed, if the circumstances of the arrest are such that the person concerned could not fail to know the reasons for arrest, then formal notification for the purposes of Article 5(2) may be unnecess-

[98] 9 E.H.R.R. 297; December 18, 1986, Series A, No. 111
[99] DR 12/14
[100] DR 12/207; and see DR 56/62
[101] DR 60/272
[102] *X* v. *U.K.* 4 E.H.R.R. 188; October 24, 1981; Series A, No. 46; and *see* DR 16/111

ary[103]. If, however, the grounds for detention change after arrest, it is required that the different grounds be notified promptly to the detainee.

In *Van der Leer* v. *Netherlands*[104] the Court found Article 5(2) to have been violated where the complainant was confined by judicial decision in a psychiatric hospital without being notified of the confinement order or indeed that she was detained and not free to leave.

Duty promptly to bring detained persons before a judicial officer and for trial within a reasonable time or release

Article 5(3) incorporates a number of separate and very important provisions. It is an essential bulwark to the presumption of innocence; if detention pending trial were the norm, then in itself it would constitute a presumption of guilt.

Article 5(3) is solely concerned with detention pursuant to Article 5(1)(c): detention in connection with a criminal offence[105].

THE DUTY TO PROMPTLY PRODUCE THE DETAINEE

The detained person must be automatically produced in person to the judicial officer. In *Koster* v. *Netherlands*[106] the complainant, a soldier, was arrested on a Wednesday whilst on military manoeuvres but not produced to a court until the following Monday. The state explained the delay by virtue of the manoeuvres and the intervening Sunday. The Court emphasised that the use in the French text of the Convention of the word 'aussitôt' with its *constraining connotation of immediacy, confirms that the degree of flexibility attaching to the notion of "promptness" is limited*. Whilst the Court accepted that "promptness" had to be assessed in each case according to its special features [107], it considered that the manoeuvres in question could not justify the delay, as they took place at periodic intervals and were therefore foreseeable and should not have prevented the army from ensuring that the Military Court sat sooner, if needs be on the Saturday or Sunday.

In *Brogan* v. *U.K.*[108] the complainants had been arrested under s.12 of the Prevention of Terrorism (Temporary Provisions) Act 1984 and held without being produced to a court for various periods, the shortest of

---

[103] DR 21/250

[104] 12 E.H.R.R. 567; February 21, 1990, Series A, No. 170

[105] E.g. DR 60/272; and DR 54/116; but *see* DR 37/113

[106] 14 E.H.R.R. 319; November 29, 1991, Series A, No. 222

[107] *De Jong, Baljet and van den Brink* v. *Netherlands* 8 E.H.R.R. 20; May 22, 1984, Series A, No. 77

[108] 11 E.H.R.R. 117; November 29, 1988, Series A, No. 145 and p. 197, *post* Article 15

which being four days and six hours. Despite the very special problems of investigating terrorist offences, the Court held that the period fell outside the strict constraints required by the notion of promptness. It should be appreciated that the Court was not laying down a rule that periods of detention less than four days would be adequate; it must be emphasised that each case must be assessed by its special features. If the case is unexceptional then a significantly shorter period would be expected.

Judge or judicial officer authorised by law to exercise judicial power

The Court and Commission have defined the powers and qualities required of a judicial officer to comply with this provision[109]. These include:

1. Complete independence (especially from the executive) when performing in the judicial capacity.
2. The detainee must be present at the hearing and the judge or judicial officer must listen to the detainee's representations or those of his/her representative.
3. The need for all the circumstances for or against release (whether or not subject to bail conditions) to be reviewed and for the judge or judicial officer to decide, by reference to established legal criteria, whether there are reasons to justify detention.
4. The power to order immediate release where continued detention is no longer justified.

Whilst there is no doubt that magistrates and judges satisfy these requirements, consideration has also been given to the tribunals that review military detentions. The Commission has held that a Military Court consisting of a civilian lawyer, President (appointed for life) and two military officers (appointed for a minimum irrevocable term of one year) satisfied the requirements of this provision[110].

A detained person's right to a trial within reasonable time

The right under this provision is closely linked with the right under Article 6(1) (the right to a public hearing within a reasonable time). Article 5(3) has, however, especial urgency as its application relates to cases where the person is detained pending trial. Whilst the Court and Commission have emphasised that detainees have a higher priority for

---

[109] *Schiesser* v. *Switzerland* 2 E.H.R.R. 417; December 4, 1979, Series A, No. 34
[110] DR 42/241

an expeditious trial, release obviously does not absolve the authorities from the obligation to arrange the trial within a reasonable time [111]. The interaction of Articles 5(3) and 6(1) means that the particular facts of a case may result in a finding that Article 5(3) has been violated but not Article 6(1) and vice versa [112].

The question of what is and what is not a reasonable time for a case to come to trial is obviously far from simple. The time is measured from the date the accused is charged to the date of the judgment at first instance[113]. The Commission and Court will review the reasons given by the state, especially the reasons given by the authorities for delay at any bail applications[114], as Article 5(3) can be violated either by an unreasonably long detention pending trial (*i.e.* by unreasonably refusing bail) or by unreasonable delay in bringing the case to trial bearing in mind that the complainant is detained.

UNREASONABLE DELAY

This can arise where the prosecution has been unduly prolonged by the manner in which the authorities have conducted the case[115], for instance, by insisting on the presence of the original documents every time a different court hears an application[116] or by failing to sever an indictment containing linked offences, where the length of linked proceedings themselves amounted to the main obstacle to an expeditious trial[117]. Whilst delay resulting from the detainee's abuse of the court process cannot be held against the state, this is not the case where the detainee has merely exercised his or her rights,[118] such as by periodically seeking a review of the refusal to grant bail.

UNREASONABLE REFUSAL TO RELEASE PENDING TRIAL

In every case where the Court and Commission are required to review unreasonable delay in the trial of a detained person, consideration is given to why release pending trial was not allowed. In such cases, the starting point is the proposition that the persistence of reasonable suspicion that the person arrested has committed the offence is fundamental to the validity of the continued detention; this

---

[11] *Wemhoff* v. *Germany* 1 E.H.R.R. 55; June 27, 1968, Series A, No. 7

[12] *See B.* v. *Austria* 13 E.H.R.R. 20; March 28, 1990, Series A, No. 175 and *see Matznetter* v. *Austria* 1 E.H.R.R. 198; November 10, 1969, Series A, No. 10 and *see* p. 147 *post*

[13] DR 60/182

[14] *Ibid.* and *see Neumeister* v. *Austria* 1 E.H.R.R. 91; June 27, 1968, Series A, No. 8; and DR 53/87

[15] DR 23/137

[16] *Toth* v. *Austria* 14 E.H.R.R. 551; December 12, 1991, Series A, No. 224

[17] *Kemmache* v. *France* 14 E.H.R.R. 520; July 3, 1991, Series A, No. 218

[18] DR 3/86

arises not by virtue of Article 5(3) but via the requirements of Article 5(1)(c) *above*. After a certain lapse of time however, suspicion no longer suffices to justify deprivation of liberty. Even where other relevant and sufficient grounds exist, the Court and Commission will nevertheless review them in light of the diligence shown by the authorities in the conduct of the proceedings[119]. The longer the delay, the greater the justification required for rejecting release pending trial. The Court and Commission have shown themselves indefatigable in analysing the logical basis for bail refusals, especially the need for these to be reassessed in the light of the passage of time since the initial arrest.

Examples of complaints alleging denial of a trial within a reasonable time include:

Toth v. *Austria*[120] where the applicant was detained for two years prior to his trial on fraud charges. The Court held this to be excessive as the proceedings were neither complex nor unusual and the delay was in large measure the responsibility of the state.

Clooth v. *Belgium*[121] where the applicant was detained for three years and two months on murder and arson charges. Although the Court accepted that aspects of the case were complicated, it found that the detention on remand had exceeded the reasonable time specified in Article 5(3).

D. v. *Germany* [122] where the applicant was detained for one year and 10 months on charges of aggravated burglary. The Commission considered the case of complexity, involving as it did summoning witnesses from another state (Yugoslavia). In the circumstances it found no violation. *V.* v. *Germany*[123] was a similar case where the applicant had been detained for one year and six months on drug trafficking charges where a witness had to be summoned from Turkey; again the Commission found no violation.

Hauschildt v. *Denmark*[124] where the applicant was detained for two years and nine months on tax evasion charges. The prosecution had to interview several hundred people in Denmark and abroad; 48 investigative sessions of the Court had to be convened and the trial lasted 18 months. In view of the complexity, the Commission found no violation.

BAIL

The Convention contains a strong presumption in favour of bail, unconditional or otherwise, pending trial; a presumption that grows

[119] *Letellier* v. *France* 14 E.H.R.R. 83; June 26, 1991, Series A, No. 207
[120] *See* note 116 *above*
[121] 14 E.H.R.R. 551; December 12, 1991, Series A, No. 224
[122] DR 53/182
[123] DR 54/116
[124] DR 49/86

stronger if the trial is delayed. In fixing appropriate bail conditions the authorities must exercise great care to ensure that they are reasonable, taking into account the person's personal circumstances such as age[125], and ability to meet any surety[126]. Whilst the detainee's co-operation is necessary to fix a sensible surety[127], a failure by the detainee to co-operate does not absolve the authorities from endeavouring to arrange appropriate bail terms.

Where forfeiture of bail results as a consequence of failure to appear before the court, the deprivation raises a possible issue under Article 1 of Protocol 1[128].

Right to a review of the legality of the detention

Habeas corpus is one of the more ancient examples of the right protected by this provision. Article 5(4) applies to each of the categories of detention listed in Article 5(1), although its application to Article 5(1)(f) (deportation) is limited and in relation to Article 5(1)(a) (post-conviction detention) is severely limited.

DEPORTATION OR EXTRADITION

The Commission considers that an appeal, provided that it is both judicial and 'speedily' convened and empowered to examine the legality of the detention, within the framework of detention pending extradition, meets the requirements of Article 5(4); the provision does not require 'a complete review on all questions of fact of the exercise of the power to detain'[129].

POST-CONVICTION DETENTION

Article 5(4) does not apply to detention for a fixed or mandatory term stemming from a court conviction. The lawfulness of the detention is the conviction and sentence. The Court has, however, considered the question of discretionary life sentences[130], and determined that:

> the principles underlying such sentences, unlike mandatory life sentences, have developed in the sense that they are composed of a punitive element and

---

[125] DR 15/211

[126] DR 23/137

[127] DR 18/100

[128] DR 42/195

[129] DR 60/272; DR 40/42; and DR 28/168 where habeas corpus was considered to comply with the requirements of Article 5(4) in relation to detention pending deportation. *See also* DR 7/123 where deportation took place so quickly that an Article 5(4) review hearing could not be convened; no violation found

[130] *Thynne, Wilson and Gunnell* v. *U.K.* 13 E.H.R.R. 666; October 25, 1990, Series A, No. 190

subsequently of a security element designed to confer on the Secretary of State the responsibility for determining when the public interest permits the prisoner's release.

After the expiry of the life sentence, the Court considers that the continuing discretionary detention is subject to the requirements of Article 5(4), by way of a right to periodic review (*see* below).

SPEEDILY

The Convention requires that the review be decided 'speedily' by a court. The speed with which the hearing is convened will depend to a degree upon the particular circumstances of the case. The word 'speedily', whilst connoting haste, does not have the same immediacy as the word 'promptly' used in Article 5(2). Cases challenging the detention without charge of a detainee in a police station will require the convening of a hearing at greater speed than a request for a periodic review of a mental health detention or a discretionary life sentence. Examples include:

De Jong v. *Netherlands*[131] where the detainees were conscript soldiers placed under arrest for refusing to obey orders; their claim for review of the legality of their detention was delayed for various periods, the shortest of which was six days. The Court held that:

> even having regard to the exigencies of military life and military justice, the length of absence of access to the court was in each case such as to deprive the applicant of his entitlement to bring proceedings to obtain a 'speedy' review of the lawfulness of his detention.

In *Egue* v. *France*[132] a delay of five days in challenging detention on suspicion of importing drugs was held by the Commission not to violate Article 5(4).

Christinet v. *Switzerland*[133] concerned a review hearing to challenge the redetention of a prisoner who had been released on parole; the Commission considered that a delay of 16 days was permissible.

Zamir v. *U.K.*[134] concerned detention with a view to deportation; the Commission considered that a delay of seven weeks between applying for habeas corpus and the hearing violated Article 5(4), which *'requires the state to organise its procedures in such a way that proceedings concerning lawfulness can be conducted with the minimum delay'*.

EQUALITY OF ARMS

The right to take proceedings to challenge the lawfulness of detention presupposes certain minimum ground rules for those proceedings.

---

[131] 8 E.H.R.R. 20; May 22, 1984, Series A, No. 77
[132] DR 57/47
[133] DR 17/35
[134] DR 40/42

In *Lamy* v. *Belgium*[135] the detainee was denied access to any part of the prosecution file and could not therefore effectively challenge the statements or prosecution submissions based upon them. The Court held that access to such documents was essential at such a crucial stage in the proceedings: *'whereas Crown Counsel had been familiar with the whole file, the procedure had not offered the applicant an opportunity of challenging appropriately the reasons relied upon to justify a remand in custody'*. As there had been no equality of arms between the prosecution and defence, it held that Article 5(4) had been violated.

The Court and Commission have commented in similar terms upon the need for the hearings to admit cross-examination of relevant prosecution evidence[136] and for legal representation[137]. The Court has also emphasised that the remit of the hearings should be wide enough *'to bear on those conditions which, according to the Convention, are essential for the "lawful" detention'*; for instance, in the case of a psychiatric detention, the review must investigate whether the particular disorder persists, and if not, have power to discharge the detainee. In short, the review should not be artificially limited to considering merely the reasonableness of the decision to detain [138].

PERIODIC REVIEWS

Where detention is prolonged, except in the case of a fixed sentence pursuant to Article 5(1)(a), the Court has confirmed that the Convention requires the availability of a process to enable the lawfulness of the detention to be reviewed at reasonable intervals[139]. The need for such a periodic review can arise for a variety of reasons, most obviously:

1. Where there is a lengthy pre-trial detention. In *Bezicheri* v. *Italy* [140] the detainee's first application for release was dismissed in June 1983 and a second application, submitted on July 6, 1983, was not heard until December 1983. The Court held that the relatively short interval between the hearing in June and the second application in July was not unreasonable since under the Convention detention on remand was assumed to be of strictly limited duration. The delay in convening the second hearing however violated the requirement that it be done 'speedily'.

---

[135] 11 E.H.R.R. 529; March 30, 1989, Series A, No. 151

[136] *Sanchez-Reisse* v. *Switzerland* 9 E.H.R.R. 71; October 21, 1986, Series A, No. 107

[137] *See Bouamar* v. *Belgium*, 11 E.H.R.R. 1; February 29, 1988, Series A, No. 129 concerning the need for legal representation in cases involving young applicants, 'it is essential not only that the individual should have the opportunity to be heard in person but that he should also have effective assistance of his lawyer'; DR 53/50 concerning legal representation at Mental Health Review hearings; DR 51/62 concerning the general question of legal representation

[138] *X* v. *U.K.* 4 E.H.R.R. 188; October 24, 1981, Series A, No. 46

[139] *Winterwerp* v. *Netherlands* 2 E.H.R.R. 387; October 24, 1979, Series A, No. 33

[140] 12 E.H.R.R. 210; October 25, 1989, Series A, No. 164

2. Where detention is upon a psychiatric ground (Article 5(1)(e)). The need for automatic periodic and full reviews in such cases is well established and decisions of the Court did much to shape the Mental Health Act 1983[141]. Where a subsequent review hearing is requested, the need for it to be convened 'speedily' applies. The Court has indicated that need for expedition in such cases is perhaps less urgent than in detention upon remand cases, but nevertheless expedition is required. A delay of four months in convening such a case is, however, unreasonable[142].

3. Discretionary life sentences. The Court has now held that in cases such as discretionary life sentences where the term of imprisonment contains a 'punitive element' and a 'security element', a right of review must exist after the punitive period has been served[143]. The Court has not, however, explained how one establishes when the punitive term has been served if it is a life sentence.

Enforceable right to compensation where Article 5 violated

Anyone detained in contravention of Article 5 shall have an enforceable right to compensation. This would normally follow in a U.K. setting where someone had been unlawfully detained contrary to domestic law, for instance, via an action for unlawful imprisonment. If for any reason no such right existed in the particular case, then this could found a complaint under Article 5(5) in its own right.

A payment of compensation in the domestic proceedings in itself does not preclude a complaint under Article 5(1-4)[144].

Where it is the European Court of Human Rights that finds a violation of an Article 5 right, this raises the question of Article 5(5) provided the violation of this right has been pleaded. As the Convention has not been incorporated into domestic law, it will almost always follow that a violation found by the Court (but not by the domestic courts) will not give rise to an enforceable right to compensation under U.K. law and therefore Article 5(5) must be pleaded in the initial complaint.

The right to compensation under Article 5(5) is distinct from the right to just satisfaction under Article 50, which applies upon winning a case.

---

[141] See for instance Winterwerp and X v. U.K. (notes 138 and 139 above); and Ashingdane v. U.K. 7 E.H.R.R. 528; May 28, 1985, Series A, No. 93

[142] Koendjbiharie v. Netherlands 13 E.H.R.R. 820; September 28, 1990, Series A, No. 185–B and see E. v. Norway August 29, 1990, Series A, No. 181–A. where a delay of eight weeks was held unreasonable

[143] See note 130 above

[144] DR 51/62 and see p. 23 above 'adequacy of domestic redress'

RIGHT TO A FAIR HEARING: ARTICLE 6

Article 6

1. *In the determination of his civil rights and obligations or of any criminal charge against him, everyone is entitled to a fair and public hearing within a reasonable time by an independent and impartial tribunal established by law. Judgment shall be pronounced publicly but the press and public may be excluded from all or part of the trial in the interests of morals, public order or national security in a democratic society, where the interests of juveniles or the protection of the private life of the parties so require, or to the extent strictly necessary in the opinion of the court in special circumstances where publicity would prejudice the interests of justice.*

2. *Everyone charged with a criminal offence shall be presumed innocent until proved guilty according to law.*

3. *Everyone charged with a criminal offence has the following minimum rights:*

   (a) *to be informed promptly, in a language which he understands and in detail, of the nature and cause of the accusation against him;*

   (b) *to have adequate time and facilities for the preparation of his defence;*

   (c) *to defend himself in person or through legal assistance of his own choosing or, if he has not sufficient means to pay for legal assistance, to be given it free when the interests of justice so require;*

   (d) *to examine or have examined witnesses against him and to obtain the attendance and examination of witnesses on his behalf under the same conditions as witnesses against him;*

   (e) *to have the free assistance of an interpreter if he cannot understand or speak the language used in court.*

Article 6 is the repository of a large bundle of rights, regulating the civil and criminal process and embracing the rule of law, natural justice, access to justice and the presumption of innocence. Where a serious and genuine question arises about a person's civil rights and obligations, Article 6 requires that the state ensure there is a court procedure available to resolve it. It follows that access to the courts must not be unreasonably obstructed by, for instance, restricting a prisoner's correspondence with his lawyer[145]. In *Philis* v. *Greece*[146] the

---

[145] *Silver* v. *U.K.* 13 E.H.R.R. 582; March 25, 1983, Series A, No. 67
[146] 13 E.H.R.R. 741; August 27, 1991, Series A, No. 209

applicant, a design engineer, was unable to sue for his fees directly, but required by Greek law to rely on a regulatory body to sue on his behalf. The Court held that the *'right of access to the court was not absolute, but might be subject to limitations . . . [these] ought not to restrict or reduce the access left to the individual in such a way or to such an extent as to impair the very essence of that right'*. It found that the restrictions imposed upon Mr Philis impaired the very essence of his right and therefore violated Article 6(1).

In *Airey* v. *Ireland*[147], the Court considered whether an effective right of access to the domestic courts required the existence of civil legal aid schemes, observing:

> To hold that so far-reaching an obligation exists would . . . sit ill with the fact that the Convention contains no provision on legal aid for those disputes . . . However, despite the absence of . . . a clause for civil litigation, Article 6(1) may sometimes compel the state to provide for the assistance of a lawyer when such assistance proves indispensable for an effective access to the court, either because legal representation is rendered compulsory, as is done by the Domestic law of certain Contracting States . . ., or by reason of the complexity of the procedure of the case.

Article 6 is invoked by more complainants than any other Article in the Convention; it contains the following elements;

Article 6(1)	CIVIL RIGHTS & OBLIGATIONS (*See below*)
	CRIMINAL OFFENCE (*See* p. 144 *post*)
	FAIR HEARING (*See* p. 145 *post*)
	PUBLIC HEARING/EXCLUSION OF PRESS (*See* p. 146 *post*)
	REASONABLE TIME (*See* p. 147 *post*)
	INDEPENDENT TRIBUNAL (*See* p. 148 *post*)
Article 6(2)	PRESUMPTION OF INNOCENCE (*See* p. 149 *post*)
Article 6(3)(a)	PROMPT INTELLIGIBLE NOTIFICATION OF CHARGES (*See* p. 149 *post*)
(b)	ADEQUATE TIME AND FACILITIES FOR DEFENCE (*See* p. 150 *post*)
(c)	RIGHT TO REPRESENTATION AND LEGAL AID (*See* p. 151 *post*)
(d)	RIGHT TO WITNESS ATTENDANCE AND EXAMINATION (*See* p. 152 *post*)
(e)	RIGHT TO INTERPRETER (*See* p. 153 *post*)

Civil rights and obligations

Article 6 ensures that civil or criminal court proceedings contain minimum standards of fairness. The safeguards are greater in criminal

---

[147] 2 E.H.R.R. 305; October 9, 1979, Series A, No. 32

than civil proceedings. Of importance therefore is the meaning of 'civil' and 'criminal' and how the two are distinguished. The Court has made it clear that it is not bound to accept the domestic court's categorisation as to whether a particular matter is civil or criminal.

It is appropriate to think of 'civil' rights in the context of 'private' rights, rather than the sense usually ascribed to it within the U.K. It includes, in addition to the torts, serious professional interferences such as the right to carry on a commercial activity[148]. Disputes involving such private rights which are not objectively trivial or purely academic[149] must comply with the fair hearing requirements of Article 6(1).

There are, however, a large number of administrative or public matters which do not amount to 'civil' determinations within the meaning of the Convention. It is not possible to give clear rules in relation to these issues as neither the Court nor the Commission have as yet formulated any clear theory to explain how the line is to be drawn. The differences are best illustrated by listing those matters which have been held to be civil and those which have not.

In some cases the difference can be seen, in practical terms, to be one of degree; for instance, a dispute relating to a planning permission is a civil matter, whereas a dispute concerning building regulations is not; disciplinary action which results in a doctor's suspension is civil, whereas if it merely results in a reprimand, it is not. Certain purely public issues, such as the payment of non-contributory benefits or criminal injuries compensation, are not civil (or 'private') whereas disputes concerning contributory pensions are. In *Feldbrugge* v. *Netherlands*[150] the Court considered whether the right to sickness benefit under the Netherlands' social security system constituted a civil right. It took the view that the private law features significantly outweighed the public law characteristics; it identified such private law features as the personal and economic nature of the benefit, its connection with the contract of employment and its similarities to insurance under the ordinary law, together with the fact that the applicant participated in the financing of the social security system by means of a deduction from her salary made for that purpose.

---

[148] *Lithgow* v. *U.K.* 8 E.H.R.R. 329; July 8, 1986, Series A, 102
[149] *Bentham* v. *Netherlands* 8 E.H.R.R. 1; October 23, 1985, Series A, No. 97
[150] 8 E.H.R.R. 425; May 29, 1986, Series A, No. 99; and *see* DR 59/5

Matters which have been held to be civil	Matters which have been held *not* to be civil
Decisions concerning paternity custody, contact, wardship, etc.	Disputes of faith or religious practice
Disputes over ownership of a patent (but not the formalities to acquire one)	Administrative proceedings to restrict immigration/entry or terminate an entry permit
Individual right to enjoy a good reputation	Right to protection of reputation against statements made in Parliament
Legal action concerning unfair trading competition	Civil servants' right to continue in employment
Proceedings concerning compulsory purchase, etc.	Taxation assessments and general taxation issues
Right to carry on practising in a profession	Disputes concerning Building Regulations approvals
Right to carry on a commercial activity	A right to non-contributory benefits
Right to planning permission	Professional disciplinary action for a minor misdemeanour
Disputes concerning contributory benefits	

Criminal matters

Practice varies throughout the Council of Europe states as to what matters are categorised as criminal. The Commission and Court have therefore developed a procedure for deciding the question independently[151]. This involves considering the following points:

DOMESTIC CLASSIFICATION

If the domestic legal system classifies the matter as criminal then that is final even if the matter in question is a misdemeanor of little consequence. The fact that a matter is classified as non-criminal (*i.e.* civil or disciplinary) is of relevance, but is not conclusive. If this were otherwise, a state could avoid its obligations under Article 6 merely by reclassifying its penal code[152]. Within a U.K. setting such matters as so-

---

[151] *Engel* v. *Netherlands* 1 E.H.R.R. 647; June 8, 1976, Series A, No. 22
[152] *Öztürk* v. *Germany* 6 E.H.R.R. 409; February 21, 1984, Series A, No. 73

called 'civil' contempt[153] of court and Community Charge enforcement proceedings in the magistrates' court could illustrate this point, as both are classified as civil proceedings, albeit in effect (considering the criteria *below*) they have a criminal character.

THE NATURE OF THE OFFENCE

If the matter in question only applies to a restricted group (for instance, a profession), then it would support the contention that the sanction is disciplinary rather than criminal; if, however, it is of general effect, a contrary presumption would apply.

THE SEVERITY OF THE PENALTY

The Court and Commission will place most weight upon the severity of the penalty that the accused risks incurring. In *Demicoli* v. *Malta*[154] for instance, the Court had no hesitation in categorising an offence which carried a maximum sentence of imprisonment for 60 days and/or a fine of 500 Maltese liri as criminal. Of relevance in determining severity is the question of whether the sanction is imposed upon a civilian or member of the armed forces. In a series of cases concerning military discipline the Court has determined that short periods of imprisonment (two to five days) do not automatically amount to a criminal sanction [155]; it might well be otherwise if a civilian faced such a sanction. In determining the severity of a sentence the Court and Commission are also prepared to consider the extent of any financial or other penalty, for instance a potential fine on a company of 5 per cent. of its annual turnover [156].

In *Campbell and Fell* v. *U.K.*[157] the Court confirmed that a disciplinary matter within a prison which resulted in a substantial loss of remission could constitute a criminal matter for the purposes of Article 6.

Fair hearings

This requirement embodies all the domestic law principles of 'natural justice'. Whilst Articles 6(2) and 6(3) detail further specific require-

---

[153] *Harman* v. *U.K.* DR 35/53
[154] 14 E.H.R.R. 47; August 27, 1991, Series A, No. 210; and *see Weber* v. *Switzerland* 12; E.H.R.R. 508; May 22, 1990, Series A, No. 177, where a fine of 500 Swiss Francs could be converted into a term of imprisonment in certain circumstances and was held by the Court to be a 'criminal' matter
[155] *See Engel* note 151 *above*; and *Eggs* v. *Switzerland* DR 15/35
[156] *Societe Stenuit* v. *France* 14 E.H.R.R. 509; February 27, 1992, Series A, No. 232-A
[157] 7 E.H.R.R. 165; June 28, 1984, Series A, No. 80; but *c.. Roelfs* v. *Netherlands* 19435/92

ments for criminal cases, these are only minimum requirements and a trial may nevertheless be 'unfair' within the meaning of Article 6(1) even though it complies with them; in similar terms, the fact that the Article 6(3) rights are only specified as applying to criminal matters does not mean that in civil cases they will not be required for a fair hearing. This may include the provision of civil legal aid (see *Airey* v. *Ireland above*), or the right to summon witnesses[158] and so on.

The Court places great importance upon 'justice being seen to be done' and is prepared to review its previous decisions in this area; in *Borgers* v. *Belgium*[159] it stated that its views on the equality of arms and the the standards for a fair trial in general had *'undergone a considerable evolution in the Court's case law, notably in respect of the importance attached to appearances and to the increased sensitivity of the public to the fair administration of justice'*.

Under the principle of 'equality of arms', any person called in whatever capacity by the defence should be examined under the same conditions as the equivalent prosecution witness[160]. The proceedings must be adversarial to the extent that each party must be given the opportunity to comment on the other's observations and cross-examine their evidence[161]. Both parties should have the right to be represented[162], a right to attend the hearing in person and in criminal cases to advance notice of the prosecution evidence[163]. A fair hearing requires reasons to be given for the final decision, and for the parties to be given sufficient notice of the date and place fixed for trial (a point worth stressing to Crown Court listing officers amongst others)[164]. A fair trial may be prejudiced by a virulent press campaign [165].

Public hearing and exclusion of the press

This is the right for a public substantive hearing of a case. Not every stage of the determination must be public; purely administrative, interlocutory matters can be disposed of in private. The party has the right to at least one public determination; if this occurs at first instance, then there is no requirement for an appeal hearing to be public if it is

[158] DR28/127

[159] 15 E.H.R.R. 92; October 30, 1991, Series A, No. 214

[160] *Brandstetter* v. *Austria* 15 E.H.R.R. 378; August 28, 1991, Series A, No. 211

[161] *Ibid.* and see *Feldbrugge* v. *Netherlands* 8 E.H.R.R. 425; May 29, 1986, Series A, No. 99; *Bönisch* v. *Austria* 9 E.H.R.R. 191; May 6, 1985, Series A, No. 92; *Bricmont* 12 E.H.R.R. 217; July 7, 1989, Series A, No. 158

[162] *Neumeister* v. *Austria* 1 E.H.R.R. 91; June 27, 1968, Series A, No. 8

[163] *Barbera, Messegue and Jabardo* v. *Spain* 11 E.H.R.R. 360; December 6, 1988, Series A, No. 146

[164] DR 28/5

[165] DR 22/100

restricted to issues of law alone [166]. Conversely a public appeal hearing can suffice provided both questions of law and fact are considered [167].

Although the requirement for a public hearing is a question of the interests of the public rather than the parties, the Court has, in civil cases, been relatively flexible in allowing parties to waive the right to a public hearing either expressly or by implication[168]. The Court has required that professional disciplinary hearings determining the right of professionals to continue practising must be held in public[169], although again, the Court has shown no consistent willingness to interpret this strictly [170].

There has been little case law on the right to exclude press and public *'in the interests of morals, public order or national security . . . [or] where the interests of juveniles or the protection of the private life of the parties so require, or to the extent strictly necessary in the opinion of the court . . . where publicity would prejudice the interests of justice'.* In view of the Court's historical lack of stringency in this area, it may be assumed that a wide margin of appreciation will be given to the state in applying this requirement, although the Commission or Court will presumably be prepared in each case to examine the factual basis for an such exclusion[170a].

Reasonable time

The reasonableness of the length of proceedings is assessed in the light of the particular circumstances of each case, including the complexity, the conduct of the applicant and the state, and what is at stake in the proceedings[171].

In X v. France[172] the applicant contracted the HIV virus from an infected blood transfusion and instituted compensation proceedings against the state. These were not determined for two years. In view of the applicant's condition and life expectancy the Court held that the time was unreasonably long; the domestic courts had failed to use their powers to expedite the hearing.

---

[66] *Helmers* v. *Sweden*, 15 E.H.R.R. 285; October 29, 1991, Series A, No. 212

[67] *Weber* v. *Switzerland* 12 E.H.R.R. 508; May 22, 1990, Series A, No. 177

[68] *Håkansson and Sturesson* v. *Sweden* 13 E.H.R.R. 1; February 21, 1990, Series A, No. 171; c.f. *H.* v. *Belgium* 10 E.H.R.R. 339; November 30, 1987, Series A, No. 127; and *Le Compte* v. *Belgium* 4 E.H.R.R. 1; June 23, 1981, Series A, No. 43

[69] DR 53/5 concerning medical practice; DR 40/100 concerning architectural practice

[70] DR 55/5 concerning a barrister's right to request a public hearing being considered sufficient to satisfy Article 6(1)

[70a] *See for instance Campbell and Fell* v. *U.K.* note 157 *above*

[71] *Buchholz* v. *Germany* 3 E.H.R.R. 597; May 6, 1981, Series A, No. 42

[72] 14 E.H.R.R. 483; March 23, 1991, Series A, No. 234–C and *see* DR 12/36 concerning the need for the applicant to take all reasonable steps to expedite a hearing

The Court has taken a similar position in relation to the hearing of cases involving children, especially parental contact applications, holding that they require exceptional diligence[173].

Time starts running in civil cases with the institution of proceedings and in criminal cases (in general[174]) with the charge. Time comes to an end at the conclusion of the proceedings at the highest instance, when the sentence or determination becomes final (*i.e.* at the conclusion of the appeal process, if applicable). It is in this respect that Article 6(1) can be most clearly contrasted to Article 5(3). In *B. v. Austria* [175] the applicant was charged in July 1980 and convicted and sentenced at first instance in November 1982. The Court held that this did not violate Article 5(3). However, his appeal against conviction and sentence was not finally disposed of until December 1985 and the Court held this to be unreasonably long and so violated Article 6(1).

The Court has had little difficulty in holding that divorce proceedings taking nine years were unreasonably long; in this case resulting from *'not so much a lack as an excess of judicial activity'*[176]. In similar terms it has held a delay of six-and-a-half years to determine a 'not particularly complex' civil dispute, excessive [177]. Where, however, the applicants have themselves been guilty of prolonging the proceedings, then a delay of seven-and-a-half years in 'not very complex' civil proceedings has been held not to violate Article 6(1)[178].

It should finally be noted that the listing of a case too soon can also violate the 'reasonable time' requirement.

Independent and impartial tribunal

The principles of impartiality and independence applied by the Commission and Court are no different to those within the domestic U.K. setting. Appearances are important; not only must the tribunal be factually independent and impartial, it must also appear so.

In *Langborger* v. *Sweden* [179] the applicant contested the composition of a housing court, alleging that two lay assessors were not independent.

---

[173] *H.* v. *U.K.* 10 E.H.R.R. 95; July 8, 1987, Series A, No. 120; and *see* DR 36/100 and DR 37/50

[174] Time runs from the day upon which the applicant is told that criminal proceedings are to be taken against him, DR17/180; and *see Deweer* v. *Belgium* 2 E.H.R.R. 439; February 27, 1980, Series A, No. 35

[175] 13 E.H.R.R. 20; March 28, 1990, Series A, No. 175

[176] 12 E.H.R.R. 247; March 29, 1989, Series A, No. 150

[177] *Neves E Silva* v. *Portugal* 13 E.H.R.R. 535; April 27, 1989, Series A, No. 153; and *see Unión Alimentaria Sanders S.A.* v. *Spain* 12 E.H.R.R. 24; July 7, 1989, Series A, No. 157 where a debt recovery case of five years' duration violated Article 6(1)

[178] *Vernillo* v. *France* 13 E.H.R.R. 881; February 20, 1991, Series A, No. 198

[179] 12 E.H.R.R. 416; June 22, 1989, Series A, No. 155

The assessors had been nominated by organisations who had an interest in the outcome of the hearing. The Court held that the composition of the tribunal gave rise to a 'possible appearance of lacking impartiality' and thus found Article 6(1) violated.

In *Hauschildt* v. *Denmark* [180] the judge involved in earlier remands of the applicant in custody, had done so on the grounds of 'a particularly confirmed suspicion' that he had committed the crime. The Court held that it violated the principle of impartiality for that judge to preside at the final hearing.

Presumption of innocence

For a tribunal to be truly impartial it must start with no preconceived notions, save only in criminal proceedings, that the accused is innocent.

The presumption requires that no representative of the state declares a person guilty of having committed an offence before guilt is established in a court[181].

In *Minelli* v. *Switzerland* [182] a prosecution of the applicant was stayed because of the expiry of the statutory limitation period. The domestic court nevertheless ordered that he pay part of the prosecution's costs as well as compensation to the alleged victim. The Court found that this violated the requirements of Article 6(1). It may be permissible for the Court to order the defendant to pay part of the costs if it is felt that his or her conduct contributed to the bringing of the prosecution, but only if in making the order the court assumes the defendant's innocence[183].

It is contrary to Article 6(1) for the defendant in criminal defamation proceedings to have to establish the truth of what was said[184].

Prompt intelligible notification of charges

The provision requires that the defendant actually receives detailed information of the charge; a mere presumption of postal service is not sufficient[185].

In *Brozicek* v. *Italy* [186] a German national was charged in Italy with various criminal offences. The Italian authorities persisted in writing to

[30] 12 E.H.R.R. 266; May 24, 1989, Series A, No. 154
[31] DR 13/73
[32] 5 E.H.R.R. 554; March 25, 1983, Series A, No. 62; and *see* DR 8/5; DR 17/5; and DR 16/56
[33] DR 16/56; and *see* DR 38/90
[34] DR 26/171
[35] DR 56/40
[36] 12 E.H.R.R. 371; December 19, 1989, Series A, No. 167

him in Italian, asserting that he had adequate knowledge of the language although he denied this. The Court found Article 6(3)(a) violated, holding that a translation should have been supplied *'unless they were in a position to establish that the applicant in fact had sufficient knowledge of Italian to understand . . . the purport of the letter notifying him of the charges brought against him'*.

In *Kamasinski* v. *Austria* [187] the applicant was a U.S.A. citizen arrested and tried in Austria on charges of fraud. Although he was not provided with a written translation of the indictment, he was provided with an English speaking lawyer who explained to him the details of the accusations he faced. The Court held that in the circumstances this was adequate, although it considered in general that *'a defendant not conversant with the court's language may in fact be put at a disadvantage if he is not also provided with a written translation of the indictment in a language he understands'*. The Court further confirmed the general requirement that the key prosecution papers be translated, although this did not extend to the whole court file [188].

There has been little case law on the amount of 'detail' to be furnished concerning the charges. It is however, clear from a comparison of the wording of Articles 6(3)(a) and 5(2) that the information required must be considerably more specific than that given at the time of an arrest.

Adequate time and facilities for defence

The right to adequate time and facilities for the preparation of the defence is *'the right of the accused to have at his disposal, for the purpose of exonerating himself or to obtain a reduction in his sentence, all relevant elements that have been or could be collected by the competent authorities'*[189]. In relation to defence access to the prosecution file, the right is not an unlimited one, although it extends to 'all relevant elements'; in cases concerning this aspect the Commission has pointed out that the word 'facilities' is qualified by 'adequate'[190]. The right does not necessarily give the defendant access to the prosecution file, it is sufficient for the defence lawyer to exercise this right on the defendant's behalf[191].

The Commission and Court consider that the ability of a defendant to confer with counsel in private is a fundamental part of preparation[192], and subject to a very high degree of scrutiny of any restriction upon the right[193]; this issue also arises under Article 6(3)(c) *below*.

[187] *Kamasinski* v. *Austria* 13 E.H.R.R. 36; December 19, 1989, Series A, No. 168
[188] *See also* DR 2/68
[189] DR 27/61
[190] DR 50/179
[191] DR 9/50
[192] DR 15/160
[193] *Campbell and Fell* v. *U.K.* 7 E.H.R.R. 165; June 28, 1984, Series A, No. 80

What constitutes 'adequate time' depends upon the particular circumstances of each case, and must take account of unexpected changes to the indictment, changes to counsel or new evidence and must be assessed upon a different basis at each stage of the proceedings[194].

Right to representation and legal aid

The three rights recited in this paragraph: the right to represent oneself, to chose one's counsel and the right to legal aid, are all qualified by being subject to 'the interests of justice'. The Commission and Court have, however, interpreted the provisions strictly. Thus any form of hindrance to a defendant communicating with counsel has been subjected to great scrutiny[195]. In *S. v. Switzerland* [196] the applicant was convicted of charges involving the use of explosives and arson. His conversations with his lawyer were listened to by the police, and he complained that this violated Article 6(3)(c). The state sought to justify this 'particularly drastic' action because of the extraordinary dangerous character of the defendant and the risk of collusion with the lawyer. The Court noted that whilst the Convention did not expressly guarantee the right of a person charged with a criminal offence to communicate with his lawyer out of hearing of other persons, it was nevertheless one of the basic requirements of a fair trial and therefore part of Article 6(3)(c). Without sufficiently cogent evidence to establish collusion (which the Swiss authorities had not provided), restrictions of the kind employed were not permitted by the Convention.

The right of a defendant to attend the trial is applied equally strictly; thus a trial should, in general, only proceed in a defendant's absence if he or she has indicated in an unequivocal manner a wish to waive the right to appear and defend him or herself.[197]

The degree of choice a legally aided party may have over counsel is unclear. The Court has preferred the French version of Article 6(3)(c), which places the word 'et' (and) between choice of counsel and access to legal assistance, whereas the English version uses the word 'or'[198]. Whatever the situation, it is clear that the lawyer appointed must be competent to act at the relevant level of complexity[199] and one in whom the defendant has confidence[200].

---

[194] DR 9/169

[195] *See for instance Golder* v. *U.K.* 1 E.H.R.R. 524; February 21, 1975, Series A, No. 18

[196] 14 E.H.R.R. 670; November 28, 1991, Series A, No. 220

[197] *F.C.B.* v. *Italy* 14 E.H.R.R. 909; August 28, 1991, Series A, No. 208-B

[198] *Pakelli* v. *Germany* 6 E.H.R.R. 1; April 25, 1983 Series A, No. 64, and *see Croissant* v. *Germany* 16 E.H.R.R. 135; September 25, 1992, Series A, No. 237-B

[199] But *see Kamasinski* v. *Austria* note 187 *above*

[200] But *see* DR 21/126 (counsel withdrawing due to defendant's bad behaviour)

Where the defendant has insufficient means, legal assistance is to be provided 'where the interests of justice so require'. Legal aid may be essential even in the case of a hopeless appeal, or for an inveterate criminal. In *Granger* v. *U.K.*[201] legal aid for an appeal against conviction for perjury and a five-year sentence was refused because counsel advised that it could not succeed, although the solicitor disagreed. The appeal went ahead with the defendant appearing in person, opposed by a Q.C. and junior counsel for the Crown. The Court had little difficulty in finding a violation of Article 6(3)(c); counsel had addressed the judges at length whereas the applicant had little comprehension of what was being said or of the technical legal arguments employed. The case was distinguished from that of *Monnell and Morris* v. *U.K.*[202] where a refusal of legal aid for an appeal was held not to violate the Convention; the appeal being by way of a written procedure in which the prosecution played no part.

In *Quaranta* v. *Switzerland*[203] the applicant, who had a long criminal record, was refused legal aid for drug-related offences for which he was then sentenced to six months' imprisonment. Although not a complicated matter, the Court held unanimously that Article 6(3)(c) had been violated. In *McDermitt* v. *U.K.*[204] the applicant was charged with breach of the peace and obstruction of a police officer; the maximum sentence for which was nine months' imprisonment. Legal aid was refused on the ground that it was not in the interests of justice. The prosecution was by a qualified lawyer and the solicitor representing the applicant continued to act for him thereby rendering the applicant liable to an account. The Commission considered the matter of sufficient merit to convene an admissibility hearing, although prior to this a friendly settlement was concluded with the applicant receiving an *ex gratia* payment of £300 and payment of his costs.

Right to witness attendance and examination

The Convention does not secure an unrestricted right to call witnesses[205] nor a right to compel the domestic court to hear a particular witness. The procedures for summonsing and hearing witnesses must be the same for the prosecution as the defence and equality of treatment is required[206]. It follows, therefore, that the applicant must establish that the failure to hear a particular witnesses prejudiced his or her case[207].

---

[201] 12 E.H.R.R. 469; March 28, 1990, Series A, No. 174
[202] 10 E.H.R.R. 205; March 2, 1987, Series A, No. 115
[203] May 24, 1991, Series A, No. 205
[204] DR 52/244; and *see R.* v. *U.K.* 15 E.H.R.R. CD 100
[205] *Bricmont* v. *Belgium* 12 E.H.R.R. 217; July 7, 1989, Series A, No. 158
[206] *Unterpertinger* v. *Austria* 13 E.H.R.R. 175; November 24, 1986, Series A, No. 110
[207] DR 28/127

In a number of cases the Court has reiterated that, in principle, evidence must be produced in the presence of the accused at a public hearing with a view to adversarial argument. This does not mean, however, that in order to be used in evidence such statements of witnesses should always be made at a public hearing in court; to use as evidence such statements obtained at the pre-trial stage is not in itself inconsistent with Article 6(3)(d), provided the rights of the defence are respected. As a rule, these rights require that an accused should be given adequate and proper opportunity to challenge and question a hostile witness either at the time the witness made his or her statement or at some later stage in the proceedings[208]. This right exists even if the defence have failed to summon the witness, relying, for instance, upon the prosecution attending to this[209].

In *Asch* v. *Austria*[210] the applicant's girlfriend made a complaint to the police that he had beaten and threatened to kill her. After criminal proceedings were instituted, a reconciliation occurred and the girlfriend asked to withdraw her complaint. The prosecution continued however, and at the trial the statement that she had made to the police was read out, the girlfriend exercising her right under Austrian law not to give evidence. The police officer who had taken the statement was available for cross-examination and medical evidence corroborating the attack was also given. In the circumstances the Court found no violation of Article 6(3)(d): the girlfriend's statement did not constitute the only item of evidence upon which the domestic court based its guilty verdict.

Where a witness is heard in the absence of the accused, but in the presence of his counsel, then this may not amount to a violation of Article 6(3)(d) if exceptionally this occurs in order to avoid attempted intimidation[211].

The Court has made it clear that expert evidence adduced by the prosecution and defence despite its non-partisan, objective nature must be accorded equal treatment within the provisions of Article 6(1) read in conjunction with Article 6(3)(d) [212].

Right to an interpreter

The right to free assistance of an interpreter is subject only to one requirement, namely that the person cannot understand or speak the

---

[208] *Kostovski* v. *Netherlands* 12 E.H.R.R. 434; November 20, 1989, Series A, No. 166; and *Windisch* 13 E.H.R.R. 281; September 27, 1990, Series A, No. 186
[209] *Delta* v. *France* December 19, 1990, Series A, No. 191
[210] *Asch* v. *Austria* 15 E.H.R.R. 597; April 26, 1991, Series A, No. 203-A and *c.f.* *Unterpertinger*, note 206 *above*
[211] DR 27/50
[212] *Brandstetter* v. *Austria* 15 E.H.R.R. 378; August 28, 1991, Series A, No. 211

language used in court. The ability to pay is of no relevance[213]. The requirement to provide such facilities extends beyond the actual trial and encompasses interpretation of relevant statements and documents, such that the defendant is able to fully understand and participate in the trial[214], although the provision of a bilingual counsel may be an adequate discharge of this obligation [215].

---

[213] DR 16/56; and DR 46/214
[214] *Luedicke, Belkacem and Koç* v. *Germany* 2 E.H.R.R. 149; November 28, 1978, Series A, No. 29
[215] *Kamasinski* v. *Austria* note 187 *above*

RETROSPECTIVE CRIMINAL LAW: ARTICLE 7

Article 7

1. *No one shall be held guilty of any criminal offence on account of any act or omission which did not constitute a criminal offence under national or international law at the time when it was committed. Nor shall a heavier penalty be imposed than the one that was applicable at the time the criminal offence was committed.*

2. *This article shall not prejudice the trial and punishment of any person for any act or omission which, at the time when it was committed, was criminal according to the general principles of law recognised by civilised nations.*

Article 7 prohibits the creation of new criminal offences which have retrospective application and likewise prohibits the retrospective application of increased sentencing powers. Article 7 is one of the non-derogable rights under Article 15 (*see* p. 197).

Whilst Article 7 expresses a well understood judicial concept, it has raised issues relating to the 're-interpretation' of existing laws by the domestic courts. It embodies the principle of legal certainty, requiring that criminal laws be framed in sufficiently clear terms so as to enable those persons to whom they are addressed to distinguish between permissible and prohibited behaviour[216]. It follows that the extension of existing offences to cover facts which previously did not constitute a criminal offence is prohibited; that the *'constituent elements of an offence may not be essentially changed by the caselaw of the domestic courts*[217].

In *Harman* v. *UK*[218] the applicant was convicted of contempt of court for having allowed a journalist to read documents, the contents of which had been read out in open court. She complained that, until the ruling of the domestic court in her case, it was not an offence to show a journalist such documents. The complaint therefore related either to a change in the law being applied retrospectively, or to the law being so imprecise that it was not possible to know whether a particular course of conduct was or was not prohibited. A friendly settlement of the complaint was effected after it had been ruled admissible.

The Commission found no violation of Article 7 where, due to a change in government policy, a prisoner serving a life sentence had his

[216] DR 38/234
[217] DR 60/256; and *c.f.* DR 41/178
[218] DR 38/53; and 46/57

assurance of parole countermanded[219]. Likewise, a system where the length of sentence depends upon the defendant's age at the time of conviction (rather than at the time the offence is committed) does not violate Article 7, provided the system was in operation at the time of the offence[220].

[219] DR 46/231
[220] DR 26/248

PRIVACY AND FAMILY LIFE: ARTICLE 8

Article 8

1. *Everyone has the right to respect for his private and family life, his home and his correspondence.*
2. *There shall be no interference by a public authority with the exercise of this right except such as is in accordance with the law and is necessary in a democratic society in the interests of national security, public safety or the economic well-being of the country, for the prevention of disorder or crime, for the protection of health or morals, or for the protection of the rights and freedoms of others.*

Article 8 is the most wide-ranging and, in many respects, elusive of the Convention rights. Its philosophical basis is that private endeavour is the well-spring of our liberal democratic tradition: a tradition that has produced the Convention itself. The starting point is therefore the principle that an individual has the right to live free from the shackles of the state; that the private is superior to the public. Where the public well-being places restrictions upon individual privacy, these restrictions must be clearly defined, logically justified and the minimum necessary to achieve the legitimate collective objective.

Where the state interferes with a person's private and family life, home or correspondence, it must justify this action by reference to one of the grounds set out in Article 8(2). No other grounds for restriction are permitted, with the sole exception of the principles set out in Article 17 (*see* p. 198), namely that a person cannot assert a right, the performance of which is aimed at the destruction of another person's Convention rights.

It is a characteristic of Article 8 that in respect of many of its rights the general public attitude is evolving; an evolution in thinking which the Commission and Court are prepared to mirror. In relation to complaints in these fields it is important to be cautious of the precedent value of the earlier reported Commission and Court cases. Examples include attitudes towards prisoners, homosexuals, transsexuals, care proceedings, etc. Areas where Article 8 might develop in the future include disabled persons' rights and the environment.

Family relationships

Family life includes not only relations between parents and their children, but also extends to grandparents[221] and grandchildren[222].

[221] DR 57/217
[222] DR 24/183

Beyond this it is a question of fact and degree. It is necessary in such cases to adduce evidence of a genuine and close family tie. Thus living in the same household in a situation of financial dependency and with a genuinely close relationship has been held sufficient[223]. In many cases an interference with a close relationship may be held an interference with 'private life' even if not 'family life'[224].

In *Marckx* v. *Belgium*[225], complex Belgian laws which discriminated against children born outside marriage, including unequal intestacy provisions, were held to violate Article 8 and to have no justification under Article 8(2). It is sometimes read from such cases that Article 8 imports to states not only a general duty to refrain from interfering in an individual's private life, but also a duty to act to protect private and family life in certain instances. Whilst the case law undoubtedly supports this contention, the Court or Commission frequently requires the state to reorganise an unfair system that it has created. In *Marckx* therefore, the discriminatory laws relating to illegitimate children required amending. In *Airey* v. *Ireland*[225a] an Irish law (and practice) restricting a woman's ability to separate from a violent spouse was held to violate Article 8; inevitably this meant that the state was required to make changes.

Public and private family law proceedings

Where the state intervenes by, for instance, removing children into care or via compulsory supervision, the Convention requires that the natural parents be properly involved in the decision-making process and that full account is taken of their views and wishes[226]. In addition, Article 6(1) requires that their civil rights to reside with, and to have contact with, their children are determined at a fair hearing within a reasonable time by an independent tribunal. The changes wrought as a result of the Court decisions in *O., H., W., B., R.* v. *U.K.*[227] have now been consolidated into the Children Act 1989.

In *Olsson* v. *Sweden*[228] the Court found Article 8 violated where siblings had been taken into care, separated and placed at considerable

---

[223] DR 13/248 which concerned foster parent/step parent relations; DR 9/57 and DR 20/168 concerning cohabitation relationships; and DR 31/241 confirming adoption is a 'family relationship'

[224] DR 32/220

[225] 2 E.H.R.R. 330; June 13, 1979, Series A, No. 31; and see also *Johnston* v. *Ireland* 9 E.H.R.R. 203; December 18, 1986, Series A, No. 112; and *Vermeire* v. *Belgium* 15 E.H.R.R. 488; November 29, 1991, Series A, No. 214-C

[225a] 2 E.H.R.R. 305; October 9, 1979, Series A, No. 32

[226] *O.,H.,W.,B.,R.* v. *U.K.* 10 E.H.R.R. 29–95; July 8, 1987, Series A, Nos. 120 and 121

[227] *Ibid.*

[228] 11 E.H.R.R. 259; March 24, 1988, Series A, No. 130

distances from the parents, thereby substantially restricting parental contact. The Court also considered in brief the question of the childrens' rights to contact with each other; an issue that has been little invoked and possibly an area requiring further development[229].

In relation to private family proceedings, the Commission has held that whilst compulsory paternity blood tests violate Article 8(1), they are justified under Article 8(2) as necessary for the protection of the rights of others[230], as are compulsory psychiatric examinations in such cases, or X-rays[231].

Article 8 requires that non-custodial parents have the right of contact with their children unless particularly serious grounds exist to the contrary [232]; the fact that the custodial parent objects to contact and that this might therefore put the child under stress, is not in itself a ground of sufficient seriousness to prevent contact[233]. The fact that the divorced non-custodial parent is serving a long prison sentence may however be a sufficiently serious ground[234].

Deportation

Article 8 protects the rights of existing families; not the right of a person to enter a country to found a new family. Deportation, or a refusal of entry, can violate Article 8 if it separates an existing family. The test in such cases is the practicability of the person's spouse or family following and all living together in another country with which they have connections,[235] safely[236]. In *Abdulaziz, Cabales and Balkandali* v. *U.K.*[237] the Court was prepared to accept that an 'existing family' could include a legally engaged couple.

In *Berrehab* v. *Netherlands* [238] the Court held that the deportation of a Moroccan, after his divorce from a Netherlands' national, violated Article 8; the deportation separated him from his daughter with whom he had regular contact and to whom he contributed significant maintenance.

Moustaquim v. *Belgium* [239] concerned a Moroccan who had lived in Belgium since three years of age. All the applicant's close relatives,

---

[229] *See also* DR 2/118; and *Eriksson* v. *Sweden* 12 E.H.R.R. 183; June 22, 1989, Series A, No. 156
[230] DR 18/154; as indeed are such tests in drinking and driving cases, DR 16/184
[231] DR 40/251
[232] DR 29/5; DR 33/9
[233] DR 18/225
[234] DR 9/166; and *see* DR 12/192
[235] DR 7/64; DR 24/98
[236] DR 60/284
[237] 7 E.H.R.R. 471; May 28, 1985, Series A, No. 94
[238] 11 E.H.R.R. 322; June 21, 1988, Series A, No. 138
[239] 13 E.H.R.R. 802; February 18, 1991, Series A, No. 193

including his parents, his seven brothers and sisters also lived in Belgium. When 19 years old he was ordered to be deported having completed a sentence of 26 months' imprisonment for a number of offences committed whilst a minor (none of them grave). The Court considered that the deportation was disproportionate in the circumstances and therefore violated the applicant's right to family life. Where, however, a complainant has been deported for serious offences such as trading in heroin, then even the separation of spouses will not stop the Commission or Court from holding it necessary 'for the prevention of disorder or crime'[240].

Abortion

The legal regulation of abortion is an intervention in a woman's private life which may or may not be justified under Article 8(2)[241]. The Commission has therefore upheld the right of a state to place limited restrictions upon the availability of abortion (by, for instance, requiring greater reasons than that the pregnancy was unwanted[242]).

The Commission has held that a father does not have the right to be consulted about a proposed termination of the mother's pregnancy; holding that whilst this may be a violation of Article 8(1), it is justified as being necessary for the protection of the rights of others[243].

Homosexuality

The Court has confirmed that sexual life forms an important part of a person's private life for the purposes of Article 8[244]. Whilst the Commission has not been prepared to extend the concept of 'family life' to include a homosexual relationship, it has confirmed that respect for such a relationship nevertheless comes within the ambit of 'private life'[245]. The degree of respect does not extend to requiring a state to enable a non-biological parent in a lesbian relationship to have parental responsibility of a child born to the couple using artificial insemination[246].

The Commission has held that the criminalisation of homosexual relations with children under the age of consent does not violate

---

[240] DR 12/197
[241] DR 5/103
[242] Ibid.
[243] DR 19/244
[244] Norris v. Ireland 13 E.H.R.R. 186; October 26, 1988, Series A, No. 142
[245] DR 32/220
[246] Kerkhoven v. Netherlands 15666/89, not yet reported in Decisions and Reports

Article 8, in that it is justified as being necessary for the protection of the rights and freedoms of others[247]. In *Dudgeon* v. *U.K.*[248] the Court held that the criminalisation of all homosexual relations between males regardless of age or consent was too wide to be justified by one of the exceptions in Article 8(2). The Commission has found however, that a total prohibition of homosexual conduct in the armed forces, even amongst consenting males over 21 years is justified as necessary for the protection of morals and the prevention of disorder[249].

Transsexuals

Article 8 protects the right of a transsexual to have his or her changed sex recognised by the state. In *Cossey* v. *U.K.*[250] the Court found that the refusal of the Government to allow the sex recorded on a birth certificate to be changed did not violate Article 8. The Court indicated that it was prepared to reconsider the question in the light of social and scientific change, but considered of greatest relevance the fact that sex change procedures did not change the person's chromosomal sex.

Eighteen months later in *B.* v. *France*[251] the Court, without changing its basic attitude on the question, nevertheless found a violation of Article 8 where the French Government refused to allow a change to the birth certificate. The Court found that whereas in the U.K. the birth certificate was viewed as a historical record of fact, in France such certificates were updated through a person's life and therefore it would be a relatively straightforward matter to include upon it a reference to a judgment ordering its amendment, not to correct an initial error, but to bring it up to date. In addition the Court found that Article 8 was violated by the French law which severely restricted a person's ability to change his or her forenames and also by the increasing use of official documents in France which recorded a person's sex and which were incapable of amendment.

The home

Article 8 cannot be used to imply a right to be provided with housing accommodation as opposed to respect for one's existing home. A home

---

[247] DR 19/66
[248] 4 E.H.R.R. 149; September 23, 1981, Series A, No. 45; and *see Norris* v. *Ireland* note 244; above
[249] DR 34/68
[250] 13 E.H.R.R. 622; September 27, 1990, Series A, No. 184
[251] 16 E.H.R.R. 1; March 25, 1992, Series A, No. 232-C

presumably includes a caravan if it is a person's only or main abode, although it is undecided if it includes a camping car[252].

A criminal [253] or civil[254] search of a home constitutes a violation of Article 8(1), even if the premises are partly used for business purposes[255]. Such searches may be justified under Article 8(2) as being for the protection of the rights of others.

The question of whether a house can remain a 'home' for the purposes of Article 8 has been examined in two complaints concerning the occupation restrictions imposed in Guernsey. In *Wiggins* v. *U.K.*[256] whilst the Commission accepted that a house remained the applicant's home despite separation from his wife, it nevertheless held that the refusal of the island authorities to grant him a licence to remain in the property was justified under Article 8(2) as being necessary for the economic well-being of the island, (by reserving low value properties for the occupation of native islanders). In *Gillow* v. *UK*[257] the Court found a violation of Article 8 despite the applicants having been away from their home for over 18 years largely by virtue of the particularly deserving nature of their claim and the inflexible and disproportionately harsh way in which the licensing authority had dealt with them.

A few applications to the Court and Commission have concerned interference with the enjoyment of property caused by excessive noise; the issues raised by these complaints are dealt with *below*.

Environmental intrusion

Whilst the Commission has asserted that *'the protection afforded by Article 8 of the Convention [cannot] extend to relationships of the individual with his entire immediate surroundings, in so far as they do not involve human relationships'*[258], the emphasis in this statement must be on the word 'entire'. Clearly interference with some aspects of a person's immediate environment would constitute a violation of Article 8.

In *G. and E.* v. *Norway*[259] the Commission considered a complaint made by two Norwegian Lapps concerning the proposed construction of a hydro-electric dam which would flood part of the land upon which

[252] DR 58/94
[253] DR 6/91
[254] *Chappell* v. *U.K.* 12 E.H.R.R. 1; March 30, 1989, Series A, No. 152 concerning an Anton Piller order; and *see* DR 57/5
[255] *Ibid.;* and *see Niemietz* v. *Germany* 16 E.H.R.R. 97; December 16, 1992, Series A, No. 251-B.
[256] DR 13/40
[257] *Gillow* v. *U.K.* 11 E.H.R.R. 335; November 24, 1986, Series A, No. 109
[258] DR 5/86
[259] DR 35/30

Lapps traditionally herded reindeer. The Commission was prepared to accept in this case that:

> the consequences, arising for the applicants from the construction of the hydro-electric plant, constitute an interference with their private life, as members of a minority, ...[and that] the environment of the plant will be affected. This could interfere with the applicants' possibilities of enjoying the right to respect for their private life.

In the circumstances of this case however, the Commission held the interference justified under Article 8(2), in that the area to be flooded was small compared to the vast areas in Northern Norway and the economic benefits from the project for Norway were considerable.

The Court and Commission have considered a series of complaints concerning the noise nuisance to houses adjoining airports. In *Powell and Rayner* v. *U.K.*[260] the Court accepted that the quality of the applicants' private lives and the scope for enjoying the amenities of their homes had been adversely affected by the noise generated by aircraft using Heathrow Airport. However, having regard to the administrative measures adopted by the Government to insulate prop-erties from noise and the economic benefits of airports, the Court found no violation of Article 8. Mr Powell lived several miles from the airport, and about half a million people experienced similar aircraft noise levels. Mr Rayner lived only one-and-a-third miles from the airport and about 6,500 persons experienced a similar noise intrusion. In *Braggs* v. *U.K.*[261] the complainant lived only a quarter of a mile from the airport and experienced noise levels of up to 127 decibels; very few people experienced similar noise intrusion. He had purchased his property before the major expansion of Heathrow and was unable to sell it due to the aircraft noise. The Commission accepted that the conditions in which Mr Braggs had been forced to live were 'truly shocking and deplorable' and declared the complaint admissible. It was subsequently the subject of a friendly settlement and thus the Court has not been required to consider a case of extreme environmental noise intrusion[262].

A 1989 complaint concerning noise from a military firing range was ruled inadmissible as it did not disclose 'intolerable nuisance in view of its actual degree and intensity'[263]. It should be appreciated however, that noise intrusion may not have to reach the appalling levels

---

[260] 12 E.H.R.R. 355; February 21, 1990, Series A, No. 172
[261] DR 44/13
[262] DR 52/29. An earlier Commission decision, also the subject of a friendly settlement, is *Arrondelle* v. *U.K.* DR 19/186 which concerned a property a mile from Gatwick and 500 feet from the M23; the noise levels were less than in *Braggs* v. *U.K.* and the decision needs to be considered in the light of the Court's decision in *Powell* and *Rayner*
[263] DR 59/186

experienced by Mr Braggs (*above*) before a violation of Article 8 occurs: Heathrow is, after all, an extraordinarily important economic enterprise, from which noise is inevitable and for which the state has made great efforts to reduce the environmental impact.

In *Ostra* v. *Spain*[263a] the applicant lived within 12 metres of a treatment works that received waste from a number of tanneries. The applicant complained that the stench and fumes affected her health and made occupation of her home intolerable. The Commission reaffirmed that states are required, not only to respect, but also to protect the rights guaranteed by Article 8(1) and that these included protection from pollution of such a degree as appeared to be disclosed by the complaint.

Prisoners

A number of important decisions have been made concerning interference with prisoners' correspondence and these are dealt with in the next section.

The Court and Commission accept that the restrictions imposed upon prisoners interfere with their Article 8(1) rights but in general have accepted such interferences as justified by virtue of Article 8(2), *i.e.* the interests of national security, public safety, the prevention of disorder or crime[264]. Complaints concerning the wearing of prison clothes[265], close surveillance during family visits[266] and restrictions on conjugal life in prison [267] have all been held justified in their particular circumstances. This is, however, an area where the Court and Commission have shown a willingness to adapt their views in line with prison reform and changing public attitudes. The Commission is prepared to review restrictions by reference to the European Prison Rules (1987)[268].

Correspondence

Any state interference with correspondence other than resulting from Post Office inefficiencies[269] violates Article 8(1) and requires

---

[263a] Application No. 16798/90 not yet reported in Decisions and Reports

[264] *See generally* the Commission decision in *McFeeley* v. *U.K.* 3 E.H.R.R. 161

[265] DR 28/5

[266] DR 14/246. A total prohibition on contact with a spouse, even for a short period, may however violate Article 8, *see* DR 25/15

[267] DR 13/241

[268] *Ibid.*, where reference was made to the previous Rules, 'The Council Of Europe Standard Minimum Rules for the Treatment of Prisoners'; the revised Rules, now called the 'European Prison Rules' were adopted by the Committee of Ministers on February 12, 1987 and without reservation by the U.K.

[269] DR 17/227; and *see Firsoff* v. *U.K.* 15 E.H.R.R. CD 11

justification under Article 8(2). Whilst most such cases have arisen in respect to prisoners, the principal of course applies to all persons, including, for instance, the monitoring of a bankrupt's correspondence by his trustee[270].

The Court and Commission consider that a prisoner has the right to correspond with his or her lawyer almost without any interference whatsoever; this extends not only to censorship of letters, but also to any restrictions, such as a refusal to allow the letter to be sent [271]. The right of contact is of course, two-way and there must not be any unjustified restriction on a lawyer's correspondence with a detainee, even if the lawyer has not been appointed by the detainee but, for instance, by his spouse and if the correspondence is advising the detainee to exercise his right of silence[272].

Whilst the prison authorities may censor non-legal correspondence, the Court and Commission will scrutinise this interference to ensure it is limited to items which might be prejudicial to security or of a criminal nature[273].

Surveillance

In *Malone* v. *UK*[274] the Court considered the (then) U.K. Governmental rules concerning the authorisation of telephone tapping and metering. The interception of calls was effected after a warrant had been granted by the Home Secretary. Although the procedure for obtaining such warrants was the subject of 'Rules', these allowed so wide a discretion as to be virtually unlimited in scope. The Court held therefore, that the U.K. system violated Article 8 by not being in accordance with the law. The Court has come to a similar decision in respect of the French system, finding that it lacked essential regulatory control[275].

In *Klass* v. *Germany*[276] the Court considered the equivalent German system and concluded that it did not violate Article 8. The system was strict, clearly drafted and the subject of administrative and judicial control. The system provided for warrants to be time-limited and for the person under investigation to be notified of the action after its

---

[270] DR 59/81

[271] *Golder* v. *U.K.* 1 E.H.R.R. 524; February 21, 1975, Series A, No. 18; and *McCallum* v. *U.K.* 13 E.H.R.R. 597; August 30, 1990, Series A, No. 183

[272] *Schöenberger and Durmaz* v. *Switzerland* 11 E.H.R.R. 202; June 20, 1988, Series A, No. 137

[273] *Silver* v. *U.K.* 5 E.H.R.R. 347; March 25, 1983, Series A, No. 61; *Boyle and Rice* v. *U.K.* 10 E.H.R.R. 425; April 27, 1988, Series A, No. 131

[274] 7 E.H.R.R. 14; August 2, 1984, Series A, No. 82

[275] *Kruslin and Huvig* v. *France* 12 E.H.R.R. 528/547; April 24, 1990, Series A, No. 176–B

[276] 2 E.H.R.R. 214; September 6, 1978, Series A, No. 28

completion as soon as this could be done without jeopardising the object of the surveillance.

The Court considers it important that a person can subsequently discover whether he or she has been the subject of surveillance and if necessary challenge its validity. Whilst subsequent notification is not an absolute requirement in every case (because in some cases 'refraining from doing so is what ensures the efficacy of the interference')[277], the Commission has held that this should only be where 'such information would risk compromising the aim and object of the telephone tapping measure' [278]. It is therefore questionable whether the Interception of Communications Act 1985, introduced as a result of the *Malone* complaint, brings the U.K. system within the requirements of Article 8.

Personal records

The collection and storage of personal information about individuals, as in a police collator system, does not in itself violate Article 8[279]; this is so even if the person has no criminal record. Where, however, there is a disclosure or publication of the information to third parties, it clearly constitutes an invasion of privacy, which violates Article 8 unless justified by reference to Article 8(2). In *Leander* v. *Sweden*[280] the disclosure of the personal information led to Mr Leander's loss of employment; the Court nevertheless found no violation as the disclosure was justified 'in the interests of national security'.

A somewhat different situation arose in *Gaskin* v. *U.K.*[281] where the applicant sought access to his social services records. The request was refused in part on the ground that some of the information had originally been given in confidence and certain of the informants did not consent to their material being disclosed. The information was important to Mr Gaskin as he had spent almost all his life in care and he wanted it for identity purposes. His was a legitimate claim, as indeed was the refusal to divulge the information which had been given to the local authority in confidence. The Court concluded that a balancing of the conflicting interests was required in such a situation; and that this required an independent adjudication system to decide whether the papers should be disclosed. As no such system existed, it found a violation of Article 8.

---

[277] DR 55/182
[278] *Ibid*.
[279] *Leander* v. *Sweden* 9 E.H.R.R. 433; March 26, 1987, Series A, No. 116; but *see H.* v. *Austria* 15 E.H.R.R. CD 71
[280] *Ibid.*; and *see Hewitt and Harman, and N.* v. *U.K.* applications 12175/86 and 12327/86 not yet reported in Decisions and Reports.
[281] 12 E.H.R.R. 36; July 7, 1989, Series A, No. 160

FREEDOM OF CONSCIENCE: ARTICLE 9

Article 9

1. *Everyone has the right to freedom of thought, conscience and religion; this right includes freedom to change his religion or belief and freedom, either alone or in community with others and in public or private, to manifest his religion or belief, in worship, teaching, practice and observance.*

2. *Freedom to manifest one's religion or beliefs shall be subject only to such limitations as are prescribed by law and are necessary in a democratic society in the interests of public safety, for the protection of public order, health or morals, or for the protection of the rights and freedoms of others.*

Article 9 permits no restriction whatsoever in relation to the private practice of a person's thought, conscience or religion. The permissible restrictions under Article 9(2) only apply to the 'freedom to manifest one's religion'. These restrictions (although similar) are less extensive than those available under Articles 8, 10 and 11.

Article 9 has been invoked in relatively few complaints; of these most have involved conscientious objection, prison restrictions and religion.

Religion

The rights under Article 9(1) extend to church bodies as representatives of their members as well as individuals[282]. A state can only restrict the freedom to manifest a religion to the extent permitted by Article 9(2); where, however, a church embarks upon a marketing exercise the primary rôle of which is commercial, it is outside the scope of the protection afforded by Article 9(2)[283].

The freedom to manifest a religion does not restrict the right of a church to expel heretics or ministers who impose separate or different rules to those of the church[284]; such persons can after all set up their own church, or pursue their own personal religious practice.

In *Darby* v. *Sweden*[285] the applicant complained that he was obliged to pay a tax for the support of the state Church (to which he did not

---

[282] DR 16/68
[283] *Ibid.*, and *see also* DR 16/85
[284] DR 5/157
[285] 13 E.H.R.R. 774; October 23, 1990, Series A, No. 187

belong) and that this, *inter alia*, violated Article 9. The Court upheld the complaint under Article 14 and Article 1 of the First Protocol without separately investigating Article 9. The issue of discrimination on grounds of religion has also arisen in respect of child custody. In *Hoffman* v. *Austria*[286] the Court found a violation of Article 8 where a mother complained that she had been denied custody of her children largely upon the ground that she was a Jehovah's Witness whereas the father was not.

The Commission has ruled that domestic laws which require everyone, including Sikhs, to wear crash helmets is justified under Article 9(1) 'in the interests of public safety'[287].

Conscientious objection and pacifism

A series of complaints have concerned the lack of respect by states for individual conscientious objection to military service. The Commission has, however, rejected all such complaints, relying upon the provisions of Article 4, which specifically envisages the possibility of military service being compulsory. Thus, in countries where compulsory military service exists, Article 9 does not require substituted civilian service[288]. It follows that where such substituted service exists, a person cannot resist it by invoking Article 9[289].

Whilst pacifism is clearly a matter of conscience or belief within the meaning of Article 9, a manifestation of this by distributing leaflets to soldiers or encouraging disaffection by distributing explicit leaflets to soldiers on the subject (rather than expressing pacifist views) is not protected by Article 9(2); such protection comes within Article 10, if at all[290].

Prisoners

The Commission has considered a number of complaints concerning the restrictions placed upon prisoners in the observance of their religious or conscientious beliefs. These include respect for the worship and dietary practices of an Orthodox Jew[291], restrictions upon access to religious or philosophical books [292], the growing of a beard, the wearing

---

[286] Application 12875/87; not yet reported in Decision and Reports; *Times*, July 27, 1993
[287] DR 14/234; for analysis and criticism of this decision, *see* Fawcett p. 248
[288] DR 38/219
[289] DR 9/196; and DR 40/203
[290] DR 19/5; and 3 E.H.R.R. 218
[291] DR 5/8
[292] DR 5/100

of prison clothes[293], and the religious objection to the cleaning of a prison floor[294]. In all such cases the Commission has been prepared to allow a sufficient margin of appreciation to the state to validate the restriction within Article 9(2). In many cases, however, the justification accepted by the Commission has strained the borders of logic and it is possible that with the development of social attitudes towards prison conditions, the Commission may be prepared to adopt a more rigorous approach to such complaints in the future.

[293] DR 28/5
[294] *Ibid.*

FREEDOM OF EXPRESSION: ARTICLE 10

Article 10

1. *Everyone has the right to freedom of expression. This right shall include freedom to hold opinions and to receive and impart information and ideas without interference by public authority and regardless of frontiers. This article shall not prevent states from requiring the licensing of broadcasting, television or cinema enterprises.*

2. *The exercise of these freedoms, since it carries with it duties and responsibilities, may be subject to such formalities, conditions, restrictions or penalties as are prescribed by law and are necessary in a democratic society, in the interests of national security, territorial integrity or public safety, for the prevention of disorder or crime, for the protection of health or morals, for the protection of the reputation or rights of others, for preventing the disclosure of information received in confidence, or for maintaining the authority and impartiality of the judiciary.*

The Court and Commission have emphasised that freedom of expression is itself a fundamental safeguard for the protection of other human rights; it is generally only through the public condemnation of human rights abuses that they are eradicated. It is also to be protected in its own right:

> Freedom of the press affords the public one of the best means of discovering and forming an opinion of the ideas and attitudes of political leaders . . . freedom of political debate is at the very core of the concept of a democratic society which prevails throughout the Convention[295].

The respect accorded to the right is not (within reason) dependent upon the acceptability of the views expressed. *'Some degree of abuse is inseparable from the proper use of everything; and in no instance is this more true than in that of the press'*[296]. In *Handyside v. U.K.*[297], which concerned the prosecution of a publisher for producing *The Little Red School Book*, the Court stated that:

> freedom of expression constitutes one of the essential foundations of . . . a [democratic] society, one of the basic conditions for its progress and for the

---

[295] *Oberschlick v. Austria* May 23, 1991, Series A, No. 204
[296] James Madison, 4 Elliot's Debates of the Federal Constitution (1876) p. 571, quoted in *Derbyshire County Council v. Times Newspapers* [1992] 1 Q.B. 770, C.A
[297] 1 E.H.R.R. 737; December 7, 1976, Series A, No. 24

development of every man. Subject to paragraph 2 of Article 10, it is applicable not only to 'information' or 'ideas' that are favourably received or regarded as inoffensive or as a matter of indifference, but also to those that offend, shock or disturb the state or any sector of the population. Such are the demands of pluralism, tolerance and broadmindedness without which there is no 'democratic society'. This means, amongst other things that every 'formality', 'condition', 'restriction' or 'penalty' imposed in this sphere must be proportionate to the legitimate aim pursued'.

Whilst the Court and Commission have repeatedly upheld the importance of the rights enshrined in Article 10, it has to be said that their decisions do not constitute a radical defence of free speech. States are generally allowed substantial leeway in interpreting the restrictions placed upon the right, by Article 10(2); the Court and Commission usually swim with the tide of liberal opinion but no more. Accordingly violations of Article 10 have not been found in cases involving the prosecution of the publisher of *The Little Red School Book* (despite the book being freely available in many other Council of Europe states)[298]; the prosecution of a journalist for asserting that two judges were not independent when objectively they were not[299]; the imprisonment of a soldier for publishing an article critical of army officers[300]; the denial of state teaching posts to persons supporting the Communist Party[301]; and the prosecution of artists for painting sexually explicit pictures in public[302].

Overlap with other Articles

Article 10 overlaps with the rights expressed in other Articles, most notably Articles 8, 9 and 11.

The right to hold opinions in Article 10 is virtually indistinguishable from the right to freedom of thought and conscience in Article 9. Where such an issue comes before the Court and Commission the violation is usually investigated under Article 9.

Where a public demonstration occurs, this is both a form of 'peaceful assembly' under Article 11 and a form of expression under Article 10. In such cases, where there is an interference with the right to demonstrate, this is first investigated from the perspective of Article 11[303].

An interference with correspondence is a potential violation of Article 8, and an interference with a person's freedom of expression; in such cases it is the Article 8 issue that is addressed first[304].

---

[298] *Ibid*.
[299] *Barford* v. *Denmark* 13 E.H.R.R. 493; February 22, 1989, Series A, No. 149
[300] *Engel* v. *Netherlands* 1 E.H.R.R. 647; June 8, 1976, Series A, No. 22
[301] *Glasenapp* v. *Germany* 9 E.H.R.R. 25; August 28, 1986, Series A, No. 104
[302] *Müller* v. *Switzerland* 13 E.H.R.R. 212; May 24, 1988, Series A, No. 133
[303] DR 21/138
[304] *Silver* v. *U.K.* 5 E.H.R.R. 347; March 25, 1983, Series A, No. 61

The permitted restrictions upon the exercise of the rights set out in Articles 8, 9, 10 and 11 are similar. In each case the Article sets out the primary right in the first paragraph. Once the complainant has established a violation of this right, it is for the state to satisfy the Commission and/or Court that the restriction is permitted by the second paragraph of the relevant Article.

Freedom to publish

On September 24, 1972 the *Sunday Times* published an article highlighting the plight of families with physically handicapped children; children whose mothers had taken the drug Thalidomide during pregnancy. At the time of publication litigation was pending (but dormant) before the High Court for compensation. Essentially the litigation concerned *quantum* rather than liability. A footnote to the article announced that a further article was to be published on the subject. The Attorney-General then obtained an injunction against the *Sunday Times* prohibiting publication of this further article; the legal basis for the injunction being expressed as the prevention of a contempt of court. The Court held that the restriction did satisfy the requirement in Article 10(2) of being 'prescribed by law', but could not be justified as being necessary in a democratic society[305]. The Court held:

> It is not sufficient that the interference involved belongs to that class of the exceptions listed in Article 10(2) which has been invoked; neither is it sufficient that the interference was imposed because its subject-matter fell within a particular category or was caught by a legal rule formulated in general or absolute terms: the Court has to be satisfied that the interference was necessary having regard to the facts and circumstances prevailing in the specific case before it.

> The Thalidomide disaster was a matter of undisputed public concern. It posed the question whether the powerful company which had marketed the drug bore legal or moral responsibility towards hundreds of individuals experiencing an appalling personal tragedy; . . . fundamental issues concerning the protection against and compensation for injuries resulting from scientific developments were raised . . .

> Article 10 guarantees not only the freedom of the press to inform the public but also the right of the public to be properly informed.

PRESCRIBED BY LAW

In the *Sunday Times* case the Court identified the characteristics a legal restriction must possess in order to be 'prescribed by law', namely:

---

[305] *Sunday Times* v. *U.K.* 2 E.H.R.R. 245; April 26, 1979, Series A, No. 30

1. It must be 'adequately accessible'; *i.e.* it must generally be known to exist.
2. It must be 'formulated with sufficient precision'; *i.e.* it must be basically as opposed to 'absolutely' predictable in effect.
3. (Where there is a discretion in applying the restriction) it must be precisely defined and limited in effect[306].

In June 1986 the *Observer, Sunday Times* and *Guardian* published articles containing extracts from the 'Spycatcher' book which included references to allegedly illegal activities by the British Security Service. The Attorney-General obtained injunctions against the newspapers; the legal basis being to restrain a breach of confidence. The injunctions were granted on July 11, 1986 and, despite applications to discharge them, remained in force until October 13, 1988. The Court held[307] that the interference with the applicants' freedom of expression was 'prescribed by law', and had a legitimate aim (the maintaining of the authority of the judiciary). It also concluded that the injunctions when first imposed were justifiably 'necessary . . . in the interests of national security' having regard to the leeway allowed to states in interpreting this restriction. Nevertheless, it held that after July 1987 (when the book was published in the U.S.A.) national security could no longer be a legitimate restriction and thereafter the newspapers' Convention rights were violated.

TV and broadcasting

Article 10(1) specifically limits the freedom of expression in respect of 'broadcasting, television or cinema enterprises' by permitting them to be the subject of state licensing systems. Article 10(1) does not constitute a right of access to such broadcasting facilities[308], but does (subject to licensing requirements) include the right not to have broadcasts jammed or otherwise interfered with[309].

Whilst the licensing permitted by Article 10(1) cannot be avoided by broadcasting from one state to another[310], the Court and Commission are prepared to scrutinise the validity of licence refusals. Thus in *Autronic A.G.* v. *Switzerland*[311] a Swiss company sought authority to

---

[306] *Malone* v. *U.K.* 7 E.H.R.R. 14; August 2, 1984, Series A, No. 82
[307] *Sunday Times* v. *U.K.* 14 E.H.R.R. 229; November 26, 1991, Series A, No. 217
[308] 4515/70 (not reported in Decisions and Reports) in this decision the Commission observed that a selective denial of broadcasting time to individuals or groups could constitute a violation of Article 10 alone or in conjunction with Article 14
[309] DR 37/236
[310] *Groppera Radio A.G.* v. *Switzerland* 12 E.H.R.R. 321; March 28, 1990, Series A, No. 173
[311] 12 E.H.R.R. 485; May 22, 1990, Series A, No. 178

show a Soviet programme which it had received via a satellite dish at a technical exhibition. The licence was refused by the Swiss authorities because the company lacked the express authority of the Soviet broadcaster. The Court ruled that limited companies as well as individuals enjoyed rights under Article 10 and that although the interference was prescribed by law and pursued a legitimate aim (the prevention of disorder in telecommunications), it was not necessary in a democratic society. In so deciding, the Court had regard to the fact that several states that had signed the European Convention of Transfrontier Television had authorised the reception of such broadcasts without requiring the broadcaster's authority; that the proposed exhibition was of limited extent and that there was no question of secret information being transmitted.

Advertising and commercial activities

The promotion of services or commodities (whether or not for profit) is itself a form of expression which is protected by Article 10. The degree of protection afforded by the Court and Commission depends in part upon the extent of the commercial involvement. The Commission has, however, held that the level of protection afforded is less than that accorded to the expression of political ideas[312]. In *Open Door Counselling Ltd. and Dublin Well Woman Centre Ltd.* v. *Ireland*[313] the Court was concerned with the injunction restraining two non-profit-making companies from informing pregnant woman about abortion facilities outside Ireland. The Court held that the absolute nature of the injunction was disproportionately wide and without justification under Article 10(2). In *Markt Intern Verlag GmbH and Beermann* v. *Germany*[314] the Court considered an injunction imposed upon a commercial publishing firm, restraining it from publishing a critical article concerning the behaviour of another company in failing to reimburse a dissatisfied customer. The Court, in an unsatisfactory judgment,[315] held that the leeway open to states in applying Article 10 in commercial matters was wide, and that the obligation to respect the privacy of others and the duty to respect the confidentiality of certain commercial information might sometimes justify prohibiting the publication of items which are true.

Special groups and individuals

As has been seen *above*, the Court and Commission in considering the degree to which interference with free expression is justified, has

[312] DR 16/68
[313] 15 E.H.R.R. 244; October 29, 1992, Series A, No. 246
[314] 12 E.H.R.R. 161; November 20, 1989, Series A, No. 164
[315] The voting was 9:9 with the casting vote of the President ruling that there had been no violation

regard to the nature of what is to be said (*i.e.* whether it is political or commercial) and the medium of communication (*i.e.* whether it is printed or broadcast). In addition the Court and Commission have taken into account the position or profession occupied by the individual in question.

PROFESSIONALS

In *Ezelin* v. *France*[316] a French lawyer took part in a public demonstration protesting against certain court decisions. He was disciplined by the Bar Council, receiving a reprimand. The Court held that the interference was prescribed by law (in that it arose out of special rules governing the profession of advocat) and pursued the legitimate aim of 'prevention of disorder'. It did however consider the interference disproportionate and not justified in a democratic society, holding that lawyers should not be discouraged, for fear of disciplinary sanctions, from making clear their beliefs on such occasions. The freedom to take part in a peaceful assembly was of such importance that it could not be restricted by such a sanction, however minimal.

There is of course a line to be drawn between a lawyer participating in a peaceful protest and the making of insulting statements about the judiciary[317].

The degree to which professional conduct rules can restrict a professional's contact with the press, by advertising or otherwise, was considered by the Court in *Barthold* v. *Germany* [318]. In this case an article appeared concerning the applicant vet which, by including certain details of his practice, was considered publicity by the professional association and therefore prohibited. The Court held that the profession's rules so severely restricted contact with the press that they amounted to an unjustifiable interference; the importance of a free press required that it have input from professionals.

POLITICIANS

Article 10(2) permits interference with the right of free expression for the protection of the reputation of others. In a series of cases however,[319] the Court has emphasised that the limits of acceptable criticism are wider in respect of politicians than in relation to private

[316] 14 E.H.R.R. 362; April 26, 1991, Series A, No. 202
[317] DR 40/214
[318] 7 E.H.R.R. 383; May 23, 1985, Series A, No. 90
[319] *Oberschlick* v. *Austria* May 23, 1991, Series A, No. 204; *Lingens* v. *Austria*, 8 E.H.R.R. 103; July 8, 1986, Series A, No. 103; *Schwabe* v. *Austria* August 28, 1992, Series A, No. 242–B, where prosecution of a journalist who had referred to to a politician's spent conviction for a traffic offence 20 years earlier was held to violate Article 10

individuals. Politicians lay themselves open to close scrutiny by the press and the public and must therefore display a greater degree of tolerance, especially when they make statements susceptible to criticism.

In *Oberschilick* v. *Austria*[320] a journalist likened a politician's policies to those pursued by the National Socialists. The politician started criminal defamation proceedings as a result of which the journalist was fined and the publication seized. The Court found that Article 10 had been violated. Freedom of the press afforded the public one of the best means of discovering and forming opinions on the ideas and attitudes of political leaders; in the circumstances of the case it held that the applicant was entitled to be provocative in order to draw the public's attention to the politician's proposals which were likely to shock many people.

In *Thorgeirson* v. *Iceland*[321] the applicant was prosecuted for defamation, having published an article containing reports of alleged police brutality. The Court held that the interference was unjustified having regard to the importance of the subject, the fact that the language used was not excessive and that the purpose of the article was to promote debate about the need for a reformed police complaints sysyem.

JUDGES

Article 10(2) permits restrictions upon free expression, not only to protect the reputations of others but also for the maintenance of the authority and impartiality of the judiciary. The Commission and Court have accordingly been less tolerant of criticism of the judiciary than of politicians. In *Barford* v. *Denmark*[322] a journalist suggested that two lay judges had decided a case on the basis of their connection with one of the parties (a local authority of which the judges were employees). The applicant was convicted of defaming the judges. On appeal the conviction was upheld, although it was agreed that the lay judges should have refrained from participating in the case. The Court found no violation of Article 10, suggesting that the applicant should have aimed his criticism at the composition of the Court without attacking the two judges personally.

In *Weber* v. *Switzerland*[323] an environmental campaigner was fined for having disclosed at a press conference details of steps taken by an investigating judge in proceedings which were pending. The Court considered that at the time of disclosure most of the relevant informa-

---

[320] *Ibid.*
[321] 14 E.H.R.R. 239; June 25, 1992, Series A, No. 239
[322] *See* note 299 *above*
[323] 12 E.H.R.R. 508; May 22, 1990, Series A, No. 177

tion was already in the public domain and that the investigating judge's enquiries were almost complete. In the circumstances it held that the restriction upon the applicant's right to free expression was not justified for the protection of the authority or impartiality of the judiciary.

Whilst a judge has the same right of free expression under Article 10, in assessing the permissible restrictions upon that right *'one must take into account the particular situation of the person exercising his freedom of expression and of the "duties and responsibilities" attached to this situation'*. Thus where a judge was reprimanded for having distributed political leaflets in his free time which criticised the administration of justice, the Commission found that the reprimand was permitted as being necessary for the maintenance and impartiality of the judiciary [324].

CIVIL SERVANTS AND TEACHERS

The Court and Commission in general have not been prepared to criticise the significant restrictions to free expression placed upon the rights of civil servants or teachers. This reticence exists even where the expression arguably takes the form of 'whistleblowing'. In *Haseldine* v. *U.K.*[325] a civil servant who was concerned about violations of the (then) sanctions against South Africa was sacked for having written a letter to the press criticising the Prime Minister. The Commission ruled that by virtue of Article 10(2) civil servants were restricted in disclosing information received in confidence, and that such restrictions were in any event inherent in their duties. In similar vein no violation was found in the case of a teacher who was disciplined for having criticised her superiors in a television broadcast as being hostile to homosexuals. The Commission considered that a 'duty of moderation' existed bearing in mind the professional responsibilities incumbent upon the applicant and the specific nature of her work.

No violation was found by the Commission on a complaint by a teacher in a non-denominational school who was dismissed for refusing to stop displaying religious and anti-abortion stickers; the restriction being justified for the protection of the rights of others (the children)[326].

Political restrictions upon the employment of civil servants were investigated by the Court in the cases of *Glasenapp* v. *Germany*[327] and *Kosiek* v. *Germany*[328]. Julia Glasenapp was dismissed from her probation-

---

[324] DR 38/124
[325] 18957/92, not yet published in Decisions and Reports
[326] DR 16/101
[327] 9 E.H.R.R. 25; August 28, 1986, Series A, No. 104; but *see also Vogt* v. *Germany* 15 E.H.R.R. CD 31
[328] 9 E.H.R.R. 328; June 28, 1986, Series A, No. 105

ry teaching post because she refused to dissociate herself from the policies of a German Communist party. Rolf Kosiek was dismissed from his lectureship because of his membership of an extreme German political party which was believed to support an extreme nationalist and racist ideology. The Court did not distinguish between the two materially different situations, and rejected the complaints on the narrow and arguably unsatisfactory issue that as *access to the civil service lies at the heart of the complaint[s]'* there was no violation as this right was not protected by the Convention.

MEMBERS OF THE ARMED FORCES

Whilst the right to free expression under Article 10 extends to servicemen and women, the Court and Commission have been prepared to allow the state a greater leeway in imposing restrictions than could be contemplated within a civilian context. *Engel* v. *Netherlands*[329] concerned the detention of five conscript soldiers, two of whom were editors of the conscript servicemen's journal; these two were detained for having published articles which the authorities considered tended to undermine military discipline. The Court held that the detention of the editors and the supression of the publication by the authorities was not disproportionate in the circumstances, and was permitted in order to ensure that military discipline was not undermined.

A prison sentence of seven months given to a protester for distributing leaflets to soldiers encouraging disaffection, although considered severe, was held by the Commission not to be out of proportion; such action serving to protect national security and the prevention of disorder[330].

EXTREMISTS

Article 10 protects the right to express views which may offend, shock or disturb the state or any sector of the population[331]. There is, of course, a limit to this freedom and this tends to be either where the expression threatens public safety, or morals under Article 10(2), or where it amounts to an objective attempt to destroy the rights and freedoms of others under Article 17. A number of cases have come before the Commission concerning restrictions upon the activities of far right wing Nationalist Socialist groups advocating, amongst other things, extreme racial discrimination[332]. In such cases the Commission

---

[9] *See note 300 above*
[0] 3 E.H.R.R. 218; DR 19/5
[1] *See for instance Handyside v. U.K. note 297 above*
[2] *See for instance DR 56/205; DR 29/194; DR 59/244*

has invoked Article 17 to prevent such persons from exploiting the Convention rights for their own interests[333].

A somewhat different situation arose in *De Becker* v. *Belgium*[334] which concerned a Belgian journalist who collaborated with the German during the Second World War. After the war he was imprisoned, but eventually released on condition that he left the country. He was, *inter alia*, prohibited from ever working or publishing again in Belgium. The Commission considered such a prohibition disproportionate, as it applied to both political and non-political expression and was imposed inflexibly for life without any provision for possible relaxation over time.

ARTISTS

Müller v. *Switzerland*[335] concerned the seizure of three paintings which Josef Müller had painted at a public exhibition and his subsequent conviction, together with the organisers, of an obscene publications offence. The paintings depicted, in a crude manner, sexual relations between men and animals. The Court confirmed that Article 10 included the freedom of artistic expression and that such expression was essential in a democratic society and upon which no undue restrictions should be allowed. Nevertheless, the leeway available to states was such that the Court was not prepared to interfere with the Swiss decision that the seizure and prosecution was necessary for the protection of public morals.

A complaint to the Commission concerning the difficulties faced by troupe of street musicians and poets in plying their trade, was declared inadmissible[336]. The Commission in so deciding took into account official tolerance of buskers, the designation of certain places for such performances and that restrictions founded upon genuine obstruction of the highway (trespass or nuisance) were justified.

Where a poet was acquitted of a criminal charge resulting from the publication of two of his poems, the requirement that he nevertheless pay the legal costs of the prosecution was held by the Commission to violate Article 10[337].

PRISONERS

Imprisonment is, by the deprivation of liberty, a punishment in itself[338] and does not therefore bring with it a denial of all rights under

---

[333] 4 E.H.R.R. 260; DR 18/187
[334] 1 E.H.R.R. 43; March 27, 1962, Series A, No. 4
[335] 13 E.H.R.R. 212; May 24, 1988, Series A, No. 133
[336] DR 34/218
[337] DR 12/103; and DR 16/56
[338] European Prison Rules 1987, Rule 64

Article 10. Indeed the European Prison Rules 1987 encourage prisoners' contact with the outside world[339]. Historically the Commission has allowed substantial leeway to states in relation to interference with prisoners' Article 10 rights, for instance: restrictions upon prisoners' contact with the press, imposed by way of a penalty for breaches of prison discipline have been permitted as necessary for the prevention of disorder[340]; the refusal of prison authorities to allow a prisoner to receive a publication that they considered offensive (in this case anti-Semitic), was deemed justified by the Commission as necessary for the prevention of disorder or crime or for the protection of the reputation or rights of others[341].

---

[9] Rules 43–45 *Ibid*.
[0] DR 20/44; 3 E.H.R.R. 161
[1] DR 59/244

FREEDOM OF ASSOCIATION: ARTICLE 11

Article 11

1. *Everyone has the right to freedom of peaceful assembly and to freedom of association with others, including the right to form and to join trade unions for the protection of his interests.*

2. *No restrictions shall be placed on the exercise of these rights other than such as are prescribed by law and are necessary in a democratic society in the interests of national security or public safety, for the prevention of disorder or crime, for the protection of health or morals or for the protection of the rights and freedoms of others. This article shall not prevent the imposition of lawful restrictions on the exercise of these rights by members of the armed forces, of the police or of the administration of the state.*

Article 11 deals with the rights of people to collect together, and to enjoy the fruits of their collective action and interaction. It is a provocative article, linking as it does two apparently simple and analogous rights, and in a single sentence arriving at the controversial issue of trade unions.

Article 11 does not protect the right to assemble *per se*, but only the right of peaceful assembly[342]. Likewise it does not protect the right to associate, but the right to freedom of association (which brings with it the concept of choice).

In respect of trade unions the Court has not as yet established any sound intellectual base; not wishing to state that the 'closed shop' violates the Convention, but being unwilling to state that it does not. The Court's difficulty is perhaps not surprising; it is at this point that the civil and political rights in the Convention and the social and economic rights in the Social Charter most obviously overlap[343].

Assembly

Article 11 obliges the state to ensure that conditions exist for demonstrations or public meetings to take place peacefully. This requires that reasonable steps be taken to allow demonstrators to

---

[42] DR 60/256; and *see H.* v. *Austria* 15 E.H.R.R. CD 70
[43] *i.e.* Social Charter Articles 5 and 6, *see* p. 213 *post*

attend without fear of being subjected to physical violence by their opponents[344].

In *Plattform 'Ärzte für das Leben'* v. *Austria*[345] a march was disrupted by counter-demonstrators despite the prior deployment of police by the authorities. The marchers, although subjected to abuse and thrown eggs and clumps of grass, did not suffer any physical violence. The organisers complained that they had received insufficient police protection for this and a subsequent rally which was similarly disrupted. The Court held that whilst there was a positive obligation upon states to take reasonable and appropriate measures to enable lawful demonstrations to proceed, it did not mean that they were obliged to guarantee this absolutely. The Court found no violation, given the leeway available to states in deciding what was appropriate protection.

States must not only safeguard the right to peacefully assemble, they must also refrain from applying unreasonable indirect restrictions upon the right. In *Ezelin* v. *France*[346] a lawyer was reprimanded by the Bar Council for taking part in a public demonstration protesting against certain judicial decisions. The Court held that this violated Article 11[347].

Article 11 is not violated by a requirement that public demonstration obtain a prior licence or other permit. The Commission views such a requirement as the corollary of the duty upon the authorities to ensure that the assembly is not disrupted[348]; so that they have adequate notice in order to deploy police and to ensure rival demonstrations are scheduled so as not to clash. Any licensing system must not overstep this aim by restricting assemblies for other purposes.

Where the circumstances are such that it is not practicable for a demonstration to proceed peacefully[349] (or exceptionally, lawfully[350]) the state may be entitled to impose a blanket ban upon public assemblies. In such situations the Commission and Court are prepared to scrutinise the reasonableness of the measures. Relevant factors will be the duration of the ban, the extent of its geographical area of application and the categories of groups to which it applies.

Freedom of association

The Convention protects the right to freedom of association; the right to choose to associate and therefore the right to choose not to do

---

[344] *Plattform 'Ärzte für das Leben'* v. *Austria* 13 E.H.R.R. 204; June 21, 1988, Series A, No 139
[345] *Ibid.*
[346] 14 E.H.R.R. 362; April 26, 1991, Series A, No. 202
[347] *See* discussion of this case at p. 176 *ante*
[348] DR 17/93
[349] DR 21/138
[350] DR 36/187

so. All European states, however, legislate compulsory membership of certain institutions, most notably the requirement that certain professionals belong to a professional body. The Court has held that such membership is not a form of association within the meaning of Article 11. It considers that these institutions are a form of public control over the profession in question, exercised for the public benefit; in the case of medicine, by the maintenance of medical ethics for the protection of public health[351]; and likewise in the case of lawyers, vets[352] and engineers[353].

Trade Unions

CLOSED SHOP AGREEMENTS

Ian Young, Noël James and Ronald Webster were employed by British Rail when in 1975 it introduced a 'closed shop' agreement, by which all existing and future employees were required to join one of three named trade unions. The three men declined to join any of them and were dismissed; refusal to join a trade union where a closed shop operated then being a valid ground for dismissal. They complained that their rights under Article 11 amongst others had been violated[354]. Whilst the Court was of the view that Article 11 did convey a right not to be compelled to join an association or union, it did not adjudicate upon this point. It did, however, find that the B.R. agreement precluded the applicants from forming or joining another union; it post-dated their employment with the company; and the threat of dismissal was such a serious form of compulsion that—taken together—Article 11 had been violated. The Court considered and rejected the possibility of the facts being justified within Article 11(2).

UNION BARGAINING RIGHTS

Article 11 does not just safeguard the individual's right to form and to join trade unions; it safeguards the right to form and join trade unions *'for the protection of his interests'*. Unions must not, therefore, be wholly impotent; the state must ensure that the régime in which they

---

[351] *Le Compte* v. *Belgium* 4 E.H.R.R. 1; June 23, 1981, Series A, No. 44

[352] *Barthold* v. *Germany* 7 E.H.R.R. 383; March 23, 1985, Series A, No. 90

[353] There is clearly a grey area between compulsory membership of associations for the public benefit and private associations for the individual/collective members' benefit; see for instance DR 9/5 which concerned a students' union

[354] *Young, James and Webster* v. *U.K.* 4 E.H.R.R. 38; June 26, 1981, Series A, No. 44; but *c.f.* *Sibson* v. *U.K.* April 20, 1993, Series A, No. 258-A

operate is not so hostile as to deprive them of any effective ability to act to protect their members' interests. Whilst the Court has confirmed that this is a logical consequence of the Article 11 right, its decisions in this area have not been characterised by any great enthusiasm. It has therefore held that trade unions have a *'right to be heard'* by their members' employers, but that this does not mean that they are automatically entitled to be included in any formal consultation procedure adopted by the employer[355], or that this right entitles them to any exclusive right to conclude collective wage agreements for their members[356]. Likewise, whilst it has confirmed its view that the right to strike is one of the most important means available to a union to protect its members' interests, it has held that this right may be the subject of restrictions[357].

Restrictions upon Article 11

Article 11(2) lists permitted restrictions upon the substantive rights, in similar terms to those applying to the three preceding Articles. It additionally permits restrictions to be placed upon the freedom of assembly, association and membership of trade unions for *'members of the armed forces, the police and of the administration of the state'*.

The extent of this additional restriction was explored in the complaint lodged by the Civil Service Unions following the Government's decision in 1984 to prohibit trade union membership amongst its civilian workers at G.C.H.Q. Cheltenham[358]. The Commission held the complaint inadmissible despite there being little objective evidence that union membership at the establishment compromised national security or was otherwise harmful to the public good. The Commission considered that the only requirement for such restrictions to be valid was that they be 'lawful'; the state was not obliged to establish that the restrictions were 'necessary in a democratic society'. If 'lawful' included the principle of proportionality which the Commission doubted, it felt that this merely extended to the question of whether the restriction was arbitrary, and in the Commission's opinion, it was not.

---

[355] *National Union of Belgium Police* v. *Belgium* 1 E.H.R.R. 578; October 27, 1975, Series A, No. 19

[356] *Swedish Engine Drivers' Union* v. *Sweden* 1 E.H.R.R. 627; February 6, 1976, Series A, No. 20

[357] *Schmidt and Dahlström* v. *Sweden* 1 E.H.R.R. 637; February 6, 1976, Series A, No. 21

[358] DR 50/228; and *see also* DR 39/237

RIGHT TO MARRY: ARTICLE 12

Article 12

Men and women of marriageable age have the right to marry and to found a family, according to the national laws governing the exercise of this right.

Article 12 may be seen as one aspect of the Article 8 right to family life. Whereas Article 8(2) details a number of restrictions upon the exercise of the substantive Article 8 right, the right to marry is subject only to the person being of marriageable age and that the exercise of the right be 'subject to the national laws governing the exercise of this right'.

The rôle of national law is to govern the exercise of the right to marriage, but the limitations imposed by the state must not have the effect of impairing the very essence of the right[359].

In *Cossey* v. *U.K.*[360] a post-operative male-to-female transsexual complained that under the U.K. law she was unable to contract a valid marriage with a man. The Court observed that the applicant's inability to marry a woman did not stem from any legal impediment. In respect of her inability to marry a man, the U.K. law was held to be in conformity with the Article 12 right, which the Court adjudged to protect 'the traditional marriage between persons of opposite biological sex'.

The right to marry does not itself require a right to divorce. Thus where after a marital separation one of the parties forms a stable relationship with another person, there is no violation of Article 12 if the state's laws prohibit divorce, and thereby deny the new partners a right to marry[361].

Whilst the Commission has held that a family can be founded by adoption[362], Article 12 does not guarantee a married couple the right to found a family by adoption[363].

Prisoners

In *Hamer* v. *U.K.*[364] the Commission considered that the U.K.'s refusal to allow prisoners to marry violated Article 12 in cases where the term

---

[359] *Cossey* v. *U.K.* 13 E.H.R.R. 622; July 27, 1990, Series A, No. 184
[360] *Ibid.*
[361] *Johnston* v. *Ireland* 9 E.H.R.R. 203; Series A, No. 112; and *see also* F. v. *Switzerland* 10 E.H.R.R. 411; December 18, 1987, Series A, No. 128
[362] DR 24/176
[363] DR 12/32; and DR 7/75
[364] DR 24/5; and *see* DR 24/72

of imprisonment was such that the exercise of the right to marry would be delayed a considerable time (in the case of Alan Hamer, two years). The Commission considered that personal liberty was not a precondition to the exercise of the right and envisaged no particular difficulties in allowing the marriage of prisoners.

In respect of the right to found a family, the Commission has indicated its sympathy for prisoners being allowed conjugal visits by their partners. It has, however, ruled all such complaints inadmissible on the basis that the refusal by the prison authorities is justified for the prevention of disorder or crime[365]. Whilst such a view is tenable in relation to conjugal visits, it is less clear in relation to a refusal by the prison authorities to allow artificial insemination facilities to a prisoner and his wife; especially if a long term of imprisonment is being served. Whilst such complaints have also been declared inadmissible, there appears to have been a change of attitude to the problem by the U.K. authorities[366].

Deportation

The principles applied to the question of deportation and its effect upon the enjoyment of the Article 12 rights, are similar to those applied to Article 8. The applicant is required to advance credible evidence[367] that if expelled the other party could not follow[368] or that marriage would not be possible in another country[369].

---

[365] DR 2/105; in such cases raising issues under Article 8 as well as Article 12, if the interference is justified under Article 8(2), no violation can be found under Article 12, DR 13/241

[366] Application 17142/90, not yet reported in Decisions and Reports, where the prisoner's wife would have been 36 on his release; the prison department permitted arrangements to be made for artificial insemination after the complaint had been lodged

[367] DR 6/138

[368] DR 6/124

[369] See also Abdulaziz, Cabales and Balkandli v. U.K. 7 E.H.R.R. 471; May 28, 1985, Series A, No. 94 where the rights of non-resident men to join their wives/prospective wives was considered under Articles 8 and 14

RIGHT TO AN EFFECTIVE REMEDY: ARTICLE 13

Article 13

> *Everyone whose rights and freedoms as set forth in this Convention are violated shall have an effective remedy before a national authority notwithstanding that the violation has been committed by persons acting in an official capacity.*

Article 13 applies not only to the rights set out in Articles 2–12 of the Convention, but also to those in the First Protocol. As a complaint can only be lodged by a 'victim'[370] of an alleged violation of the Convention and Protocol, it follows that a complaint can only allege a violation of Article 13 ancillary to a violation of one of the substantive rights. The Court is not, however, precluded from finding a violation of Article 13 alone[371].

Where an individual considers that he or she has been a victim of a violation of one of the substantive rights (and the alleged violation is objectively 'arguable')[372] Article 13 requires an effective domestic remedy. To be effective, the remedy must involve the determination of the claim as well as providing for the possibility of redress[373]. What is required therefore, is a domestic process for adjudicating upon arguable claims. It follows that the lack of such a mechanism will result in a violation of Article 13 even if the 'arguable violation' is found, upon examination, not to be a violation.

Unfortunately the practical application of Article 13 has been undermined by the Court finding 'unarguable' many alleged violations declared admissible by the Commission; the Court being much sterner in assessing what is arguable than the Commission.

The limitations imposed upon Article 13 by the Court have therefore made it virtually redundant. *Abdulaziz, Cabales and Balkandali v. U.K.*[374] is a rare example of a violation of the Article being found. The case concerned the fact that it was easier for a man settled in the U.K., than for a woman, to obtain permission for his or her non-national spouse to enter and remain in the country. The Court found that this violated Article 8 in conjunction with Article 14. It also held that there was no

---

[370] Article 25(1)
[371] *Klass* v. *Germany* 2 E.H.R.R. 214; September 6, 1978, Series A, No. 28
[372] *Boyle and Rice* v. *U.K.* 10 E.H.R.R. 425; April 27, 1988, Series A, No.131
[373] *See* note 371 *above*
[374] 7 E.H.R.R. 471; May 28, 1985, Series A, No. 94

way that such sex discrimination could be argued in a domestic U.K. setting and therefore Article 13 had been violated.

Limitations upon Article 13

The Court has developed certain implied limitations to Article 13. It cannot, for instance require a domestic remedy for a violation stemming directly from legislation[375]. If this were otherwise it would be tantamount to requiring that the Convention be entrenched into domestic law and that domestic Courts have the power to set aside inconsistent legislation as is the case with EEC law[376].

A further example of an implied limitation on the scope of Article 13 relates to the field of state security and police surveillance. Where, for instance, an individual's privacy is being compromised by surveillance, a strict interpretation of Article 13 would require that he or she have a right to challenge the surveillance, and for a domestic court to adjudicate upon the point. For this to occur the individual would have to know of the alleged violation, which could make the surveillance ineffective. The Court has therefore required that in such cases the domestic remedy be as effective as it can be given the particular nature of the problem[377]. In the case of telephone interceptions this has been held to include the person being notified as soon as this can be done without jeopardising the surveillance[378]. In the case of secret police registers (less satisfactorily) this has been held to include the supervision of the process by an independent ombudsman[379].

Overlap with other Articles

Article 6(1) requires that in the determination of everyone's civil rights and obligations as well as any criminal charges, there be an effective remedy. The Court takes the view that the requirements of Article 13 are less strict than those imposed by Article 6(1) and therefore if a violation of Article 6(1) is found, that it is unnecessary to investigate Article 13[380]. In similar fashion the Court considers that if Article 5(4) is found to have been violated there is no purpose in then examining Article 13[381].

---

[375] *Young, James and Webster* v. *U.K.* 4 E.H.R.R. 38; June 26, 1981, Series A, No. 44

[376] *See for instance Factortame Ltd.* v. *Secretary of State for Transport (No. 2)* [1991] 1 All E.R. 70

[377] *Leander* v. *Sweden* 9 E.H.R.R. 433; March 26, 1987, Series A, No. 116

[378] *See* note 371 *above*

[379] *See* note 377 *above*

[380] *See for instance Granger* v. *U.K.* 12 E.H.R.R. 460 at p. 467, *c.f. W* v. *U.K.* 10 E.H.R.R. 29; July 8, 1987, Series A, No. 121

[381] *See for instance, Brogan* v. *U.K.* 11 E.H.R.R. 117; November 29, 1988, Series A, No. 145–B

Judicial review

As has been stated earlier (*see* p. 28) the effectiveness of judicial review as a remedy remains a controversial issue with the Court and Commission. In *Soering* v. *U.K.*[382] the Court considered judicial review an effective remedy for the purposes of Article 13, holding that a U.K. Court would have jurisdiction to quash a challenged decision that there was a serious risk of inhuman or degrading treatment (by being exposed to the death row phenomena), on the ground that the decision was one that no reasonable minister could take; a view that any practitioner regularly appearing in the Crown Office List might find hard to believe, given the excessive deference generally shown by the Divisional Court to the Executive. In the subsequent case of *Vilvarajah* v. *U.K.*[383] although a majority of the judges upheld this view, two judges expressed dissenting opinions[384]; highlighting the fact that judicial review does not allow a review of the merits of a decision, but only the decision-making process. An effective remedy requires more than the mere control of procedure; an effective remedy must enable an investigation of the merits of the impugned decision. The two judges distinguished the *Soering* judgment thus:

> the [*Soering*] judgment can only be understood in the light of the circumstances of that case because there was no essential question of fact in issue and if there had been judicial review it would not have involved any disputed question of fact or any of the merits of that case.

Whilst for the present therefore the Court considers judicial review an effective remedy for the purposes of Article 13, it does not of course follow that this is the case for the purposes of Article 6(1).

---

[382] 11 E.H.R.R. 439; July 7, 1989, Series A, No. 161
[383] 14 E.H.R.R. 248; October 30, 1991, Series A, No. 215
[384] Judge Walsh and Judge Russo

FREEDOM FROM DISCRIMINATION: ARTICLE 14

Article 14

The enjoyment of the rights and freedoms set forth in this Convention shall be secured without discrimination on any ground such as race, colour, language, religion, political or other opinion, national or social origin, association with a national minority, property, birth or other status.

A major omission from the Convention is a substantive Article protecting the rights of minorities. Article 14, like Article 13, can only be invoked in relation to one of the substantive rights set out in Articles 2–12 of the Convention and in the First Protocol. Article 14 requires that in the delivery of the substantive rights there be no discrimination. Unlike Article 13, it does not require an arguable violation of a substantive right before it applies; merely the existence of real and unjustified discrimination between the way certain individuals are permitted to enjoy that right.

The list of grounds of possible discrimination given in Article 14 is illustrative and not in any way exhaustive.

In 1967 the Court gave judgment in the 'Belgian Linguistic' case[385], a case which concerned the rights of French-speaking Belgians living, in general, in primarily Dutch-speaking municipalities, to have their children instructed in French. In its judgment the Court laid down basic principles for approaching the question of Article 14, stating:

> the principle of equality of treatment is violated if the distinction has no objective and reasonable justification. The existence of such a justification must be assessed in relation to the aim and effects of the measure under consideration, regard being had to the principles which normally prevail in democratic societies. A difference of treatment in the exercise of a right laid down in the Convention must not only pursue a legitimate aim: Article 14 is likewise violated when it is clearly established that there is no reasonable relationship of proportionality between the means employed and the aim sought to be realised.

A checklist of principles can be extracted from the judgment, applicable to most Article 14 situations.

---

[385] 1 E.H.R.R. 241; February 9, 1967, Series A, No. 5; the case is referred to by its general title as it originated from several hundred complaints by parents and children

Checklist for Article 14

1. IS THERE DIFFERENT TREATMENT?

Is like being compared to like? Are the situations really comparable? Discrimination in this context means treating people differently in similar situations[386].

In *Van der Mussele* v. *Belgium*[387] the applicant barrister complained that his profession was required to provide free legal work contrary to Article 4 whilst the mandatory provision of unpaid work was not applied to other professions such as doctors, vets and dentists; that accordingly there was discrimination against barristers as opposed to other professions in respect of Article 4. Although the Court found no violation of Article 4 alone, it confirmed that this did not preclude a violation of Article 4 in conjunction with Article 14. Upon analysis the Court considered that there were fundamental differences between the way in which the various professions operated and accordingly 'like' was not being compared with 'like'.

2. DOES THE DIFFERENT TREATMENT AFFECT THE ENJOYMENT OF A CONVENTION RIGHT?

Whilst Article 14 can be violated without the Court finding a violation of a substantive Convention right, it is necessary to establish that the discriminatory treatment does not fall completely outside the ambit of one of the Convention rights. Thus the complaint of an Irish loyalist prisoner that he had been the victim of discriminatory treat-ment—because he was not segregated from republican prisoners whereas in another prison such segregation existed—was rejected by the Commission, holding that the Convention contained no right to be detained under segregated conditions[388].

3. DOES THE DIFFERENCE IN TREATMENT PURSUE A LEGITIMATE AIM?

What is the reason for the different treatment? What is its aim? Is it objectively and reasonably justified? In *Wiggins* v. *U.K.*[389] the applicant complained that, because of the Housing Control (Guernsey) Law 1969, he was not allowed to live in his house in Guernsey. The Commission considered that the legislation pursued the legitimate aim

---

[386] *See for instance Fredin* v. *Sweden* 13 E.H.R.R. 784; February 18, 1991, Series A, No. 192
[387] 6 E.H.R.R. 163; November 23, 1983, Series A, No. 70
[388] DR 46/182
[389] DR 13/40

of preventing the over-population of the island which would be harmful to its economy. Such an aim was objectively and reasonably justifiable.

In *Abdulaziz, Cabales and Balkandali* v. *U.K.*[390] the Court did not accept the state's argument that there were justifiable reasons for imposing more severe restrictions upon non-native husbands joining their wives in the U.K. than vice versa.

In *Darby* v. *Sweden*[391] the applicant worked in Sweden for many years without formally registering his residence. He was required to pay a church tax for a church to which he did not belong whereas persons in a similar situation who had registered their residence were exempt from the tax. The Court found no legitimate aim for this unequal treatment and accordingly found Article 14 violated in conjunction with Article 1 of the First Protocol.

In certain situations the unequal treatment of different persons is in fact merely treatment designed to counteract an existing inequality. Thus groups which occupy a privileged position may be required to compensate for this by accepting additional burdens or restrictions upon their rights[392].

4. ARE THE MEANS EMPLOYED TO ACHIEVE THE AIM PROPORTIONATE?

Whilst a difference in treatment may be justified in many situations, this cannot justify any unfair discrimination. There must be a sensible relationship between the two. In *Wiggins* v. *U.K.*[393] the legislation stipulated that only low value properties be reserved for the occupation of (primarily) native islanders. This was found to be a proportionate restriction given the objective of restricting over-population of the island[394].

5. DOES THE DEGREE OF UNEQUAL TREATMENT IN ANY EVENT EXCEED THE LEEWAY GIVEN TO STATES IN APPLYING THE CONVENTION?

The application of Article 14 is not a precise art, and the state is therefore accorded a certain leeway or 'benefit of the doubt' in deciding whether a violation exists. The degree of latitude allowed depends

---

[390] 7 E.H.R.R. 471; May 28, 1985, Series A, No. 94
[391] 13 E.H.R.R. 774; October 23, 1990, Series A, No. 187; and *see also Pine Valley Developments* v. *Ireland* 14 E.H.R.R. 319; November 29, 1991, Series A, No. 222
[392] DR 18/216 where the Commission found that because of the monopoly enjoyed by notaries, it was not discriminatory to impose upon them obligations which were not required of other professions
[393] *See* note 389 *above*
[394] But *see Gillow* v. *U.K.* 11 E.H.R.R. 335; November 24, 1986, Series A, No. 109 where on slightly different facts a violation was found by virtue of the inflexible and harsh way the provisions were interpreted in that case

upon the nature of the matter in issue; in such matters as taxation, the margin given to a state will usually be wide[395], whereas the latitude on questions involving family life[396] or in cases of clear racial bias[397] will inevitably be restricted.

Dyer v. *U.K.*[398] provides an example of the application of the above principles. Graham Dyer was a soldier who was very seriously injured in a road accident whilst on a training exercise. He was unable to obtain compensation from the vehicle driver in tort, as the M.O.D. invoked Crown immunity. In his application to the Commission he claimed that he was a victim of a violation of Article 14. He pointed out that members of the police and fire services ran the risk of injury or death in the performance of their profession, but that they were not precluded from bringing such proceedings.

The Commission agreed that there was a difference of treatment, and that this related to a substantive Convention right (Article 6(1): the determination of a civil claim). It considered, however, that it was legitimate to single out servicemen because of the high risks of injury and death in the profession, and that these risks were higher than those of other professional groups. In lieu of their right to sue for compensation, servicemen had an automatic right to a no-fault disablement pension. The Commission considered that in view of this there was a *'reasonable relationship of proportionality between the means chosen, that is, the pension scheme replacing the civil action for tort, and the aim of making special provision for injured servicemen'*. The Commission looked at certain aspects of the pension scheme which it considered could be thought harsh, including the fact that the total amount of the pension award might be considerably less than the amount of damages that could be awarded by a court. It however concluded that *'the national authorities must enjoy a wide discretion in deciding on the limits of the scheme'* and accordingly found no violation of Article 14.

---

[395] DR 58/163; DR 60/194
[396] *See for instance Marckx* v. *Belgium* 2 E.H.R.R. 330; June 13, 1979, Series A, No. 31; and DR 36/130
[397] *East African Asians* v. *U.K.* 3 E.H.R.R. 40
[398] DR 39/246

ARTICLES 15–18

Article 15

POWER TO DEROGATE

(For full text *see* p. 233)

Article 15 permits a state to suspend the application of certain parts of the Convention and Protocol in times of war or other public emergency threatening the life of the nation, but only *'to the extent strictly required by the exigencies of the situation'*.

No derogation at all is permitted from Article 2 (except in respect of deaths resulting from lawful acts of war) or from Articles 3, 4(1) and 7.

States do not have a free hand in deciding whether or not to derogate from their obligations under the Convention, and the Court has confirmed that, together with the Commission, it is empowered to investigate the validity of derogations. It is however, an area where politics come strongly into the Court's assessment; historically (if less so today) the Court has been particularly aware that a rejection of a state's purported use of Article 15 might result in the state withdrawing from the Convention.

It is beyond the scope of this text to examine in detail the issues raised by Article 15[399]. The U.K. Government has, however, invoked Article 15, most recently in relation to the troubles in Northern Ireland. After being found to have violated the Convention in respect of the detention of terrorist suspects under the Prevention of Terrorism (Temporary Provisions) Act 1984[400], the U.K. Government announced on 23 December 1988 that it would be derogating from the requirements of the Court decision in view of the public emergency in Northern Ireland threatening the life of the nation[401].

---

[399] For a detailed and critical examination of Article 15, see van Dijk and van Hoof 2nd p. 548 *et seq*. *See also Lawless* v. *Ireland (No. 3)* 1 E.H.R.R. 15; July 1, 1961, Series A, No. 3 and *Ireland* v. *U.K.* 2 E.H.R.R. 25; January 18, 1978, Series A, No. 25

[400] *Brogan* v. *U.K.* 11 E.H.R.R. 117; November 29, 1988, Series A, No. 145

[401] The validity of the derogation was challenged unsuccessfully in *Brannigan and McBride* v. *U.K.*, *The Times*, May 28, 1993

197

Article 16

RESTRICTIONS ON THE POLITICAL ACTIVITY OF ALIENS

(For full text *see* p. 233)

Article 16 allows a state to place virtually unlimited restrictions, in respect of Articles 10, 11 and 14, upon the political activity of aliens. In practice this provision does not appear to have been invoked; possibly because where such an issue might arise, deportation or the threat of it is considered a more efficacious remedy[402].

Article 17

ACTIVITIES AIMED AT THE DESTRUCTION OF CONVENTION RIGHTS AND FREEDOMS ARE NOT PROTECTED BY THE CONVENTION

(For full text *see* p. 233)

The exercise of many of the rights and freedoms protected by the Convention inevitably interfere with the rights and freedoms of others. This is, however, unavoidable in a pluralistic democratic society.

The Convention Articles which contain the most potential for affecting the enjoyment of others—freedom of speech and assembly, right to family life and to the enjoyment of possessions—are in each case subject to permissible restrictions. It is perhaps for this reason that Article 17 is so seldom invoked.

The purpose of Article 17 is to deny the right of (primarily) extremists to exercise a particular freedom, the exercise of which is aimed at destroying the rights of others. Thus, Article 17 was invoked against a journalist who complained to the Commission that he had been prosecuted for publishing an anti-semitic pro-National Socialist Party pamphlet[403]. Article 17 does not however give states a right to ignore the rights and freedoms of extremists; it cannot, for instance, be used as a ground for denying members of the IRA a right to liberty under Article 5 or a right to a fair hearing under Article 6[404].

Article 17 is expressed as applying not only to persons and groups, but also to 'any state'. In extreme cases it could apply to a partisan government which chose to make certain civic values sacrosanct, whilst at the same time legislating against alternative values; in a European

---

[402] *See for instance Agee* v. *U.K.* DR 7/164
[403] DR 56/205
[404] *Lawless* v. *Ireland (No. 3),* note 399 *above*

setting one might (provocatively) put into this context the plight of the nomadic gypsy as against the settled population.

Article 18

RESTRICTIONS PERMITTED BY THE CONVENTION UPON THE RIGHTS AND FREEDOMS CAN NOT BE APPLIED FOR ANY OTHER PURPOSE

(For full text *see* p. 233)

Article 18 is aimed primarily at the ulterior motive; it would, for instance, prohibit prison authorities isolating a prisoner on the purported ground of the prevention of disorder and crime, when the isolation is in fact designed to break his will[405].

---

[405] DR 20/44 where this ulterior motive was alleged but not substantiated

Protocol 1

Enjoyment of Possessions: Article 1, Protocol 1

Article 1

> *Every natural or legal person is entitled to the peaceful enjoy-*
> *ment of his possessions. No one shall be deprived of his*
> *possessions except in the public interest and subject to the*
> *conditions provided for by law and by the general principles of*
> *international law.*
>
> > *The preceding provision shall not, however, in any way*
> > *impair the right of a state to enforce such laws as it deems*
> > *necessary to control the use of property in accordance with the*
> > *general interest or to secure the payment of taxes or other*
> > *contributions or penalties.*

Article 1 of the First Protocol is frequently invoked, but violations are seldom found; given that the permissible restrictions are so widely drawn this is perhaps not surprising. In such cases it is not uncommon for a violation to be found of an ancillary Article, most frequently Article 6(1); the Court then finds the interference justified, but not the way in which it was carried out.

Article 1 comprises three principles:

1. The principle of the peaceful enjoyment of property.
2. The principle that deprivation of property can only occur subject to specific conditions (as set out in the second sentence of the first paragraph).
3. The principle of interference; that states are entitled to control of the use of property in accordance with the general interest (as set out in the second paragraph).

The three principles are connected: the second and third rules are concerned with particular instances of interference with the right to peaceful enjoyment of property and are therefore to be construed in the light of the general right enunciated in the first principle[406].

Whilst the first paragraph delimits the situations in which deprivation of possessions is permitted, the second paragraph almost amounts to a presumption that some form of control over the enjoyment of possessions is inevitable. The Court and Commission are therefore

---

[406] DR 60/128

alive to attempts to suggest that an 'interference' is in fact a 'deprivation'. This usually occurs where a complaint attempts to hive off one aspect of the whole and seek to have it viewed in isolation. Thus the loss of a licence to sell alcohol was held not to be a deprivation of a licence, but an interference in the enjoyment of the wider business of running a restaurant to which it applied[407]. In a similar fashion, the Court held that a substantial reduction in rents resulting from the imposition of rent control was not a 'deprivation', even though it deprived the landlords of part of their income from their properties; it was in fact an 'interference' in the enjoyment of the wider asset, the land[408]. By the same principle, the loss of the right to live in one's own house is an interference with the enjoyment of the property rather than a deprivation of the right to occupy[409].

POSSESSIONS

The Court and Commission have taken a reasonably pragmatic view on the subject of what constitutes a possession. Beyond the more obvious items such as chattels and land, there is, in general, a necessity that the item have an economic value[410]. Goodwill[411], fishing rights[412] and the ownership of a debt[413] have all been held to be possessions within the meaning of Article 1.

Whether a licence amounts to a possession depends upon the licence-holder having a *'reasonable and legitimate expectation as to the lasting nature of the licence and as to the possibility to continue to draw benefits from the exercise of the licensed activity'*[414]. A driving licence has been held not to be a possession under Article 1[415].

The right to an inheritance is not a possession[416] until it is acquired, regardless of whether distribution has occurred[417]. Trust monies are owned by the beneficiaries, not the trustee, and accordingly a trustee cannot complain in his or her own right of an interference in the enjoyment of trust property[418].

The obligation to pay contributions to a social security scheme may, in certain circumstances, give an individual a property right over a

---

[407] *Tre Traktörer Aktiebolag* v. *Sweden* 13 E.H.R.R. 309; July 7, 1989, Series A, No. 159
[408] *Mellacher* v. *Austria* 12 E.H.R.R. 391; December 19, 1989, Series A, No. 169
[409] *Wiggins* v. *U.K.* DR 13/40
[410] DR 29/64
[411] *See Van Marle* v. *Netherlands* 8 E.H.R.R. 483; June 26, 1986, Series A, No. 101; *Tre Traktörer 407 above;* and DR 55/157
[412] DR 60/128
[413] DR 58/63, provided that the debt has crystallised—as opposed to a liability action which has not concluded in a final judgment
[414] DR 40/234; and *see Tre Traktörer 407 above*
[415] DR 26/255
[416] *Marckx* v. *Belgium* 2 E.H.R.R. 330; June 13, 1979, Series A, No. 31
[417] *Inze* v. *Austria* 10 E.H.R.R. 394; October 28, 1987, Series A, No. 126
[418] DR 19/233

portion of the assets thus constituted[419]. To amount to a 'possession' however, there needs to be at any given time an identifiable share in a fund claimable by the applicant as belonging to him or her[420]. Obviously this situation will most commonly arise in relation to private pension schemes, although it will also exist where, as part of the employment contract, an employer makes specific pension contributions for the employee[421].

DEPRIVATION

As detailed *above*, not all deprivations of property constitute a 'deprivation' for the purposes of Article 1. The Commission has, for example, held that the adjudication bankruptcy is an interference rather than a deprivation, in that it amounts to a form of control in the general public interest[422].

In *James* v. *U.K.* [423] the Trustees of the Duke of Westminster's estate complained that the leasehold enfranchisement provisions of the Leasehold Reform Act 1967 constituted an unjustified deprivation contrary to Article 1. Whilst no violation was found by the Court, it laid down certain principles for the consideration of such questions, including:

1. The deprivation must be justified as being in the public interest, which requires
   (a) it must be for a legitimate purpose;
   (b) the achievement of that purpose must strike a fair balance between the demands of the general interest of the community and the requirements of the protection of the individual's fundamental rights and does not impose an excessive burden on the latter;
   (c) although there is a leeway available to the state in these matters, the measures imposed must not be arbitrary, or 'manifestly without reasonable foundation'.
2. Whilst Article 1 does not explicitly guarantee a right to compensation, the taking of property in the public interest without payment of compensation reasonably related to its value could only be justified in exceptional circumstances.

The deprivation of property most frequently considered by the Court and Commission concerns the question of the compulsory purchase of land, although a number of complaints have arisen out of the state nationalisation of industries, including the computation of appropriate compensation[424] and the forfeiture of possessions in the criminal process[425]. In considering the justification for compulsory purchases

---

[419] DR 1/46
[420] DR 34/153
[421] DR 57/131
[422] DR 24/198
[423] 8 E.H.R.R. 123; February 21, 1986, Series, A, No. 98
[424] *Lithgow* v. *U.K.* 8 E.H.R.R. 329; July 8, 1986, Series A, No. 102
[425] *See for instance* forfeiture of smuggled goods, *AGOSI* v. *U.K.* 9 E.H.R.R. 1; October 24, 1986, Series A, No. 108; obscene publications DR 32/231; and bail DR 42/195

and the reasonableness of subsequent compensation, the Commission has made it clear that the state retains a wide leeway in determining these matters[426]. In considering a complaint concerning the justification for the compulsory purchase of land for a new road, for instance, the Commission stated *'because of their direct knowledge of their society and needs, the national authorities are in principle better placed to appreciate what is in the "public interest". In their assessment in this respect, the national authorities enjoy a margin of appreciation'*[427]. In relation to compensation the Commission has stated that it is not prepared to interfere unless it falls outside the state's *'wide margin of appreciation; [the Commission] will respect the legislature's judgment in this connection unless that judgment was manifestly without reasonable foundation'*[428].

The reference in the first paragraph of Article 1 to 'the general principles of international law' refers primarily to the principle that where a state appropriates property belonging to a national of another state, this creates a general right to compensation. This provision is of little relevance, given the Court's view that a general right in such cases exists in all but the most exceptional circumstances.

INTERFERENCE

Not every interference with the enjoyment of possessions amounts to an 'interference' for the purposes of Article 1. Interferences which stem from private law rules for instance are deemed to be part of the envelope of attributes that go with the particular possession. In this context can be included the suspension of a person's pension permitted in the employment contract[429], an attachment or other charging order in civil proceedings[430] and the division of possessions as a result of a matrimonial dispute[431].

The relevant principles to be applied when judging the reasonableness of an interference contrary to Article 1 have been listed as:

1. Although the margin of appreciation available to the national legislature under Article 1 is a wide one, the measure imposed must have a legitimate aim, in the sense of not being 'manifestly without foundation'.
2. Where the measure has a legitimate aim, there must be a reasonable relationship of proportionality between the means employed and the aim sought to be realised.
3. A fair balance must be struck between the demands of the general interest of the community and the requirements of the protection of the individual's fundamental

---

[426] *See for instance* DR 60/44; DR 56/254; and DR 56/268
[427] DR 59/281
[428] *Lithgow* v. *U.K.*, note 424 *above*
[429] DR 56/20
[430] DR 8/161
[431] DR 53/234, 'the transfer of title . . . in case of a dissolution of marriage . . . effected by . . . a court . . . continues to be the result of obligations stemming from general private law rules governing the conclusion and dissolution of marriages and their legal consequences'

rights, and this balance will not be struck if the measure results in a person or a section of the public having an individual and excessive burden[432].

An interference may be indirect, such as results from planning blight by virtue of the land being designated for a future development[433]. In *Sporrong and Lönnroth* v. *Sweden*[434] the applicants owned property in Stockholm upon which an expropriation permit was granted which designated the land for the construction of a viaduct and a car parking area; the permit prohibited construction (including renovation). Although the applicants were able to continue to let and otherwise use their properties, the Court held that their enjoyment of them was interfered with because they were left for an unreasonably long period in complete uncertainty as to the fate of their properties, and the permits were so inflexible that they did not enable any of the applicants' difficulties during this period to be taken into account by the Government. It held therefore that the applicants had unnecessarily borne an individual and excessive burden.

The 'general interest' includes the refusal of planning permission for a development[435] or a change of use[436] contrary to the development plan; and has been held to include the protection of the environment[437].

TAXATION

The leeway available to states in relation to taxation is extremely wide, although not immune to review by the Court and Commission[438]. Whilst a tax may in itself be justified under Article 1, it may, by virtue of its discriminatory effect, amount to a violation in conjunction with Article 14[439].

---

[432] DR 58/163
[433] *See for instance* DR 55/205
[434] 5 E.H.R.R. 35; September 23, 1982, Series A, No. 52
[435] DR 56/215
[436] DR 52/250
[437] DR 59/127
[438] DR 23/203; and *see* DR 58/163
[439] *Darby* v. *Sweden* 13 E.H.R.R. 774; October 23, 1990, Series A, No. 187

Right of Education: Article 2, Protocol 1

Article 2

> *No person shall be denied the right to education. In the exercise of any functions which it assumes in relation to education and to teaching, the State shall respect the right of parents to ensure such education and teaching in conformity with their own religious and philosophical convictions.*

U.K. RESERVATION

(by virtue of Article 64 of the Convention)

> *At the time of signing the present Protocol, I declare that, in view of certain provisions of the Education Acts in force in the United Kingdom, the principle affirmed in the second sentence of Article 2 is accepted by the United Kingdom only so far as it is compatible with the provision of efficient instruction and training and the avoidance of unreasonable expenditure.*
> *Anthony Eden, March 20, 1952.*

Article 2 enshrines the right to education. It does not however oblige the state to provide this education. Article 2 is concerned with restricting state interference in education and the consequent requirement that the state respect the right of parents to ensure that their children are educated in conformity with their religious and philosophical convictions.

Article 2 does not require the state to establish any specific educational system. It guarantees however that persons subject to the jurisdiction of the state should have the right to avail themselves of the educational institutions existing at a given time[440]. Article 2 is primarily (but not exclusively) concerned with the right of access to elementary education[441] rather than to the arena of advanced or technical education.

Article 2 does not require the state to organise at its own expense or to subsidise education of any specific form or level. It cannot for instance be used as a means for insisting that a child be given a grammar school place, rather than one at a comprehensive[442], or that

---

[440] Belgian Linguistic Case (No. 1) 1 E.H.R.R. 241; February 9, 1967, Series A, No. 5; and *see* DR 51/125
[441] DR 2/50; and DR 9/185
[442] DR 37/96

207

Government subsidy of education be extended to Steiner schools[443]. In the Belgium Linguistics case[444] the Court found that the refusal of the Belgian state to establish or subsidise, in the Dutch unilingual region, primary education in which French was employed as the language of instruction, did not of itself violate Article 2.

REGULATION OF EDUCATION BY THE STATE

Whilst the state must not by any action in the educational system prevent parents from exercising their right to ensure that their children are taught in conformity with their religious and philosophical convictions, this does not restrict the right of a state to make compulsory the elementary education of children[445].

The Court has held that the right to education presupposes some regulation by the state, *regulation which may vary in time and space according to the needs and resources of the community and of individuals*[446]. Whilst Article 2 guarantees the right to start and run a private school, this does not mean that this is a right without conditions; most obviously, conditions as to the minimum quality of the education provided[447]. The same of course applies to 'education otherwise' than at school[448]. Whilst there is therefore a wide discretion in making regulations for public education, the state is required to abstain from any indoctrination which could offend the parents' religious or philosophical convictions[449].

RELIGIOUS AND PHILOSOPHICAL CONVICTIONS

Article 2 does not guarantee an absolute right to have children educated in accordance with their parents' religious and philosophical convictions—but a right to respect for those convictions[450].

Campbell and Cosans v. U.K.[451] concerned complaints that the corporal punishment was still practised in the state schools attended by the sons of Mrs Campbell and Mrs Cosans. The Court held that:

> the word 'convictions' taken on its own, is not synonymous with the words 'opinions' and 'ideas' such as are used in Article 10 . . . and denotes views that attain a certain level of cogency, seriousness and importance[452].

---

[443] DR 45/143; and DR 31/210
[444] *See* 440 *above*
[445] DR 37/105
[446] *See* 440 *above*
[447] DR 51/125
[448] Section 36 of the Education Act 1944, which requires that it be efficient full-time education suitable to his age and ability and aptitude and to any special educational needs he may have either by regular attendance at school or otherwise
[449] *Kjeldsen, Busk Madsen and Pedersen* v. *Denmark* 1 E.H.R.R. 711; December 7, 1976, Series A, No. 23
[450] DR 37/105
[451] *Campbell and Cosans* v. *U.K.* 4 E.H.R.R. 293; February 25, 1982, Series A, No. 48
[452] *See also* in this respect DR 31/50

the expression 'philosophical convictions' in the present context denotes . . . such convictions as are worthy of respect in a democratic society . . . and are not incompatible with human dignity; in addition they must not conflict with the fundamental right of the child to education.

The Court held that the parents' objection to corporal punishment amounted to a philosophical conviction within the meaning of Article 2, and that this had therefore been violated.

The Court however felt that it had to look further into the application. Not only had there been a lack of respect for the parents' philosophical convictions (contrary to the second sentence of the Article), but Jeffrey Cosans had been suspended from school for almost a whole school year because his mother refused to accept that he be liable to such punishment. He had accordingly been denied the right to education, contrary to the first sentence of the Article and the Court held that this constituted a separate violation.

A failure of the U.K. to give assurances to parents that their children would not be the possible subjects of corporal punishment in state schools (in contravention of the parents' firmly held philosophical convictions) led to a number of further complaints being declared admissible on this point, to subsequent friendly settlements[453] and eventually to a change in the law[454].

Kjeldsen v. *Denmark* [455] concerned complaints made by parents against the imposition in Denmark of compulsory, integrated sex education. Whilst the Court found that the particular system operating in Denmark did not violate Article 2, it commented upon the practical limitations upon the state's obligation to ensure respect for the parents' philosophical convictions, stating:

the second sentence of Article 2 does not prevent states from imparting through teaching or education information or knowledge of a directly or indirectly religious or philosophical kind. It does not even permit parents to object to the integration of such teaching or education in the school curriculum, for otherwise all institutionalised teaching would run the risk of proving impracticable. In fact, it seems very difficult for many subjects taught at school not to have, to a greater or lesser extent, some philosophical complexion or implications. The same is true of religious affinities if one remembers the existence of religions forming a very broad dogmatic and moral entity which has or may have answers to every question of a philosophical, cosmological or moral nature.

The second sentence of Article 2 implies on the other hand that the state, in fulfilling the functions assumed by it in regard to education and teaching, must take care that information or knowledge included in the curriculum is conveyed in an objective, critical and pluralistic manner. The state is forbidden to pursue an aim of indoctrination that might be considered as not respecting parents' religious and philosophical convictions. That is the limit that must not be exceeded.

---

[453] *See for instance* DR 50/36; DR 52/13; DR 52/21; DR 56/181; and DR 60/5
[454] Sections 47 and 48 of the Education (No. 2) Act 1986
[455] *See* 449 *above*

U.K. RESERVATION

As seen *above*, the U.K. upon signing the First Protocol entered a reservation concerning the extent to which it was able to comply with the second sentence of Article 2. In the *Campbell and Cosans* complaint, the U.K. sought to argue that the failure to respect the parents' wishes was a matter covered by the reservation. The Court rejected this assertion, pointing out that under Article 64 of the Convention a reservation in respect of any provision is permitted only to the extent that any law in force in the state's territory at the time when the reservation is made is not in conformity with the provision (the legislation in issue was enacted in 1962); in any event the Court stated that it did not consider that other means of respecting the applicants' convictions could not have been devised, which would not have involved unreasonable public expenditure.

Duty to hold free elections: Article 3, Protocol 1

Article 3

The High Contracting parties undertake to hold free elections at reasonable intervals by secret ballot, under conditions which will ensure the free expression of the opinion of the people in the choice of the legislature.

When in 1987 the Court gave judgment in the first (and to date, only) complaint it had considered under Article 3, it commented with approval upon how the Commission's attitude to the Article had changed over time:

> from the idea of an 'institutional' right to the holding of free elections, the Commission has moved to the concept of 'universal sufffrage' and then, as a consequence, to the concept of subjective rights of participation—the 'right to vote' and the 'right to stand for election to the legislature'[456].

The case, *Mathieu-Mohin and Clerfayt* v. *Belgium*[457] concerned the complex rules that existed in Belgium to balance the interests of the French and Dutch speaking communities. The complainants were French speaking Belgians who could only stand for election in the particular municipality if they were prepared to take their oath in Dutch and then sit on the Flemish Council. In giving judgment the Court used the opportunity to make certain general comments upon the application of the Article, including:

> The rights in question are not absolute . . . In their internal legal orders the Contracting States may make the right to vote and to stand for election subject to conditions . . . they have a wide margin of appreciation in this sphere, but it is for the Court to determine in the last resort whether the requirements of Protocol 1 have been complied with; it has to satisfy itself that the conditions do not curtail the rights in question to such an extent as to impair their very essence and deprive them of their effectiveness; that they are imposed in pursuit of a legitimate aim; and that the means employed are not disproportionate. In particular, such conditions must not thwart 'the free expression of the opinion of the people in the choice of the legislature'.

> Article 3 applies only to the election of the 'legislature', or at least one of its chambers if it has two or more.

> Electoral systems seek to fulfil objectives which are sometimes scarcely compatible with each other: on the one hand, to reflect fairly faithfully the opinions of the

[456] *Mathieu-Mohin and Clerfayt and* v. *Belgium* 10 E.H.R.R. 1; March 2, 1987, Series A, No. 113
[457] *Ibid*

211

people, and on the other, to channel currents of thought so as to promote the emergence of a sufficiently clear and coherent political will. In these circumstances the phrase 'conditions which will ensure the free expression of the opinion of the people in the choice of the legislature' implies essentially—apart from freedom of expression—the principle of equality of treatment of all citizens in the exercise of their right to vote and their right to stand for election.

It does not follow, however, that all votes must necessarily have equal weight as regards the outcome of the elections or that all candidates must have equal chances of victory. Thus no electoral system can eliminate 'wasted votes'.

LEGISLATURE

The Commission has held that the European Parliament (even after the Single European Act) is not a legislative body for the purposes of Article 3, but that this is something that may change as it obtains greater powers[458]. It has also ruled that the phrase does not include the former Metropolitan County Councils[459] but that it does encompass the Regional Councils at the heart of the complaint in *Mathieu-Mohin and Clerfayt* v. *Belgium*.

CONDITIONS

The Commission has approved of the following conditions imposed upon the right to vote and/or the right to stand for election: conditions of residence and the restriction of overseas nationals' voting rights[460]; restrictions upon convicted persons voting (even in cases involving relatively minor misdemeanours)[461]; electoral deposits returnable only if a certain share of the vote is obtained[462]; the requirement that a minimum number of nomination signatures be obtained before a person can qualify to stand in an election[463]. The Commission has also held that the payment of political party subsidies (paid according to the votes obtained by parties) does not violate Article 3[464].

[458] DR 55/130
[459] DR 43/236
[460] DR 24/192; and DR 15/259
[461] DR 18/250; and DR 33/242
[462] DR 55/130
[463] DR 6/120
[464] DR 5/90

9 Other Human Rights Procedures Available in the U.K.

SOCIAL CHARTER

The European Social Charter is an international treaty drafted by the Council of Europe, first signed in 1961, which came into force in 1965[1]. The U.K. is a full signatory to the Social Charter. Its aim is the protection of key social rights in much the same way that the Convention protects civil and political rights. The principal Articles of the Charter are:

1. Right to work.
2. Right to just conditions of work (*i.e.* pay, hours, holiday).
3. Right to safe and healthy working conditions.
4. Right to fair remuneration.
5. Right of workers to form unions, etc.
6. Right to collective bargaining.
7. Protection of children and young persons at work.
8. Protection of women at work.
9. Right to vocational guidance.
10. Right to vocational training.
11. Right to protection of health (generally).
12. Right to social security.
13. Right to social and medical assistance.
14. Right to benefit from social welfare services.
15. Right of physically or mentally disabled persons to vocational training and rehabilitation.
16. Right of family to social, legal and economic protection.
17. Right of mothers and children to social and economic protection.
18. Right of workers to work in other Social Charter States.
19. Right of workers working in other Social Charter States to equivalent protection.

States upon signing the Social Charter do not have to accept all of its provisions, and the U.K. has not accepted the following:

[1] For the full text of the Social Charter, *see* Brownlie p. 363

ARTICLES

2(1). Reasonable working hours and their progressive reduction.

4(3). Equal pay for men and women for work of equal value.

7(1). Minimum age for child employment to be 15 years.

7(4). Limiting the working hours for persons under 16 years.

7(7). Persons under 18 years to have minimum of three weeks' holiday, per annum.

7(8). Restricting night working for persons under 18 years.

8(2). Prohibiting dismissal of women during maternity leave.

8(3). Provision of sufficient leave to nursing mothers.

8(4). Restriction or prohibition of certain work for women (night work, mining work, etc).

12(2). Maintenance of social security system to a minimum level.

12(3). Aim of progressive improvement of social security system.

12(4). Harmonisation of, and reciprocal arrangements for, social security arrangements for nationals in other Social Charter States.

The Social Charter contains an Appendix which provides interpretation for certain of the rights, and an additional protocol has been drafted and was opened for signature in 1988.

The Charter lacks an effective enforcement mechanism, and as a result its impact has been limited. There is however evidence that legislation is now drafted so as to accord with its principles. Amendments to legislation protecting young people at work; s.89 of the Shipping Act 1970; Scottish law on the status of children born outside marriage; and the union closed shop are claimed to have resulted from the Charter[2].

Enforcement of the rights protected by the Charter is by way of a reporting system. There is no individual right of petition and no possibility of binding judgments. Article 21 stipulates that every two years each state must send to the Secretary-General of the Council of Europe a report concerning the application of the provisions in the Charter which it has accepted[3].

The format of the report is prescribed by the Committee of Ministers. In addition to sending the report to the Secretary-General, the state is required to send a copy to major trade union and employers' organisations, whose comments are invited and sent direct to Strasbourg. It is at this stage that an individual can have the greatest input into the process. By liaising with an appropriate trade union or employers'

---

[2] European Social Charter: origin, operation and results. Council of Europe 1991

[3] Article 22 requires states to submit 'at appropriate intervals' reports upon the provisions which they have not accepted. The intervals are determined by the Committee of Ministers and have tended to be 10 yearly

organisation, detailed comments and factual information can be incorporated into their submissions.

The state's report and the union or employers' organisations' comments are then passed by the Secretary-General to the 'Committee of Experts'. The Committee consists of not more than seven independent experts of the highest integrity and of recognised competence in international social questions[4], together with one nominee of the International Labour Organisation who sits in a consultative capacity.

The Committee considers the report and the unions' or employers' comments with a view to determining the extent to which the state has complied with the provisions of the Charter. The Committee's report (its 'conclusions'), is then examined by a sub-committee of the Governmental Committee of the Council of Europe. The sub-committee includes (in addition to representatives from the Social Charter States) representatives from two international trade union organisations and two international employers' organisations.

The sub-committee report (to which the Committee of Expert's report is appended) is then sent to the Committee of Ministers and to the Parliamentary Assembly, whose comments are communicated to the Committee of Ministers. The Committee of Ministers may then make recommendations (subject to a two-thirds majority) to the individual state.

The enforcement procedure is thus long and complicated, containing ample opportunity at each stage for criticisms to be diluted or diverted; the end product being no more than a 'recommendation'.

The Charter does however contain a clear set of important social rights to which the U.K. has put its name. There is scope for using the process of regular reports to highlight shortcomings in domestic law. An individual or group wishing to challenge violations of the Charter should liaise with the relevant trade union or employers' organisation so that the state's report is copied to them as soon as it is available. The complaints of violations can then be incorporated and forwarded to the Secretary-General.

CONFERENCE ON SECURITY AND CO-OPERATION IN EUROPE: (CSCE)

The CSCE[5] is a creature of the Cold War that has developed an important rôle in the turbulent post-Communist era, especially in

Article 25
For a comprehensive analysis, see R. Brett *The Development of the Human Dimension Mechanism of the Conference on Security and Co-operation in Europe,* Human Rights Centre, Essex University, 1992

relation to the fragmentation of the USSR and Yugoslavia. In 1972, at the instigation of the then seven Warsaw Pact countries, preparatory talks took place between them, the 16 NATO countries, and 12 non-aligned European states with a view to promoting peace and security in Europe. The talks culminated in 1975 with the parties agreeing at Helsinki a declaration of common purpose, the 'Helsinki Final Act[6]'. The Final Act recorded that the parties had agreed to co-operate in the fields of security, economics, science and technology. In addition it was agreed that the parties would respect human rights and act in accordance with the Universal Declaration of Human Rights. Implementation of the Final Act was left to the individual states but a follow-up meeting was arranged, which was held in Belgrade in 1977.

The CSCE has developed to the stage that it now contains a small Secretariat in Prague *(see below)*, and it holds annual meetings of foreign ministers, to discuss the progress of the Final Act and interstate co-operation. At the Vienna meeting of the CSCE (1989), it was agreed to establish a permanent human rights monitoring procedure, known as the Human Dimension Mechanism. Meetings solely concerned with the Human Dimension now occur annually. Three practical human rights procedures have been evolved, the third of the most potential relevance within the U.K.:

1. At the Vienna meeting of the CSCE, the states agreed to a procedure whereby they would upon request provide other states with information about individuals or situations within their country; this is known as the Vienna mechanism, and was much used to ascertain the well-being of East European dissidents.
2. At the Moscow meeting of the Human Dimension, the states agreed to a procedure whereby individual states would permit, upon request, a CSCE fact-finding mission to visit their country to investigate a particular human rights situation; this is known as the Moscow mechanism.
3. The CSCE has created a High Commissioner for National Minorities, whose remit is to visit CSCE states, discuss and conciliate in relation to cases of actual or potential conflict involving national minorities.

Whilst the degree of human rights abuses occurring in what used to be Yugoslavia and the USSR are such as to occupy these mechanisms at present, it remains to be seen whether they may in the future be of use to U.K. individuals or groups. The position of a national minority might be ameliorated (or at least highlighted) by recourse to the Commissioner for National Minorities.

---

[6] For the full text of the Helsinki Final Act, *see* Brownlie p. 391

At the Copenhagen meeting of the Human Dimension, the final document contained as strong a statement of minority rights as may be found in almost any other international document[7]. The issue of minority rights may therefore prove to be the major contribution of the CSCE to human rights; the past and present violations of the rights of minorities being a major cause of the turmoil in Europe. The European Convention on Human Rights does not of course contain a primary article dealing with this issue.

At the Copenhagen meeting it was also stated that future meetings would be open to the media and non-governmental organisations (NGOs); and that the media and NGOs would have unimpeded access to delegates[8]. The most straightforward procedure therefore for raising human rights issues with the CSCE will be through the lobbying of the annual Human Dimension meetings. The Foreign Office CSCE unit is charged with disseminating information about the CSCE process (including the details of forthcoming meetings).

The CSCE Secretariat address:
Thunovskà 12
Malà Strana
11000
Prague 1
Tel: 42–23–119793/4
Fax: 42–23–116215

The Foreign Office CSCE Unit address:
Foreign & Commonwealth Office
London SW1A 2AH
Tel: 071–270–2428
Fax: 071–270–3884

EUROPEAN CONVENTION FOR THE PREVENTION OF TORTURE AND INHUMAN OR DEGRADING TREATMENT OR PUNISHMENT (ECT)

The ECT[9] was drafted by the Council of Europe in 1987 and came into force on February 1, 1989; the U.K. being an original signatory. The importance of the ECT is it's rôle in seeking out evidence of torture

---

[7] Document of the Copenhagen meeting of the Conference on the Human Dimension of the CSCE June 5–29, 1992; HMSO Cm. 1324
[8] Chairman's Statement on Access of Non-Governmental Organisations, *ibid*.
[9] For the full text of the Convention *see* 9 E.H.R.R. 161

and other ill-treatment within the signatory States, rather than waiting for a complaint to be lodged under the European Convention on Human Rights.

The ECT system is based upon a Committee[10] which consists of experts, one for each state party to the ECT. The Committee is required to carry out periodic visits to the ECT states. In general the visits are by at least two of the Committee members, assisted as necessary by experts and interpreters. The state is required to facilitate the visits without restriction and provide all necessary information; only in exceptional circumstances can a state request a visit be deferred, and in such cases the ECT stipulates the procedure to be followed for resolving the conflicting interests.

After each visit the Committee prepares a factual report on its findings, taking into account any observations made by the state concerned. The report, which may contain any recommendations the Committee considers necessary, is then transmitted to the state in confidence. If the state fails to co-operate or refuses to improve the situation, the Committee may decide to publish the report (subject to the Committee approving this course by a two-thirds majority).

The Committee aims, subject to any special demands, to make biennial visits to each state signatory. In relation to Turkey the Committee has shown especial concern and organised three visits in a relatively short period [11]. In spite of sending confidential reports to the authorities after the first two visits, and arranging follow-up meetings with the authorities, the Committee concluded on its third visit that the authorities had failed to act upon the recommendations; that the practice of torture and other forms of severe ill-treatment remained widespread in Turkey. The Committee accordingly voted to publish a statement of its findings, which it did on December 21, 1992[12].

The purpose of the ECT requires that the Committee members have the right to interview detainees in private and unlimited access to places of detention. The ECT also stipulates that the Committee can communicate freely with any person whom it believes can provide relevant information. A small Secretariat based in Strasbourg services the Committee and any communications should be directed via the Secretary-General. An investigation by the Committee of torture or other inhuman or degrading treatment or punishment does not preclude the victim from making a complaint under Article 3 of the European Convention on Human Rights [13], subject of course to satisfying the admissibility requirements.

[10] European Committee for the Prevention of Torture and Inhuman or Degrading Treatment or Punishment

[11] The first visit took place from September 9–21, 1990; the second from September 29, 1991–October 7, 1991 and the third from November 22, 1992–December 3, 1992

[12] The text can be found at 15 E.H.R.R. 309

[13] Article 17 of the European Convention for the Prevention of Torture and Inhuman or Degrading Treatment or Punishment

UNITED NATIONS MECHANISMS

The historical importance of the Universal Declaration of Human Rights (UDHR) and the UN Covenants (*see* p. 1) has been their example; the European Convention on Human Rights was itself inspired by, and based upon, the UDHR. The European Convention was always intended to be an enforceable set of principles, whereas the UDHR contains no enforcement mechanisms. It was drafted as a free-standing international standard.

The structure and functions of the United Nations is a subject of labyrinthine complexity; the UN's involvement in the area of human rights is no exception. There is little logic to the distribution of duties amongst the various UN bodies responsible for human rights supervision, nor to their respective importance; subsidiary bodies may have greater authority than those to which they report.

UNITED NATIONS MECHANISMS

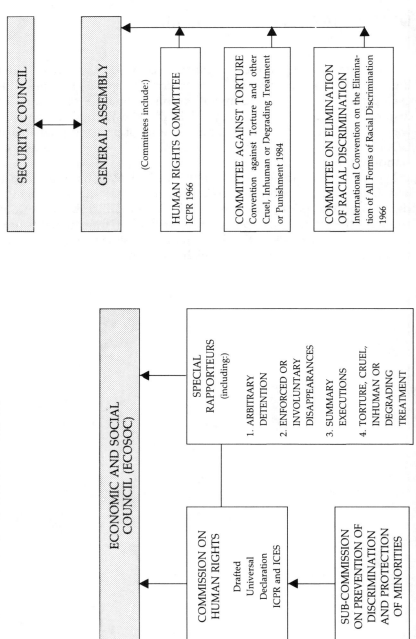

The UN structure, so far as it applies to human rights, involves three primary bodies.

1. SECURITY COUNCIL

The Security Council contains five permanent members (China, France, Russia, the U.K. and the U.S.A.) and 10 other members elected from the General Assembly. Whilst the Security Council has primary responsibility for international peace and security, this has inevitably led to it becoming involved in human rights questions when these impinge upon security and peace.

2. GENERAL ASSEMBLY

The General Assembly comprises all members of the UN. Under the United Nations Charter of 1945 its primary human rights functions are to draft human rights conventions, initiate human rights studies, co-ordinate, discuss and make recommendations.

3. ECONOMIC AND SOCIAL COUNCIL (ECOSOC)

ECOSOC comprises 54 members elected by the General Assembly. Although a primary body of the UN, it reports to the General Assembly. It has now lost most of its importance and in the arena of human rights acts largely as a conduit between the Human Rights Commission and the General Assembly.

Under the UN Charter a respect for human rights was to be engendered, and in pursuance of this goal various agencies were created and the UDHR drafted. These subsidiary agencies are explained *below*.

The Commission on Human Rights

Article 68 of the UN Charter required ECOSOC to create a human rights Commission (amongst others). In pursuance of this, the Commission on Human Rights was established. Today it has 53 members, elected from the General Assembly. The Human Rights Commission is the most important UN human rights body, although it is very much a political organ. The Commission was responsible for the actual drafting of the UDHR and subsequently the International Covenant on Civil and Political Rights 1966 and the International Covenant on Economic, Social, and Cultural Rights 1966.

The Sub-Commission on Prevention of Discrimination and Protection of Minorities

The Commission created in 1947 a Sub-Commission on the Prevention of Discrimination and Protection of Minorities. The Sub-Commission has 26 members elected by the Commission on a regional basis. The remit of the Sub-Commission has long since ceased to be limited to discrimination and minorities and now extends to all areas involving gross human rights violations. In many respects the Sub-Commission has become a more influential body than the full Commission to which it reports.

The Sub-Commission is empowered to investigate 'situations which reveal a consistent pattern of gross violations of human rights and fundamental freedoms'. There is a procedure for correspondence concerning such violations to be vetted by a committee of the Sub-Commission and then (depending upon the procedure) considered in open or closed session[14]. Whilst the Commission can receive correspondence concerning such human rights violations, the correspondent has little or no feedback thereafter as to what if any action is taken in response. Human rights involvement in the Commissions is very much a specialist activity conducted by non-governmental organisations such as Amnesty International[15].

Special rapporteurs

Under the wing of the Commission on Human Rights are a number of special rapporteurs (or in the case of enforced or involuntary disappearances, a 'working group'), appointed by the UN to deal with specific temporary or ongoing human rights problems. The remit of these rapporteurs depends upon the nature of the problem they have to tackle. In the case of the working group on enforced or involuntary disappearances, their primary activity is contacting individual states for details of named persons within their juridiction whose whereabouts are uncertain. Rapporteurs have powers to take evidence, conduct visits and prepare reports upon the areas of their concern; they submit annual reports to the Commission on their findings[15].

The rôle of the special rapporteur on summary executions is to receive details of, and to investigate, 'extra-legal executions'; essentially state-permitted or inspired kilings outside the state's judicial process. It was to this rapporteur that the deaths of the three IRA members killed in Gibraltar in July 1988 was reported (see p. 110).

A number of special rapporteurs exist whose remit includes torture, religious intolerance and arbitrary detention.

---

[14] The closed session consideration is known as the 1503 procedure, and in open session, the 1235 procedure. For a full and practical guide to these (and other UN procedures), see Hurst Hannum, 2nd Edn

[15] Further details (including Human Rights Facts Sheets) can be obtained from the UN Centre for Human Rights, 1211 Geneva 10, Switzerland

UN Committees

Certain UN human rights covenants and conventions provide for the creation of special committees to oversee their performance. Individual states are in general required to submit periodic reports to these committees to record how the provisions of the covenant or convention are being implemented within their jurisdiction.

UN Committee against torture

The U.K. is a signatory to the UN Convention against Torture and Other Cruel, Inhuman or Degrading Treatment or Punishment (UNTC)[16], which has been in force since 1987. The U.K. has not however signed an additional protocol which would enable the Committee[17] set up by the UNTC to consider individual complaints. The Committee may nevertheless act on its own initiative where it receives well-founded indications that torture is being systematically practised in the territory of a state party[18] by initiating an investigation[19].

Of most relevance to the U.K. however is the procedure for scrutinising the reports which the states are required to submit to the Committee every four years. The reports set out the measures taken by the states to give effect to their undertakings under the UNTC. The reports are copied to the other state parties to the UNTC and are then scrutinised by the Committee; part of the process being a meeting where the report is presented by the government which is then subject to detailed questions put by the Committee members. The Committee members may be briefed by relevant NGOs, and ask detailed questions regarding the state's actions where there is concern about any form of ill-treatment. The consideration of a state's report at such meetings takes about a day, depending upon the degree of interrogation by the Committee. The meetings therefore provide a periodic forum whereby a state's record on treatment of detainees or others can be the subject of public examination; with the state being required to justify its action. Thus in November 1991 when the Committee considered the U.K.'s report in Geneva, it subjected the Government representatives to detailed questions upon the treatment of detainees at interrogation centres in Northern Ireland, and the question of the number of U.K. prison suicides.

---

[16] For the full text of the Convention *see* Brownlie, 3rd Edn p. 38

[17] The Committee against Torture, whose composition and functions are detailed in Part II of the UN Convention against Torture and other Cruel, Inhuman or Degrading Treatment or Punishment

[18] Article 20 of the UNTC

[19] A state may, on signing the UNTC, exclude the Committee from such initiatives, but the U.K. has not

For action in this sphere it is essential to liaise with a NGO, such as Amnesty International.

UN Human Rights Committee

The Human Rights Committee is charged with overseeing the implementation of the International Covenant on Economic, Social, and Cultural Rights[20]. Whilst an individual right of complaint to the Committee exists, this procedure is not available to persons within the jurisdiction of the U.K. as it only arises if an optional protocol[21] has been signed by the relevant state; which the U.K. has not. The present relevance of the Committee to the U.K. is therefore its scrutiny of the periodic (four yearly) reports which individual states are required to submit to the Committee (and in respect of which much the same comments apply as made in relation to the UN Committee against Torture, detailed *above*).

Other UN 'reporting' conventions

The U.K. is required to file periodic reports in relation to a number of UN Covenants, in addition to those required by the Committee against Torture and the Human Rights Committee (as detailed *above*). These include:[22]

Committee on Economic, Social and Cultural Rights
Pursuant to the International Covenant on Economic, Social and Cultural Rights 1966[23]

Committee on the Rights of the Child
Pursuant to the Convention on the Rights of the Child 1989[24]

Committee on the Elimination of Racial Discrimination
Pursuant to the International Convention on the Elimination of all Forms of Racial Discrimination 1966[25]

Committee on the Elimination of Discrimination against Women
Pursuant to the Convention on the Elimination of All Forms of Discrimination against Women 1979[26]

---

[20] For the full text of the ICPR *see* Brownlie p. 114
[21] Optional Protocol to the International Covenant on Civil and Political Rights 1966, *see* Brownlie p. 144 for full text
[22] For further details *see* H. Hannum
[23] For the full text *see* p. 114 Brownlie, 3rd Edn
[24] *Ibid.* p. 182
[25] *Ibid.* p. 148
[26] *Ibid.* p. 169

INDEX TO APPENDICES

Appendix 1

EUROPEAN CONVENTION ON HUMAN RIGHTS AND PROTOCOL 1

CONVENTION FOR THE PROTECTION OF HUMAN RIGHTS AND FUNDAMENTAL FREEDOMS

Rome, November 4, 1950
Entry into force: September 3, 1953, in accordance with Article 66
Text amended according to the provisions of Protocol No. 3, which entered into force on September 21, 1970, of Protocol No. 5, which entered into force on December 20, 1971 and of Protocol No. 8, which entered into force on January 1, 1990, and comprising also the text of Protocol No. 2 which, in accordance with Article 5, paragraph 3 thereof, has been an integral part of the Convention since its entry into force on September 21, 1970.

The Governments signatory hereto, being Members of the Council of Europe,

Considering the Universal Declaration of Human Rights proclaimed by the General Assembly of the United Nations on December 10, 1948;

Considering that this Declaration aims at securing the universal and effective recognition and observance of the rights therein declared;

Considering that the aim of the Council of Europe is the achievement of greater unity between its Members and that one of the methods by which that aim is to be pursued is the maintenance and further realisation of Human Rights and Fundamental Freedoms;

Reaffirming their profound belief in those Fundamental Freedoms which are the foundation of justice and peace in the world and are best maintained on the one hand by an effective political democracy and on the other by a common understanding and observance of the Human Rights upon which they depend;

Being resolved, as the Governments of European countries which are like-minded and have a common heritage of political traditions, ideals, freedom and the rule of law, to take the first steps for the collective enforcement of certain of the rights stated in the Universal Declaration;

Have agreed as follows:

Article 1

The High Contracting Parties shall secure to everyone within their jurisdiction the rights and freedoms defined in Section I of this Convention.

SECTION I

Article 2

1. Everyone's right to life shall be protected by law. No one shall be deprived of his life intentionally save in the execution of a sentence of a court following his conviction of a crime for which this penalty is provided by law.
2. Deprivation of life shall not be regarded as inflicted in contravention of this Article when it results from the use of force which is no more than absolutely necessary:
   a. in defence of any person from unlawful violence;
   b. in order to effect a lawful arrest or to prevent the escape of a person lawfully detained;
   c. in action lawfully taken for the purpose of quelling a riot or insurrection.

Article 3

No one shall be subjected to torture or to inhuman or degrading treatment or punishment.

Article 4

1. No one shall be held in slavery or servitude.
2. No one shall be required to perform forced or compulsory labour.
3. For the purpose of the Article the term 'forced or compulsory labour' shall not include:
   a. any work required to be done in the ordinary course of detention imposed according to the provisions of Article 5 of this Convention or during conditional release from such detention;

b. any service of a military character or, in case of conscientious objectors in countries where they are recognised, service exacted instead of compulsory military service;

c. any service exacted in case of an emergency or calamity threatening the life or well-being of the community;

d. any work or service which forms part of normal civic obligations.

Article 5

1. Everyone has the right to liberty and security of person. No one shall be deprived of his liberty save in the following cases and in accordance with a procedure prescribed by law:

   a. the lawful detention of a person after conviction by a competent court;

   b. the lawful arrest or detention of a person for non-compliance with the lawful order of a court or in order to secure the fulfilment of any obligation prescribed by law;

   c. the lawful arrest or detention of a person effected for the purpose of bringing him before the competent legal authority on reasonable suspicion of having committed an offence or when it is reasonably considered necessary to prevent his commiting an offence or fleeing after having done so;

   d. the detention of a minor by lawful order for the purpose of educational supervision or his lawful detention for the purpose of bringing him before the competent legal authority;

   e. the lawful detention of persons for the prevention of the spreading of infectious diseases, of persons of unsound mind, alcoholics or drug addicts or vagrants;

   f. the lawful arrest or detention of a person to prevent his effecting an unauthorised entry into the country or of a person against whom action is being taken with a view to deportation or extradition.

2. Everyone who is arrested shall be informed promptly, in a language which he understands, of the reasons for his arrest and of any charge against him.

3. Everyone arrested or detained in accordance with the provisions of paragraph 1(c) of of this Article shall be brought promptly before a judge or other officer authorised by law to exercise judicial power and shall be entitled to trial within a reasonable time or to release pending trial. Release may be conditioned by guarantees to appear for trial.

4. Everyone who is deprived of his liberty by arrest or detention shall be entitled to take proceedings by which the lawfulness of

his detention shall be decided speedily by a court and his release ordered if the detention is not lawful.

5. Everyone who has been the victim of arrest or detention in contravention of the provisions of this Article shall have an enforceable right to compensation.

Article 6

1. In the determination of his civil rights and obligations or of any criminal charge against him, everyone is entitled to a fair and public hearing within a reasonable time by an independent and impartial tribunal established by law. Judgment shall be pronounced publicly but the press and public may be excluded from all or part of the trial in the interest of morals, public order or national security in a democratic society, where the interests of juveniles or the protection of the private life of the parties so require, or to the extent strictly necessary in the opinion of the court in special circumstances where publicity would prejudice the interests of justice.
2. Everyone charged with a criminal offence shall be presumed innocent until proved guilty according to law.
3. Everyone charged with a criminal offence has the following minimum rights:
   a. to be informed promptly, in a language which he understands and in detail, of the nature and cause of the accusation against him;
   b. to have adequate time and facilities for the preparation of his defence;
   c. to defend himself in person or through legal assistance of his own choosing or, if he has not sufficient means to pay for legal assistance, to be given it free when the interests of justice so require;
   d. to examine or have examined witnesses against him and to obtain the attendance and examination of witnesses on his behalf under the same conditions as witnesses against him;
   e. to have the free assistance of an interpreter if he cannot understand or speak the language used in court.

Article 7

1. No one shall be held guilty of any criminal offence on account of any act or omission which did not constitute a criminal offence under national or international law at the time when it was

committed. Nor shall a heavier penalty be imposed than the one that was applicable at the time the criminal offence was committed.

2. This Article shall not prejudice the trial and punishment of any person for any act or omission which, at the time when it was committed, was criminal according to the general principles of law recognised by civilised nations.

Article 8

1. Everyone has the right to respect for his private and family life, his home and his correspondence.
2. There shall be no interference by a public authority with the exercise of this right except such as in accordance with the law and is necessary in a democratic society in the interests of national security, public safety or the economic well-being of the country, for the prevention of disorder or crime, for the protection of health or morals, or for the protection of the rights and freedoms of others.

Article 9

1. Everyone has the right to freedom of thought, conscience and religion; this right includes freedom to change his religion or belief and freedom, either alone or in community with others and in public or in private, to manifest his religion or belief, in worship, teaching, practice and observance.
2. Freedom to manifest one's religion or beliefs shall be subject only to such limitations as are prescribed by law and are necessary in a democratic society in the interests of public safety, for the protection of public order, health or morals, or for the protection of the rights and freedoms of others.

Article 10

1. Everyone has the right to freedom of expression. This right shall include freedom to hold opinions and to receive and impart information and ideas without interference by public authority and regardless of frontiers. This Article shall not prevent states from requiring the licensing of broadcasting, television or cinema enterprises.
2. The exercise of these freedoms, since it carries with it duties and responsibilities, may be subject to such formalities, conditions,

restrictions or penalties as are prescribed by law and are necessary in a democratic society, in the interests of national security, territorial integrity or public safety, for the prevention of disorder or crime, for the protection of health or morals, for the protection of the reputation or rights of others, for preventing the disclosure of information received in confidence, or for maintaining the authority and impartiality of the judiciary.

Article 11

1. Everyone has the right to freedom of peaceful assembly and to freedom of association with others, including the right to form and to join trade unions for the protection of his interests.
2. No restrictions shall be placed on the exercise of these rights other than such as are prescribed by law and are necessary in a democratic society in the interests of national security or public safety, for the prevention of disorder or crime, for the protection of health or morals or for the protection of the rights and freedoms of others. This Article shall not prevent the imposition of lawful restrictions on the exercise of these rights by members of the armed forces, of the police or of the administration of the State.

Article 12

Men and women of marriageable age have the right to marry and to found a family, according to the national laws governing the exercise of this right.

Article 13

Everyone whose rights and freedoms as set forth in this Convention are violated shall have an effective remedy before a national authority notwithstanding that the violation has been committed by persons acting in an official capacity.

Article 14

The enjoyment of the rights and freedoms set forth in this Convention shall be secured without discrimination on any ground such as sex, race, colour, language, religion, political or other opinion, national or social origin, association with a national minority, property, birth or other status.

Article 15

1. In time of war or other public emergency threatening the life of the nation any High Contracting Party may take measures derogating from its obligations under this Convention to the extent strictly required by the exigencies of the situation, provided that such measures are not inconsistent with its other obligations under international law.
2. No derogation from Article 2, except in respect of deaths resulting from lawful acts of war, or from Articles 3, 4 (paragraph 1) and 7 shall be made under this provision.
3. Any High Contracting Party availing itself of this right of derogation shall kep the Secretary General of the Council of Europe fully informed of the measures which it has taken and the reasons therefor. It shall also inform the Secretary General of the Council of Europe when such measures have ceased to operate and the provisions of the Convention are again being fully executed.

Article 16

Nothing in Articles 10, 11, and 14 shall be regarded as preventing the High Contracting Parties from imposing restrictions on the political activity of aliens.

Article 17

Nothing in this Convention may be interpreted as implying for any state, group or person any right to engage in any activity or perform any act aimed at the destruction of any of the rights and freedoms set forth herein or at their limitation to a greater extent than is provided for in the Convention.

Article 18

The restrictions permitted under this Convention to the said rights and freedoms shall not be applied for any purpose other than those for which they have been prescribed.

Protocols to the Convention for the Protection of Human Rights and Fundamental Freedoms

PROTOCOL NO. 1 TO THE CONVENTION FOR THE PROTECTION OF HUMAN RIGHTS AND FUNDAMENTAL FREEDOMS, SECURING CERTAIN RIGHTS AND FREEDOMS OTHER THAN THOSE ALREADY INCLUDED IN THE CONVENTION

Paris, March 20, 1952

Entry into force: May 18, 1954, in accordance with Article 6

The Governments signatory hereto, being Members of the Council of Europe,

Being resolved to take steps to ensure the collective enforcement of cetain rights and freedoms other than those already included in Section I of the Convention for the Protection of Human Rights and Fundamental Freedoms signed at Rome on November 4, 1950 (hereinafter referred to as 'the Convention'),

Have agreed as follows:

Article 1

Every natural or legal person is entitled to the peaceful enjoyment of his possessions. No one shall be deprived of his possessions except in the public interest and subject to the conditions provided for by law and by the general principles of international law.

The preceding provisions shall not, however, in any way impair the right of a state to enforce such laws as it deems necessary to control the use of property in accordance with the general interest or to secure the payment of taxes or other contributions or penalties.

Article 2

No person shall be denied the right to education. In the exercise of any functions which it assumes in relation to education and to teaching, the state shall respect the right of parents to ensure such education and teaching in conformity with their own religious and philosophical convictions.

Article 3

The High Contracting Parties undertake to hold free elections at reasonable intervals by secret ballot, under conditions which will ensure the free expression of the opinion of the people in the choice of the legislature.

Article 4

Any High Contracting Party may at the time of signature of ratification or at any time thereafter communicate to the Secretary General of the Council of Europe a declaration stating the extent to which it undertakes that the provisions of the present Protocol shall apply to such of the territories for the international relations of which is responsible as are named therein.

Any High Contracting Party which has communicated a declaration in virtue of the preceding paragraph may from time to time communicate a further declaration modifying the terms of any former declaration or terminating the application of the provisions of this Protocol in respect of any territory.

A declaration made in accordance with the Article shall be deemed to have been made in accordance with paragraph 1 of Article 63 of the Convention.

Article 5

As between the High Contracting Parties the provisions of Articles 1, 2, 3 and 4 of this Protocol shall be regarded as additional Articles to the Convention and all the provisions of the Convention shall apply accordingly.

Article 6

This Protocol shall be open for signature by the Members of the Council of Europe, who are the signatories of the Convention; it shall be ratified at the same time as or after the ratification of the Convention. It shall enter into force after the deposit of instruments of ratification. As regards any signatory ratifying subsequently, the Protocol shall enter into force at the date of the deposit of its instrument of ratification.

The instruments of ratification shall be deposited with the Secretary General of the Council of Europe, who will notify all Members of the names of those who have ratified.

Done at Paris, this 20th day of March 1952, in English and French, both texts being equally authentic, in a single copy which shall remain deposited in the archives of the Council of Europe. The Secretary General shall transmit certified copies to each of the signatory Governments.

Appendix 2

UNIVERSAL DECLARATION OF HUMAN RIGHTS

Adopted and proclaimed by General Assembly Resolution 217 A (III) of 10 December 1948

Preamble

Whereas recognition of the inherent dignity and of the equal and inalienable rights of all members of the human family is the foundation of freedom, justice and peace in the world,

Whereas disregard and contempt for human rights have resulted in barbarous acts which have outraged the conscience of mankind, and the advent of a world in which human beings shall enjoy freedom of speech and belief and freedom from fear and want has been proclaimed as the highest aspiration of the common people,

Whereas it is essential, if man is not to be compelled to have recourse, as a last resort, to rebellion against tyranny and oppression, that human rights should be protected by the rule of law,

Whereas it is essential to promote the development of friendly relations between nations,

Whereas the peoples of the United Nations have in the Charter reaffirmed their faith in fundamental human rights, in the dignity and worth of the human person and in the equal rights of men and women and have determined to promote social progress and better standards of life in larger freedoms,

Whereas Member States have pledged themselves to achieve, in co-operation with the United Nations, the promotion of universal respect for and observance of human rights and fundamental freedoms,

Whereas a common understanding of these rights and freedoms is of the greatest importance for the full realisation of this pledge,

Now, therefore,

The General Assembly,

Proclaims this Universal Declaration of Human Rights as a common standard of achievement for all peoples and all nations, to the end that every individual and every organ of society, keeping this Declaration constantly in mind, shall strive by teaching and education to promote respect for these rights and freedoms and by progressive measures, national and international, to secure their universal and effective recognition and observance, both among the peoples of Member States themselves and among the peoples of territories under their jurisdiction.

Article 1

All human beings are born free and equal in dignity and rights. They are endowed with reason and conscience and should act towards one another in a spirit of brotherhood.

Article 2

1. Everyone is entitled to all the rights and freedoms set forth in this Declaration, without distinction of any kind, such as race, colour, sex, language, religion, political or other opinion, national or social origin, property, birth or other status.
2. Furthermore, no distinction shall be made on the basis of the political, jurisdictional or international status of the country or territory to which a person belongs, whether it be independent, trust, non-self-governing or under any other limitation of sovereignty.

Article 3

Everyone has the right to life, liberty and security of person.

Article 4

No one shall be held in slavery or servitude; slavery and the slave trade shall be prohibited in all their forms.

Article 5

No one shall be subjected to torture or to cruel, inhuman or degrading treatment or punishment.

Article 6

Everyone has the right to recognition everywhere as a person before the law.

Article 7

All are equal before the law and are entitled without any discrimination to equal protection of the law. All are entitled to equal protection against any discrimination in violation of this Declaration and against any incitement to such discrimination.

Article 8

Everyone has the right to an effective remedy by the competent national tribunals for acts violating the fundamental rights granted him by the constitution or by law.

Article 9

No one shall be subjected to arbitrary arrest, detention or exile.

Article 10

Everyone is entitled in full equality to a fair and public hearing by an independent and impartial tribunal, in the determination of his rights and obligations and of any criminal charge against him.

Article 11

1. Everyone charged with a penal offence has the right to be presumed innocent until proved guilty according to law in a public trial at which he has had all the guarantees necessary for his defence.
2. No one shall be held guilty of any penal offence on account of any act or omission which did not constitute a penal offence, under national or international law, at the time when it was committed. Nor shall a heavier penalty be imposed than the one that was applicable at the time the penal offence was committed.

Article 12

No one shall be subjected to arbitrary interference with his privacy, family, home or correspondence, nor to attacks upon his honour and reputation. Everyone has the right to the protection of the law against such interference or attacks.

Article 13

1. Everyone has the right to freedom of movement and residence within the borders of each State.
2. Everyone has the right to leave any country, including his own, and to return to his country.

Article 14

1. Everyone has the right to seek and to enjoy in other countries asylum from persecution.
2. This right may not be invoked in the case of prosecutions genuinely arising from non-political crimes or from acts contrary to the purposes and principles of the United Nations.

Article 15

1. Everyone has the right to a nationality.
2. No one shall be arbitrarily deprived of his nationality nor denied the right to change his nationality.

Article 16

1. Men and women of full age, without any limitation due to race, nationality or religion, have the right to marry and to found a family. They are entitled to equal rights as to marriage, during marriage and at its dissolution.
2. Marriage shall be entered into only with free and full consent of the intending spouses.
3. The family is the natural and fundamental group unit of society and is entitled to protection by society and the State.

Article 17

1. Everyone has the right to own property alone as well as in association with others.
2. No one shall be arbitrarily deprived of his property.

Article 18

Everyone has the right to freedom of thought, conscience and religion; this right includes freedom to change his religion or belief, and freedom, either alone or in community with others and in public or private, to manifest his religion or belief in teaching, practice, worship and observance.

Article 19

Everyone has the right to freedom of opinion and expression; this right includes freedom to hold opinions without interference and to seek, receive and impart information and ideas through any media and regardless of frontiers.

Article 20

1. Everyone has the right to freedom of peaceful assembly and association.
2. No one may be compelled to belong to an association.

Article 21

1. Everyone has the right to take part in the government of his country, directly or through freely chosen representatives.
2. Everyone has the right to equal access to public service in his country.
3. The will of the people shall be the basis of the authority of government; this will shall be expressed in periodic and genuine elections which shall be by universal and equal suffrage and shall be held by secret vote or by equivalent free voting procedures.

Article 22

Everyone, as a member of society, has the right to social security and is entitled to realisation, through national effort and international co-operation and in accordance with the organisation and resources of each State, or the economic, social and cultural rights indispensable for his dignity and the free development of his personality.

Article 23

1. Everyone has the right to work, to free choice of employment, to just and favourable conditions of work and to protection against unemployment.

2. Everyone, without any discrimination, has the right to equal pay for equal work.
3. Everyone who works has the right to just and favourable remuneration ensuring for himself and his family an existence worthy of human dignity, and supplemented, if necessary, by other means of social protection.
4. Everyone has the right to form and to join trade unions for the protection of his interests.

Article 24

Everyone has the right to rest and leisure, including reasonable limitation of working hours and periodic holidays with pay.

Article 25

1. Everyone has the right to a standard of living adequate for the health and well-being of himself and of his family, including food, clothing, housing and medical care and necessary social services, and the right to security in the event of unemployment, sickness, disability, widowhood, old age or other lack of livelihood in circumstances beyond his control.
2. Motherhood and childhood are entitled to special care and assistance. All children, whether born in or out of wedlock, shall enjoy the same social protection.

Article 26

1. Everyone has the right to education. Education shall be free, at least in the elementary and fundamental stages. Elementary education shall be compulsory. Technical and professional education shall be made generally available and higher education shall be equally accessible to all on the basis of merit.
2. Education shall be directed to the full development of the human personality and to the strengthening of respect for human rights and fundamental freedoms. It shall promote understanding, tolerance and friendship among all nations, racial or religious groups, and shall further the activities of the United Nations for the maintenance of peace.
3. Parents have a prior right to choose the kind of education that shall be given to their children.

Article 27

1. Everyone has the right freely to participate in the cultural life of the community, to enjoy the arts and to share in scientific advancement and its benefits.

2. Everyone has the right to the protection of the moral and materia
interests resulting from any scientific, literary or artistic production of which he is the author.

Article 28

Everyone is entitled to a social and international order in which the
rights and freedoms set forth in this Declaration can be fully realised.

Article 29

1. Everyone has duties to the community in which alone the free
and full development of his personality is possible.
2. In the exercise of his rights and freedoms, everyone shall be
subject only to such limitations are are determined by law solely
for the purpose of securing due recognition and respect for the
rights and freedoms of others and of meeting the just require
ments of morality, public order and the general welfare in a
democratic society.
3. These rights and freedoms may in no case be exercised contrary
to the purposes and principles of the United Nations.

Article 30

Nothing in this Declaration may be interpreted as implying for any
state, group or person any right to engage in any activity or to perform
any act aimed at the destruction of any of the rights and freedoms se
forth herein.

Appendix 3

RULES OF PROCEDURE OF THE EUROPEAN
COMMISSION OF HUMAN RIGHTS
(*Revised on January 7, 1992*)

TITLE III PROCEDURE

CHAPTER I

General rules

Rule 30

1. The official languages of the Commission shall be English and French.
2. The President may authorise a member to speak in another language.
3. The President may permit the use by a party or a person representing that party of a language other than English or French, either in hearings or documents. Any such document shall be submitted in an original and at least two copies.
4. The Secretary is authorised, in correspondence with an applicant, to employ a language other than English or French.

Rule 31

The High Contracting Parties shall be represented before the Commission by their agents who may have the assistance of advisers.

Rule 32

1. Persons, non-governmental organisations, or groups of individuals, may present and conduct applications under Article 25 of

the Convention on their own behalf or through a representative appointed under paragraph 2 of this Rule.

2. Any such applicant may appoint, and be represented in proceedings before the Commission by, a lawyer or any other person, resident in a Convention country, unless the Commission at any stage decides otherwise.

3. Any such applicant or representative shall appear in person before the Commission:

    a. to present the application in a hearing fixed by the Commission; or

    b. for any other purpose, if invited by the Commission.

4. In the other provisions of these Rules the term 'applicant' shall, where appropriate, include the applicant's representative.

Rule 33

The Commission shall deal with applications in the order in which they become ready for examination. It may, however, decide to give precedence to a particular application.

Rule 34

1. The Commission may, *proprio motu* or at the request of a party, take any action which it considers expedient or necessary for the proper performance of its duties under the Convention.

2. The Commission may delegate one or more of its members to take any such action in its name, and in particular to hear witnesses or experts, to examine documents or to visit any locality. Such member or members shall duly report to the Commission.

3. In case of urgency when the Commission is not in session, the President or one of the Vice-Presidents may take any necessary action on behalf of the Commission. As soon as the Commission is again in session, the President or the Vice-President concerned shall report to it on any action which has been taken under this paragraph.

Rule 35

The Commission may, if it considers necessary, order the joinder of two or more applications.

Rule 36

The Commission or, when it is not in session, the President may indicate to the parties any interim measure the adoption of which seems desirable in the interest of the parties or the proper conduct of the proceedings before it.

CHAPTER II

Hearings

Rule 37

1. Hearings before the Commission shall be held *in camera*. Unless the Commission decides otherwise, no person shall be admitted, other than:
   a. the persons referred to in Rule 31 or 32;
   b. the individual applicant;
   c. any person being heard by the Commission as a witness;
   d. the persons referred to in Rule 17, paragraph 1.
2. If the applicant is a non-governmental organisation or group of individuals, the Commission shall ensure that those appearing are entitled to represent it.
3. When it considers it in the interest of the proper conduct of a hearing, the Commission may limit the number of the parties' representatives or advisers who may appear.
4. The parties shall inform the Commission at least ten days before the date of the opening of the hearing of the names and functions of the persons who will appear on their behalf at the hearing.
5. The provisions of the present Rule shall apply *mutatis mutandis* to hearings before delegates of the Commission.

Rule 38

1. Any individual applicant, expert or other person whom the Commission decides to hear as a witness, shall be summoned by the Secretary. The summons shall indicate:
   a. the parties to the application;
   b. the facts or issues regarding which the person concerned will be heard;
   c. the arrangements made, in accordance with Rule 42, paragraph 1 or 2, to reimburse the persons concerned for any expenses incurred by them.
2. Any such persons may, if they have not sufficient knowledge of English or French, be authorised by the President to speak in any other language.

Rule 39

1. After establishing the identity of the witnesses or experts the President or the principal delegate mentioned in Rule 34, paragraph 2, shall request them to take the following oath:
   a. for witnesses: 'I swear that I will speak the truth, the whole truth and nothing but the truth.'
   b. for experts: 'I swear that my statement will be in accordance with my sincere belief.'
2. Instead of taking the oath in the terms set out in paragraph 1 of this Rule, the witnesses or experts may make the following declaration:
   a. for witnesses: 'I solemnly declare upon my honour and conscience that I will speak the truth, the whole truth and nothing but the truth.'
   b. for experts: 'I solemnly declare upon my honour and conscience that my statement will be in accordance with my sincere belief.'

Rule 40

1. The President, or the principal delegate, shall conduct the hearing or examination of any persons heard. Any member may put questions to the parties or to the persons heard with the leave of the President or the principal delegate.
2. A party may, with the permission of the President or of the principal delegate, also put questions to any person heard.

Rule 41

1. The Secretary shall be responsible for the production of verbatim records of hearings before the Commission.
2. The parties or, where appropriate, their representatives shall receive a draft verbatim record of their submissions in order that they may propose corrections to the Secretary within a time limit laid down by the President. After necessary corrections, if any, the text shall constitute certified matters of record.

Rule 42

1. The expenses incurred by any person who is heard by the Commission as a witness at the request of a party shall be borne either by that party or by the Council of Europe, as the Commis-

sion may decide. Where it is decided that the expenses shall be borne by the Council of Europe, the amount shall be fixed by the President of the Commission.

2. The expenses incurred by any such person whom the Commission hears *proprio motu* shall be fixed by the President and be borne by the Council of Europe.

3. Where the Commission decides to obtain written experts' opinions, the costs, as agreed by the President, shall be borne by the Council of Europe.

4. Where the Commission decides to obtain written evidence, any costs incurred by the party who submits it shall be borne either by that party or by the Council of Europe, as the Commission may decide. Where it is decided that the costs shall be borne by the Council of Europe, the amount shall be agreed by the President of the Commission.

CHAPTER III

nstitution of proceedings

Rule 43

1. Any application made under Articles 24 or 25 of the Convention shall be submitted in writing and shall be signed by the applicant or by the applicant's representative.

2. Where an application is submitted by a non-governmental organisation or by a group of individuals, it shall be signed by those persons competent to represent such organisation or group. The Commission shall determine any question as to whether the persons who have signed an application are competent to do so.

3. Where applicants are represented in accordance with Rule 32 of these Rules, a power of attorney or written authorisation shall be supplied by their representative or representatives.

Rule 44

1. Any application under Article 25 of the Convention shall be made on the application form provided by the Secretariat, unless the President decides otherwise. It shall set out:

   a. the name, age, occupation and address of the applicant;

    b. the name, occupation and address of the representative, if any;
    c. the name of the High Contracting Party against which the application is made;
    d. the object of the application and the provision of the Convention alleged to have been violated;
    e. a statement of the facts and arguments;
    f. any relevant documents and in particular the decision, whether judicial or not, relating to the object of the application.
2. Applicants shall furthermore:
    a. provide information enabling it to be shown that the conditions laid down in Article 26 of the Convention have been satisfied;
    b. indicate whether they have submitted their complaints to any other procedure of international investigation or settlement;
    c. indicate in which of the official languages they wish to receive the Commission's decisions;
    d. indicate whether they do or do not object to their identity being disclosed to the public;
    e. declare that they will respect the confidentiality of the proceedings before the Commission.
3. Failure to comply with the requirements set out under paragraphs 1 and 2 above may result in the application not being registered and examined by the Commission.
4. The date of introduction of the application shall in general be considered to be the date of the first communication from the applicant setting out, even summarily, the object of the application. The Commission may nevertheless for good cause decide that a different date be considered to be the date of introduction.
5. Applicants shall keep the Commission informed of any change of their address and of all circumstances relevant to the application.

CHAPTER IV

Proceedings on admissibility

Rule 45

1. Where, pursuant to Article 24 of the Convention, an application is brought before the Commission by a High Contracting Party, the President of the Commission shall give notice of such application to the High Contracting Party against which the claim

is made and shall invite it to submit to the Commission its observations in writing on the admissibility of such application. The observations so obtained shall be communicated to the High Contracting Party which brought the application and it may submit written observations in reply.

2. The Commission shall designate one or more of its members to submit a report on admissibility. Rule 47, paragraph 3, is, by analogy, applicable to this report.

3. Before deciding upon the admissibility of the application the Commission may invite the parties to submit further observations, either in writing or at a hearing.

Rule 46

In any case of urgency, the Secretary to the Commission may, without prejudice to the taking of any other procedural steps, inform a High Contracting Party concerned in an application, by any available means, of the introduction of the application and of a summary of its objects.

Rule 47

1. Any application submitted pursuant to Article 25 of the Convention shall be referred to a member of the Commission who, as *rapporteur*, shall examine the application and submit a report to the Commission on its admissibility and a proposal on the procedure to be adopted.

2. *Rapporteurs*, in their examination of the application:
   a. may request relevant information on matters connected with the application from the applicant or the High Contracting Party concerned;
   b. shall communicate any information so obtained from the High Contracting Party to the applicant for comments;
   c. shall decide whether to refer the application to a Committee.

3. The report of the *rapporteur* on the admissibility of the application shall contain:
   a. a statement of the relevant facts, including any information or comments obtained under paragraph 2 of this Rule;
   b. if necessary, an indication of the issues arising under the Convention in the application;
   c. a proposal on admissibility and on any other action to be taken, as the case may require.

Rule 48

1. The Commission shall consider the report of the *rapporteur* and may declare at once that the application is inadmissible or to be struck off its list.

2. Alternatively, the Commission may:
   a. request relevant information on matters connected with the application from the applicant or the High Contracting Party concerned. Any information so obtained from the High Contracting Party shall be communicated to the applicant for comments;
   b. give notice of the application to the High Contracting Party against which it is brought and invite that Party to present to the Commission written observations on the application. Any observations so obtained shall be communicated to the applicant for any written observations in reply.

Rule 49

1. An application shall be referred to a Chamber unless it has been referred to a Committee under Rule 47, paragraph 2(c), or its examination by a Chamber is excluded under Article 20, paragraph 2, of the Convention.
2. Applications shall normally be referred to the Chamber which includes the member of the Commission elected in respect of the High Contracting Party against which the application has been made.
3. If there is a reasoned request from a party that the application should be referred to the Plenary Commission, that request shall be considered by the Plenary Commission.
4. The members of the Commission shall be informed of the decisions of the Chambers.

Rule 50

Before deciding upon the admissibility of the application, the Commission may invite the parties:
   a. to submit further observations in writing;
   b. to submit further observations orally at a hearing on issues of admissibility and at the same time, if the Commission so decides, on the merits of the application.

Rule 51

Time limits shall be fixed by the *rapporteur* for any information or comments requested under Rule 47, paragraph 2, and by the Commission for any information, observations or comments requested under Rule 48, paragraph 2, and under Rule 50.

Rule 52

1. The decision of the Commission shall be communicated by the Secretary of the Commission of the applicant and to the High Contracting Party or Parties concerned. However, in the case provided for in paragraph 1 of Rule 48 or where information has been obtained from the applicant only, the decision shall be communicated to the High Contracting Party or Parties concerned only at their request and provided that the Commission does not decide otherwise.
2. The decision of the Commission shall state whether it was taken unanimously or by majority and shall be accompanied or followed by reasons.

CHAPTER V

Procedure after the admission of an application

Rule 53

1. After deciding to admit an application, the Commission shall decide on the procedure to be followed:
   a. for the examination of the application under Article 28, paragraph 1(a), of the Convention;
   b. with a view to securing a friendly settlement under Article 28, paragraph 1(b), of the Convention.
2. In order to accomplish its tasks under Article 28, paragraph 1(a), of the Convention, the Commission may invite the parties to submit further evidence and observations.
3. The Commission shall decide in each case whether observations should be submitted in writing or orally at a hearing.
4. The President shall lay down the time limits within which the parties shall submit evidence and written observations.

Rule 54

1. The Commission shall appoint one or more of its members as *rapporteur*.
2. The *rapporteur* may at any stage of the examination of an application under Article 25 of the Convention invite the parties to submit further written evidence and observations.

3. The *rapporteur* shall:
   a. draft such memoranda as may be required by the Commission for its consideration of the case before it;
   b. draft a Report for the Commission in accordance with Rule 57, Rule 60 or Rule 62, as the case may be.

Rule 55

The Commission may, when it sees fit, deliberate with a view to reaching a provisional opinion on the merits of the case.

Rule 56

Where the Commission decides to reject an application under Article 29 of the Convention, its decision shall be accompanied by reasons. The Secretary shall communicate the decision to the parties.

CHAPTER VI

The Report of the Commission

Rule 57

1. The Report provided for in Article 28, paragraph 2, of the Convention shall contain:
   a. a description of the parties, their representatives and advisers;
   b. a statement of the facts;
   c. the terms of the settlement reached.
2. The Report shall also contain the names of the President and members participating and shall be signed by the President and the Secretary.
3. The Report shall be sent to the High Contracting Party or Parties concerned, to the Committee of Ministers and to the Secretary General of the Council of Europe for publication. It shall also be sent to the applicant.

Rule 58

1. When the Commission has found that no friendly settlement in accordance with Article 28, paragraph (b), of the Convention can

be reached, it shall consider a draft Report drawn up by the *rapporteur* on the basis of any provisional opinion reached by the Commission in its deliberations under Rule 55.

2. Where the Commission has been divided in its provisional opinion, the draft Report shall include alternative opinions, if the Commission so decides.

Rule 59

1. When the Commission considers the draft Report referred to in Rule 58, it shall adopt in the first place the parts of the Report in which it establishes the facts.

2. It shall then deliberate and vote on whether the facts found disclose any violation by the State concerned of its obligations under the Convention.

3. Only those members who have participated in the deliberations and votes provided for in this Rule shall be entitled to express their separate opinion in the Report.

Rule 60

1. The Report provided for in Article 31 of the Convention shall contain:
   a. a description of the parties, their representatives and advisers;
   b. a statement of the proceedings followed before the Commission;
   c. a statement of the facts established;
   d. the complaints declared admissible;
   e. the opinion of the Commission, with an indication of the number of members forming the majority, as to whether or not the facts found disclose any breach by the State concerned of its obligations under the Convention;
   f. the reasons upon which that opinion is based;
   g. any separate opinion of a member of the Commission.

2. The Report shall contain the names of the President and the members participating in the deliberations and vote provided for in Rule 59, paragraph 2. It shall be signed by the President and by the Secretary.

3. It shall be sent, together with any proposal under Article 31, paragraph 3, of the Convention, to the Committee of Ministers and to the High Contracting Party or Parties concerned.

Rule 61

1. After the adoption of the Report, drawn up under Article 31 of the Convention, the Plenary Commission shall decide whether or

not to bring the case before the European Court of Human Rights under Article 48(a) of the Convention.

2. Where the Commission decides to bring the case before the Court, it shall file its request with the Registry of the Court within three months after the transmission of the Report to the Committee of Ministers. It shall also inform the Committee of Ministers and parties to the application.

3. Where the Commission decides not to bring the case before the Court, it shall so inform the Court, the Committee of Ministers and the parties to the application.

Rule 62

1. The Report provided for in Article 30, paragraph 2, of the Convention shall contain:
   a. a description of the parties, their representatives and advisers;
   b. a statement of the facts;
   c. a brief account of the proceedings;
   d. the terms of the decision striking out the application together with the reasons therefor.

2. The Report shall contain the names of the President and members who participated in the decision striking out the application. It shall be signed by the President and by the Secretary.

3. It shall be communicated to the Committee of Ministers of the Council of Europe for information and to the parties. The Commission may publish it.

TITLE IV

Relations of the Commission with the Court

Rule 63

1. The Commission shall assist the European Court of Human Rights in any case brought before the Court. When a case is referred to the Court the Commission shall appoint, at a plenary session, one or more delegates to take part in the consideration of

the case before the Court. These delegates may be assisted by any person appointed by the Commission. In discharging their functions they shall act in accordance with such directives as they may receive from the Commission.

2. Until delegates have been appointed, the President may, if consulted by the Court, express views upon the procedure to be followed before the Court.

Rule 64

1. When, in pursuance of Article 48(a) of the Convention, the Commission decides to bring a case before the Court, it shall draw up a request indicating in particular:
   a. the parties to the proceedings before the Commission;
   b. the date on which the Commission adopted its Report;
   c. the date on which the Report was transmitted to the Committee of Ministers;
   d. the object of the request;
   e. the names and addresses of its delegates.
2. The Secretary of the Commission shall transmit to the Registry of the Court forty copies of the request referred to in paragraph 1 of this Rule.

Rule 65

When, in pursuance of Article 48(b), (c) or (d) of the Convention, a High Contracting Party brings a case before the Court, the Secretary of the Commission shall communicate to the Registry of the Court as soon as possible:
   a. the names and addresses of the Commission's delegates;
   b. any other information wihch the Commission may consider appropriate.

Rule 66

The Secretary to the Commission shall, as soon as the request referred to in Rule 64, paragraph 2, *above*, has been transmitted or the communication mentioned in Rule 33, paragraph 1(c), of the Rules of Court, has been received, file with the Registry of the Court an adequate number of copies of the Commission's Report.

Rule 67

The Commission shall communicate to the Court, at its request, any memorial, evidence, document or information concerning the case, with the exception of documents relating to the attempt to secure a friendly settlement in accordance with Article 28, paragraph 1(b), of the Convention. The communication of those documents shall be subject in each case to a decision of the Commission.

Appendix 4

RULES ADOPTED BY THE COMMITTEE OF MINISTERS ARTICLES 32 AND 54

Strasbourg, February 1, 1991

[RULES ADOPTED BY THE COMMITTEE OF MINISTERS FOR THE APPLICATION OF ARTICLE 32 OF THE EUROPEAN CONVENTION ON HUMAN RIGHTS]

(Text approved by the Committee of Ministers at the 181st meeting of the Ministers' Deputies in June 1969 (1) and amended at the 215th (November 1972) 24th (May 1975), 307th (September 1979), 409th (June 1987), 449th (December 1990) and 451st (January 1991) meetings)
[The text approved at the 181st meeting of the Ministers' Deputies contained a restatement of the Rules previously adopted at the 68th (January 1959), 94th (January 1961), 99th (May 1961), 140th (April 1965) and 164th (October 1967) meetings.]

Rules of substance

Rule 1

When exercising its functions under Article 32 of the Convention, the Committee of Ministers is entitled to discuss the substance of any case on which the Commission has submitted a report, for example by considering written or oral statements of the parties and hearing of witnesses (*see* Rule 4).

Rule 2

The representative of any Member State on the Committee of Ministers shall be fully qualified to take part in exercising the functions and powers set forth in Article 32 of the Convention, even if that State has not yet ratified the Convention.

Rule 3

Each representative on the Committee of Ministers has an intrinsic right to make submissions and deposit documents. Consequently, the representative on the Committee of Ministers of a government which was not a party to the proceedings before the Commission, may play a full part in the proceedings before the Committee of Ministers (*see* Appendix, para. 1).

Rule 4

While the Committee of Ministers must have all the necessary powers to reach a decision on a report of the Commission, nevertheless, it may not itself wish to undertake the task of taking evidence, etc., should the need arise. The procedure to be followed in such a case will be decided *ad hoc* (*see* Appendix, para. 2).

Rule 5

The provisions of paragraph 2 of Article 32 enable the Committee of Ministers, in cases where it has decided that there has been a violation, to give advice or make suggestions or recommendations to the state concerned, provided that these are closely related to the violation. Such advice, suggestions or recommendations, whether based on proposals made by the Commission or not, would not be binding on the government to which they are addressed because they would not constitute decisions within the meaning of paragraph 4 of Article 32 (*see* Appendix, para. 2).

Rule 6

The Committee of Ministers considers that the Commission is not entitled to make proposals under Article 31, paragraph 3, of the Convention in cases where it considers that there has not been a violation of the Convention.

Rule 6*bis*

Prior to taking a decision under Article 32, paragraph 1, of the Convention, the Committee of Ministers may be informed of a friendly settlement, arrangement or other fact of a kind to provide a solution of the matter. In that event, it may decide to discontinue its examination of the case, after satisfying itself that the solution envisaged is based on respect for human rights as defined in the Convention.

Procedural Rules

Rule 7

If the chairmanship of the Committee of Ministers is held by the representative of a state which is party to a dispute referred to the Committee of Ministers, that representative shall step down from the chair during the discussion of the Commission's report.

Rule 8

The Chairman of the Committee shall obtain the opinion of the representatives of the State Party or States Parties to the dispute in regard to the procedure to be followed, and the Committee shall specify, if necessary, in what order and within what time limits any written submissions or other documents are to be deposited (this Rule applies not only to interstate disputes but also when the Committee of Ministers is considering the report of the Commission on an individual application).

Rule 9

1. During the examination of the case and before taking the decision mentioned in Article 32, paragraph 1, of the Convention, the Committee of Ministers may, if it deems advisable, request the Commission for information on particular points in the report which it has transmitted to the Committee.
2. After taking a decision under Article 32, paragraph 1, to the effect that there has been a violation of the Convention, the Committee of Ministers may request the Commission to make proposals concerning in particular the appropriateness, nature and extent of just satisfaction for the injured party.

Rule 9*bis*

When a vote is taken in accordance with Article 32, paragraph 1, and the majority required to decide whether there has been a violation of the Convention has not been attained, a second and final vote shall be taken at one of the three following meetings of the Committee of Ministers.

Rule 9*ter*

1. The Commission's report shall be published when the Committee of Ministers has completed consideration of the case under Article 32, paragraph 1.
2. The Committee of Ministers may, by way of exception and without prejudice to Article 32, paragraph 3, decide not to publish a report of the Commission or a part thereof upon a reasoned request of a Contracting Party or of the Commission.

Rule 10

In the matter of voting, the Rules laid down in Article 20 of the Statute should, in general, apply. (In the case of a decision by the Committee of Ministers on the question whether there has been a violation of the Convention, paragraph 1 of Article 32 of the Convention already provides that 'the Committee of Ministers shall decide by a majority of two-thirds of the members entitled to sit on the Committee whether there has been a violation of the Convention'). In particular:
  a. the parties to the dispute shall have the right to vote;
  b. any advice, suggestions or recommendations offered or made in accordance with Rule 5 above and decisions taken in pursuance of Rule 6 *bis* require a two-thirds majority of the representatives casting a vote and a majority of the representatives entitled to sit on the Committee;
  c. certain questions of procedure, such as in what order and within what time limits any written submissions or other documents are to be deposited, shall be determined by a simple majority of the representatives entitled to sit on the Committee.

Rule 11

The decision taken under Article 32, paragraph 1, will be published in the form of a Resolution adopted by a two-thirds majority of the representatives casting a vote and a majority of the representatives entitled to sit on the Committee.

APPENDIX

Other points discussed by the Committee of Ministers

1. With reference to Rule 3 *above*, the Committee of Ministers reserved its position on the possibility that the representative of a government which had not been a party to the proceedings before the Commission might make a request to the Committee of Ministers which had not been made before the Commission (for example, a request for damages).

2. In connection with Rule 4, the Committee of Ministers considered that while it must have all the necessary powers to reach a decision on a case submitted to it, nevertheless it is not well-equipped to take evidence, etc., and ought not normally to undertake such tasks. If therefore it should become necessary for the Committee of Ministers to take evidence, etc., when it is considering a case under Article 32, there are the following possibilities:

    a. to conclude a Protocol to the Convention conferring on the Commission the power to undertake such tasks on behalf of the Committee of Ministers;

    b. to invite the Commission to undertake these tasks on its behalf, since the Commission is in its nature better equipped to do so, if the Commission agrees to this procedure;

    c. the Committee of Ministers could take evidence, etc., in plenary sessions (possibly with alternate members) or appoint a sub-committee for the purpose;

    d. under Article 17 of the Statute, the Committee of Ministers may set up advisory and technical committees for specific purposes.

The Committee of Ministers decided not to adopt the first of these possibilities but to leave the choice open for a decision *ad hoc* should the need arise.

2. *bis* In connection with Rule 5, the Committee of Ministers decided that in every case in which it finds there has been a violation of the Convention, it would consider, taking into account any proposals from the Commission, whether just satisfaction should be afforded to the injured party and, if necessary, indicate measures on this subject to the State concerned.

3. *a.* The Committee of Ministers decided not to establish a procedure permitting the communication to an applicant of the report of the Commission on his application, or the communication to the Committee of Ministers of the applicant's observations on the report.

    b. The communication to an individual applicant of the complete text or extracts for the report of the Commission should take place only as an exceptional measure (for example, where the Committee of Ministers wishes to obtain the observations of the applicant), only on a strictly confidential basis, and only with the consent of the State against which the application was lodged.

    c. Since the individual applicant is not a party to the proceedings before the Committee of Ministers under Article 32 of the Convention, he has no right to be heard by the Committee of Ministers or to have any written communication considered by the Committee.

       This should be explained by the Secretary General to the applicant when he writes to inform him that the report of the Commission on his case has been transmitted to the Committee of Ministers in accordance with the provisions of Article 31 of the Convention.

    d. If communications from the individual applicant intended for the Committee of Ministers are nevertheless received, the Secretary General should acknowledge their receipt and explain to the applicant why they will not form part of the proceedings before the Committee of Ministers and cannot be considered as a document in the case. In appropriate cases, the Secretary General might add that it is possible for the applicant to submit a new application to the Commission if he wishes to invoke important new information.

4. The Committee of Ministers decided not to make provisions in its Rules for participation by delegates of the Commission in its proceedings, since the Commission considered that such participation would be outside its powers as defined in the Convention (at the 245th meeting of the Ministers' Deputies (May 1975), the Deputies agreed, unless otherwise decided in a particular case, to transmit to the European Commission of Human Rights, at the end of their discussions on a case referred to the Committee of Ministers in accordance with Article 32 of the European Convention on Human Rights, the texts of every decision appearing in their Conclusions, on the understanding that these texts are not made public; they agreed also that this decision cannot be regarded as a precedent with regard to other decisions of the Committee).

* * *

The Committee of Ministers at the 307th meeting of the Ministers' Deputies (September 1979) adopted the following additional Rules:

a. an individual applicant ought normally to be informed of the outcome of the examination of his case before the Committee of Ministers. It would be for the Committee of Ministers to decide in each particular case on the information to be communicated and on the procedure to be followed;

b. a decision to inform an individual applicant about the outcome of his case should be taken, in accordance with Article 21.b of the Statute, by unanimous vote;

c. the Committee of Ministers could indicate in its communication to the applicant if any of the information conveyed to him is to be treated as confidential.

[RULES ADOPTED BY THE COMMITTEE OF MINISTERS CONCERNING THE APPLICATION OF ARTICLE 54 OF THE EUROPEAN CONVENTION ON HUMAN RIGHTS]

(Text approved by the Committee of Ministers of the 254th Meeting of the Ministers' Deputies in February 1976)

Rule 1

When a judgment of the Court is transmitted to the Committee of Ministers in accordance with Article 54 of the Convention, the case shall be inscribed on the agenda of the Committee without delay.

Rule 2

a. When, in the judgment transmitted to the Committee of Ministers in accordance with Article 54 of the Convention, the Court decides that there has been a violation of the Convention and/or affords just satisfaction to the injured party under Article 50 of the Convention, the Committee shall invite the state concerned to inform it of the measures which it has taken in consequence of the judgment, having regard to its obligation under Article 53 of the Convention to abide by the judgment (at the 215th meeting of the Ministers' Deputies (November 1972), it was agreed that the Committee of Ministers is entitled to consider a communication from an individual who claims that he has not received damages in accordance with a decision of the Court under Article 50 of the Convention affording him just satisfaction as an injured party, as well as any further information furnished to it concerning the execution of such a judgment of the Court, and that, consequently, any such communication should be distributed to the Committee of Ministers).

b. If the State concerned informs the Committee of Ministers that it is not yet in a position to inform it of the measures taken, the case shall be automatically inscribed on the agenda of a meeting of the Committee taking place not more than six months later, unless the Committee of Ministers decides otherwise; the same Rule will be applied on expiration of this and any subsequent period.

Rule 3

The Committee of Ministers shall not regard its functions under Article 54 of the Convention as having been exercised until it has taken note of the information supplied in accordance with Rule 2 and, where just satisfaction has been afforded, until it has satisfied itself that the State concerned has awarded this just satisfaction to the injured party

Rule 4

The decision in which the Committee of Ministers declares that its functions under Article 54 of the Convention have been exercised shall take the form of a Resolution.

Appendix 5

RULES OF THE EUROPEAN COURT OF HUMAN RIGHTS

As in force of April 20, 1992
The European Court of Human Rights,
Having regard to the Convention for the Protection of Human Rights
and Fundamental Freedoms and the Protocols thereto,
Makes the present Rules:

CHAPTER IV

The working of the court

Rule 15

SEAT OF THE COURT

The seat of the European Court of Human Rights shall be at the seat
of the Council of Europe at Strasbourg. The Court may, however, if it
considers it expedient, exercise its functions elsewhere in the territories
of the Member States of the Council of Europe.

Rule 16

SESSIONS OF THE PLENARY COURT

The plenary sessions of the Court shall be convened by the President
whenever the exercise of its functions under the Convention and under
these Rules so requires. The President shall convene a plenary session
if at least one third of the members of the Court so request, and in any
event once a year to consider administrative matters.

Rule 17

QUORUM

1. The quorum of the plenary Court shall be 12 judges.
2. If there is no quorum, the President shall adjourn the sitting.

Rule 18

PUBLIC CHARACTER OF THE HEARINGS

The hearings shall be public unless the Court shall in exceptional circumstances decide otherwise.

Rule 19

DELIBERATIONS

1. The Court shall deliberate in private. Its deliberations shall remain secret.
2. Only the judges shall take part in the deliberations. The Registrar or his substitute, as well as such other officials of the registry and interpreters whose assistance is deemed necessary, shall be present. No other person may be admitted except by special decision of the Court.
3. Each judge present at such deliberations shall state his opinion and the reasons therefor.
4. Any question which is to be voted upon shall be formulated in precise terms in the two official languages and the text shall, if a judge so requests, be distributed before the vote is taken.
5. The minutes of the private sittings of the Court for deliberations shall remain secret; they shall be limited to a record of the subject of the discussions, the votes taken, the names of those voting for and against a motion and any statements expressly made for insertion in the minutes.

Rule 20

VOTES

1. The decisions of the Court shall be taken by the majority of judges present.

2. The votes shall be cast in the inverse order to the order of precedence provided for in Rule 5.
3. If the voting is equal, the President shall have a second and casting vote.

CHAPTER V

THE CHAMBERS

Rule 21

COMPOSITION OF THE COURT WHEN CONSTITUTED IN A CHAMBER

1. [As amended by the Court on May 23, 1990.] When a case is brought before the Court either by the Commission or by a Contracting State having the right to do so under Article 48 of the Convention, the Court shall be constituted in a Chamber of nine judges.
2. On the reference of a case to the Court, the Registrar shall notify all the judges, including the newly-elected judges, that such a Chamber is to be constituted. If any judge, upon receiving such notification, believes that for one of the reasons set out in Rule 24 he will be unable to sit, he shall so inform the Registrar. The President shall then draw up the list of judges available to constitute the Chamber.
3. There shall sit as members *ex officio* of the Chamber:
   (a) in accordance with Article 43 of the Convention, every judge who has the nationality of a Party;
   (b) the President of the Court, or, failing him, the Vice-President, provided that they do not sit by virtue of the preceding sub-paragraph.
4. The other judges named on the list provided for in paragraph 2 shall be called upon to complete the Chamber, as members or as substitutes, in the order determined by a drawing of lots effected by the President of the Court in the presence of the Registrar.
5. The President of the Chamber shall be the judge sitting by virtue of paragraph 3(b) or, failing one, a judge appointed under paragraph 4 as a member of the Chamber, in accordance with the order of precedence provided for in Rule 5.

   If the President of the Chamber is unable to sit or withdraws, he shall be replaced by the Vice-President or, if the same applies

267

to him, by a judge appointed under paragraph 4 as a member of the Chamber, in accordance with the said order of precedence. However, where he is unable to to sit or withdraws less than twenty-four hours before the opening of, or during or after, the hearings, his place shall be taken, in accordance with the said order of precedence, by one of the judges called upon to be present or present at the hearings.

6. If the President of the Court finds that two cases concern the same Party or Parties and raise similar issues, he may refer the second case to the Chamber already constituted, or in the course of constitution, for the consideration of the first case or, if there is none, proceed to the constitution of one Chamber to consider both cases.

Rule 22

SUBSTITUTE JUDGES

1. The substitute judges shall be called upon, in the order determined by the drawing of lots, or replace the judges appointed as members of the Chamber by virtue of Rule 21, paragraph 4.
2. Judges who have been so replaced shall cease to be members of the Chamber.
3. The substitute judges shall be supplied with the documents relating to the proceedings. The President may convoke one or more of them, according to the above order of precedence, to attend the hearings and deliberations.

Rule 23

AD HOC JUDGES

1. If the Court does not include an elected judge having the nationality of a Party or if the judge called upon to sit in that capacity is unable to sit or withdraws, the President of the Court shall invite that Party to inform him within 30 days whether it wishes to appoint to sit as judge either another elected judge or, as an *ad hoc* judge, any other person possessing the qualifications required under Article 39, paragraph 3 of the Convention and, if so, to state at the same time the name of the person so appointed. The same rule shall apply if the person so appointed is unable to sit or withdraws.

2. The Party concerned shall be presumed to have waived such right of appointment if it does not reply within 30 days.
3. An *ad hoc* judge shall, at the opening of the first sitting fixed for the consideration of the case after he has been appointed, take the oath or make the solemn declation provided for in Rule 3. This act shall be recorded in minutes.

Rule 24

NABILITY TO SIT, WITHDRAWAL OR EXEMPTION

1. Any judge who is prevented from taking part in sittings for which he has been convoked shall, as soon as possible, give notice thereof to the President of the Chamber or to the Registrar.
2. A judge may not take part in the consideration of any case in which he has a personal interest or has previously acted either as the agent, advocate or adviser of a Party or of a person having an interest in the case, or as member of a tribunal or commission of enquiry, or in any other capacity.
3. If a judge withdraws for one of the said reasons, or for some special reason, he shall inform the President who shall exempt him from sitting.
4. If the President considers that a reason exists for a judge to withdraw, he shall consult with the judge concerned; in the event of disagreement, the Court shall decide.
5. Any judge who has been called upon to sit on one or more recent cases may, at his own request, be exempted by the President from sitting on a new case.

Rule 25

COMMON INTEREST

1. [As amended by the Court on May 23, 1991.] If several Parties have a common interest, the President of the Court may invite them to agree to appoint a single elected judge or *ad hoc* judge in accordance with Article 43 of the Convention. If the Parties are unable to agree, the President shall choose by lot, from among the persons proposed as judges by these Parties, the judge called upon to sit *ex officio*. The names of the other judges and substitute judges shall then be chosen by lot by the President from among the elected judges who are not nationals of any of these Parties.

2. In the event of dispute as to the existence of a common interest, the plenary Court shall decide.

TITLE II

Procedure

CHAPTER I

General rules

Rule 26

POSSIBILITY OF PARTICULAR DEROGATIONS

The provisions of this Title shall not prevent the Court from derogating from them for the consideration of a particular case with the agreement of the Party or Parties and after having consulted the Delegates of the Commission and the applicant.

Rule 27

OFFICIAL LANGUAGES

1. The official languages of the Court shall be English and French.
2. A Party may, not later than the consultation provided for in Rule 38, apply to the President for leave to use another language at the oral hearings. If such leave is granted by the President, the Party concerned shall be responsible for the interpretation into English or French of the oral arguments or statements made by its Agent, advocates or advisers and shall, to the extent which the President may determine in each case, bear the other extra expense involved in the use of a non-official language.
3. The President may grant the applicant, as well as any person assisting the Delegates under Rule 29, paragraph 1, leave to use a non-official language. In that event, the Registrar shall make th

necessary arrangements for the translation or interpretation into English and French of their comments or statements.

4. Any witness, expert or other person appearing before the Court may use his own language if he does not have sufficient knowledge of either of the two official languages. The Registrar shall, in that event, make the necessary arrangements for the interpretation into English and French of the statements of the witness, expert or other person concerned.

5. All judgments shall be given in English and in French; unless the Court decides otherwise, both texts shall be authentic.

Rule 28

REPRESENTATION OF THE PARTIES

The Parties shall be represented by Agents who may have the assistance of advocates or advisers.

Rule 29

RELATIONS BETWEEN THE COURT AND THE COMMISSION AND RELEASE OF THE REPORT OF THE COMMISSION

1. The Commission shall delegate one or more of its members to take part in the consideration of a case before the Court. The Delegates may be assisted by other persons.
2. The Court shall, whether a case is referred to it by a Contracting Party or by the Commission, take into consideration the report of the latter.
3. Unless the President decides otherwise, the said report shall be made available to the public through the Registrar as soon as possible after the case has been brought before the Court.

Rule 30

REPRESENTATION OF THE APPLICANT

1. The applicant shall be represented by an advocate authorised to practice in any of the Contracting States and resident in the

territory of one of them, or by any other person approved by the President. The President may, however, give leave to the applicant to present his own case, subject, if need be, to his being assisted by an advocate or other person as aforesaid.

2. Unless the President decides otherwise, the advocate or other person representing or assisting the applicant, or the applicant himself if he seeks leave to present his own case, must have an adequate knowledge of one of the Court's official languages.

Rule 31

COMMUNICATIONS, NOTIFICATIONS AND SUMMONSES ADDRESSED TO PERSONS OTHER THAN THE AGENTS OF THE PARTIES OR THE DELEGATES OF THE COMMISSION

1. If, for any communication, notification or summons addressed to persons other than the Agents of the Parties or the Delegates of the Commission, the Court considers it necessary to have the assistance of the Government of the State on whose territory such communication, notification or summons is to have effect, the President shall apply directly to that Government in order to obtain the necessary facilities.

2. The same rule shall apply when the Court desires to make or arrange for the making of an investigation on the spot in order to establish the facts or to procure evidence or when it orders the appearance of a person resident in, or having to cross, that territory.

CHAPTER II

Institution of proceedings

Rule 32

FILING OF THE APPLICATION OR REQUEST

1. Any Contracting Party which intends to bring a case before the Court under Article 48 of the Convention shall file with the registry an application, in forty copies, indicating:

(a) the parties to the proceedings before the Commission;

(b) the date on which the Commission adopted its report;

(c) the date on which the report was transmitted to the Committee of Ministers;

(d) the object of the application;

(e) the name and address of the person appointed as Agent.

2. If the Commission intends to bring a case before the Court under Article 48 of the Convention, it shall file with the registry a request, in forty copies, signed by its President and containing the particulars indicated in sub-paragraphs (a), (b), (c) and (d) of paragraph 1 of this Rule together with the names and addresses of the Delegates of the Commission.

Rule 33

COMMUNICATION OF THE APPLICATION ON REQUEST

1. On receipt of an application or request, the Registrar shall transmit a copy thereof:

(a) to the President, Vice-President and judges; and also, as the case may be,

(b) to any Contracting Party mentioned in Article 48 of the Convention;

(c) to the Commission;

(d) to the person, non-governmental organisation or group of individuals who lodged the complaint with the Commission under Article 25 of the Convention.

He shall also inform the Committee of Ministers, through the Secretary General of the Council of Europe, of the filing of the application or request.

2. The communications provided for in sub-paragraphs (a), (b) and (d) of paragraph 1 shall include a copy of the report of the Commission.

3. When making the communications provided for in sub-paragraphs (b), (c) and (d) of paragraph 1, the Registrar shall invite:

(a) the Contracting Party against which the complaint has been lodged before the Commission to notify him within two weeks of the name and address of its Agent;

(b) any other Contracting Party which appears to have the right, under Article 48 of the Convention, to bring a case before the Court and which has not availed itself of that right, to inform him within four weeks whether it wishes to take part in the proceedings and, if so, to notify him at the same time of the name and address of its Agent;

(c) the Commission to notify him as soon as possible of the names and addresses of its Delegates;

(d) the person, non-governmental organisation or group of individuals who lodged the complaint with the Commission under Article 25 of Convention to notify him within two weeks:

- whether he or it wishes to take part in the proceedings pending before the Court;
- if so, of the name and address of the person appointed by him or it in accordance with Rule 30.

Rule 34

QUESTION WHETHER A CONTRACTING PARTY HAS THE RIGHT TO BRING A CASE BEFORE THE COURT

In the event of doubt or dispute as to whether a Contracting Party has the right under Article 48 of the Convention to bring a case before the Court, the President shall submit that question to the plenary Court for decision.

Rule 35

NOTICE OF THE COMPOSITION OF THE CHAMBER

As soon as a Chamber has been constituted for the consideration of a case, the Registrar shall communicate its composition to the judges, to the Agents of the Parties, to the Commission and to the applicant.

Rule 36

INTERIM MEASURES

1. [As amended by the Court on January 26, 1989.] Before the constitution of a Chamber, the President of the Court may, at the request of a Party, of the Commission, of the applicant or of any other person concerned, or *proprio motu*, indicate to any Party and, where appropriate, the applicant, any interim measure which it is advisable for them to adopt. The Chamber when

constituted or, if the Chamber is not in session, its President shall have the same power.

Notice of these measures shall be immediately given to the Committee of Ministers.

2. Where the Commission, pursuant to Rule 36 of its Rules of Procedure, has indicated an interim measure as desirable, its adoption or maintenance shall remain recommended to the Parties and, where appropriate, the applicant after the case has been brought before the Court, unless and until the President or the Chamber otherwise decides or until paragraph 1 of this Rule is applied.

CHAPTER III

Examination of cases

Rule 37

WRITTEN PROCEDURE

1. [As amended by the Court on January 26, 1989 and May 23, 1991.] The proceedings before the Court shall, as a general rule, comprise as their first stage a written procedure in which memorials are filed by the Parties, the applicant and, if it so wishes, the Commission.

As soon as possible after the reference of a case to the Court, the President shall consult the Agents of the Parties, the applicant and the Delegates of the Commission, or, if the latter have not yet been appointed, the President of the Commission, as to the organisation of the procedure; unless, with their agreement, he directs that a written procedure is to be dispensed with, he shall lay down the time limits for the filing of the memorials.

No memorial or other document may be filed except within such time limit (if any) or with the authorisation of the President or at his or the Chamber's request.

2. The President may, in the interest of the proper administration of justice, invite or grant leave to any Contracting State which is not a Party to the proceedings to submit written comments within a time limit and on issues which he shall specify. He may extend such an invitation or grant such leave to any person concerned other than the applicant.

3. Where two cases have been referred to the same Chamber under Rule 21, paragraph 6, the President of the Chamber may, in the interest of the proper administration of justice and after consulting the Agents of the Parties, the Delegates of the Commission and the applicants, order that the proceedings in both cases be conducted simultaneously, without prejudice to the decision of the Chamber on the joinder of the cases.

4. Memorials, comments and documents annexed thereto shall be filed with the registry; they shall be filed in forty copies when they are submitted by a Party, by another state or by the Commission. The Registrar shall transmit copies thereof to the judges, to the Agents of the Parties, to the Delegates of the Commission and to the applicant, as the case may be.

Rule 38

FIXING OF THE DATE OF THE OPENING OF THE ORAL PROCEEDINGS

The President of the Chamber shall, after consulting the Agents of the Parties, the Delegates of the Commission and the applicant, fix the date of the opening of the oral proceedings. The Registrar shall notify them of the decision taken in this respect.

Rule 39

CONDUCT OF THE HEARINGS

The President of the Chamber shall direct the hearings. He shall prescribe the order in which the Agents, advocates or advisers of the Parties, the Delegates of the Commission, any person assisting the Delegates in accordance with Rule 29, paragraph 1 and the applicant shall be called upon to speak.

Rule 40

FAILURE TO APPEAR AT THE HEARINGS

[Inserted by the Court on January 26, 1989. As a result, the subsequent Rules were renumbered and certain cross-references amended.]

Where, without showing sufficient cause, a Party or the applicant fails to appear, the Chamber may, provided that it is satisfied that such a course is consistent with the proper administration of justice, proceed with the hearings.

Rule 41

MEASURES FOR TAKING EVIDENCE

1. The Chamber may, at the request of a Party, of the Delegates of the Commission, of the applicant or of a third party invited or granted leave to submit written comments under Rule 37, paragraph 2, or *proprio motu*, obtain any evidence which it considers capable of providing clarification on the facts of the case. The Chamber may, *inter alia*, decide to hear as a witness or expert or in any other capacity any person whose evidence or statements seem likely to assist it in the carrying out of its task.

   When the Chamber is not in session, the President of the Chamber may exercise, by way of preparatory measure, the powers set forth in the immediately foregoing sub-paragraph, without prejudice to the decision of the Chamber on the relevance of the evidence so taken or sought.
2. The Chamber may ask any person or institution of its choice to obtain information, express an opinion or make a report, upon any specific point.
3. Where a report drawn up in accordance with the preceding paragraphs has been prepared at the request of a Party, the costs relating thereto shall be borne by that Party unless the Chamber decides otherwise. In other cases, the Chamber shall decide whether such costs are to be borne by the Council of Europe, or awarded against an applicant, or a third party, at whose request the report was prepared. In all cases, the costs shall be taxed by the President.
4. The Chamber may, at any time during the proceedings, depute one or more of its members to conduct an enquiry, carry out an investigation on the spot or take evidence in some other manner.

Rule 42

CONVOCATION OF WITNESSES, EXPERTS AND OTHER PERSONS; COSTS OF THEIR APPEARANCE

1. Witnesses, experts or other persons whom the Chamber or the

277

President of the Chamber decides to hear shall be summoned by the Registrar. If they appear at the request of a Party, the costs of their appearance shall be borne by that Party unless the Chamber decides otherwise. In other cases, the Chamber shall decide whether such costs are to be borne by the Council of Europe or awarded against an applicant, or a third party within the meaning of Rule 41, paragraph 1, at whose request the person summoned appeared. In all cases, the costs shall, if need be, be taxed by the President.

2. The summons shall indicate:
   - the case in connection with which it has been issued;
   - the object of the enquiry, expert opinion or other measure ordered by the Chamber or the President of the Chamber;
   - any provisions for the payment of the sum due to the person summoned.

Rule 43

OATH OR SOLEMN DECLARATION BY WITNESSES AND EXPERTS

1. After the establishment of his identity and before giving evidence, every witness shall take the following oath or make the following solemn declaration:

   'I swear'–or 'I solemnly declare upon my honour and conscience'–'that I will speak the truth, the whole truth and nothing but the truth.'

This act shall be recorded in minutes.

2. After the establishment of his identity and before carrying out his task, every expert shall take the following oath or make the following solemn declaration:

   'I swear'—or 'I solemnly declare–that I will discharge my duty as expert honourably and conscientiously'.

This act shall be recorded in minutes.

This oath may be taken or this declaration made before the President of the Chamber, or before a judge or any public authority nominated by the President.

Rule 44

OBJECT TO A WITNESS OR EXPERT; HEARING OF A PERSON FOR PURPOSE OF INFORMATION

The Chamber shall decide in the event of any dispute arising from an objection to a witness or expert. It may hear for the purpose of information a person who cannot be heard as a witness.

Rule 45

QUESTIONS PUT DURING THE HEARINGS

1. The President or any judge may put questions to the Agents, advocates or advisers of the Parties, to the witnesses and experts, to the Delegates of the Commission, to the applicant and to any other persons appearing before the Chamber.
2. The witnesses, experts and other persons referred to in Rule 41, paragraph 1 may, subject to the control of the President, be examined by the Agents, advocates or advisers of the Parties, by the Delegates of the Commission, by any person assisting the Delegates in accordance with Rule 29, paragraph 1, and by the applicant. In the event of an objection as to the relevance of a question put, the Chamber shall decide.

Rule 46

FAILURE TO APPEAR OR FALSE EVIDENCE

When, without good reason, a witness or any other person who has been duly summoned fails to appear or refuses to give evidence, the Registrar shall, on being so required by the President, inform that Contracting Party to whose jurisdiction such witness or other person is subject. The same provisions shall apply when a witness or expert has, in the opinion of the Chamber, violated the oath or solemn declaration provided for in Rule 43.

Rule 47

VERBATIM RECORD OF HEARINGS

1. The Registrar shall be responsible for the making of a verbatim record of each hearing. The verbatim record shall include:
   (a) the composition of the Chamber at the hearing;
   (b) a list of those appearing before the Court, that is to say, Agents, advocates and advisers of the Parties, Delegates of the

Commission and persons assisting them, applicants, Contracting States and other persons referred to in Rule 37, paragraph 2;

(c) the surnames, forenames, description and residence of each witness, expert or other person heard;

(d) the text of statements made, questions put and replies given;

(e) the text of any decision delivered by the Chamber during the hearing.

2. The Agents, advocates and advisers of the Parties, the Delegates of the Commission, the applicant and the witnesses, experts and other persons mentioned in Rules 29, paragraph 1 and 41, paragraph 1 shall receive the verbatim record of their arguments, statements or evidence, in order that they may, subject to the control of the Registrar or the President of the Chamber, make corrections, but in no case may such corrections affect the sense and bearing of what was said. The Registrar, in accordance with the instructions of the President, shall fix the time limits granted for this purpose.

3. [As amended by the Court on January 26, 1989.] The verbatim record, once so corrected, shall be signed by the President and the Registrar and shall then constitute certified matters of record.

Rule 48

PRELIMINARY OBJECTIONS

1. A Party wishing to raise a preliminary objection must file a statement setting out the objection and the grounds therefor not later than the time when that Party informs the President of its intention not to submit a memorial or, alternatively, not later than the expiry of the time limit laid down under Rule 37, paragraph 1 for the filing of its first memorial.

2. Unless the Chamber decides otherwise, the filing of a preliminary objection shall not have the effect of suspending the proceedings on the merits. In all cases, the Chamber shall, after following the procedure provided for under Chapter III herein, give its decision on the objection or join the objection to the merits.

Rule 49

STRIKING OUT OF THE LIST

1. When the Party which has brought the case before the Court

notifies the Registrar of its intention not to proceed with the case and when the other Parties agree to such discontinuance, the Chamber shall, after consulting the Commission and the applicant, decide whether or not it is appropriate to approve the discontinuance and accordingly to strike the case out of its list.

2. When the Chamber is informed of a friendly settlement, arrangement or other fact of a kind to provide a solution of the matter, it may, after consulting, if necessary, the Parties, the Delegates of the Commission and the applicant, strike the case out of the list.

3. The striking out of a case shall be effected by means of a judgment which the President shall forward to the Committee of Ministers in order to allow them to supervise, in accordance with Article 54 of the Convention, the execution of any undertakings which may have been attached to the discontinuance or solution of the matter.

4. The Chamber may, having regard to the responsibilities of the Court under Article 19 of the Convention, decide that, notwithstanding the notice of discontinuance, friendly settlement, arrangement or other fact referred to in paragraphs 1 and 2 of this Rule, it should proceed with the consideration of the case.

Rule 50

QUESTION OF THE APPLICATION OF ARTICLE 50 OF THE CONVENTION

1. [As amended by the Court on January 26, 1989.] Any claims which the applicant may wish to make under Article 50 of the Convention shall, unless the President otherwise directs, be set out in his memorial or, if he does not submit a memorial, in a special document filed at least one month before the date fixed pursuant to Rule 38 for the opening of the oral proceedings.

2. The Chamber may, at any time during the proceedings, invite any Party, the Commission and the applicant to submit comments on this question.

Rule 51

RELINQUISHMENT OF JURISDICTION BY THE CHAMBER IN FAVOUR OF THE PLENARY COURT

1. Where a case pending before a Chamber raises one or more

serious questions affecting the interpretation of the Convention, the Chamber may, at any time during the proceedings, relinquish jurisdiction in favour of the plenary Court. The relinquishment of jurisdiction shall be obligatory where the resolution of such question or questions might have a result inconsistent with a judgment previously delivered by a Chamber or the plenary Court. Reasons need not be given for the decision to relinquish jurisdiction.

2. The plenary Court, when the case has been referred to it, may either retain jurisdiction over the whole case or may, after deciding the said question or questions, order that the case be referred back to the Chamber which shall, in regard to the remaining part of the case, recover its original jurisdiction.

3. Any provisions governing the Chambers shall apply, *mutatis mutandis*, to proceedings before the plenary Court.

4. When a case pending before a Chamber is referred to the plenary Court under paragraph 1 above, any *ad hoc* judge who is a member of that Chamber shall sit as a judge on the plenary Court.

CHAPTER IV

Judgments

Rule 52

PROCEDURE BY DEFAULT

Where a Party fails to appear or to present its case, the Chamber shall, subject to the provisions of Rule 49, give a decision in the case.

Rule 53

CONTENTS OF THE JUDGMENT

1. The judgment shall contain:
   (a) the names of the President and the judges constituting the Chamber, and also the names of the Registrar and, where appropriate, the Deputy Registrar;

(b) the dates on which it was adopted and delivered;

(c) a description of the Party or Parties;

(d) the names of the Agents, advocates or advisers of the Party or Parties;

(e) the names of the Delegates of the Commission and of the persons assisting them;

(f) the name of the applicant;

(g) an account of the procedure followed;

(h) the final submissions of the Party or Parties and, if any, of the Delegates of the Commission and of the applicant;

(i) the facts of the case;

(j) the reasons in point of law;

(k) the operative provisions of the judgment;

(l) the decision, if any, in respect of costs;

(m) the number of judges constituting the majority;

(n) where appropriate, a statement as to which of the two texts, English or French, is authentic.

2. Any judge who has taken part in the consideration of the case shall be entitled to annex to the judgment either a separate opinion, concurring with or dissenting from that judgment, or a bare statement of dissent.

Rule 54

JUDGMENT ON THE APPLICATION OF ARTICLE 50 OF THE CONVENTION

1. [As amended by the Court on January 26, 1989.] Where the Chamber finds that there is a breach of the Convention, it shall give in the same judgment a decision on the application of Article 50 of the Convention if that question, after being raised under Rule 50, is ready for decision; if the question is not ready for decision, the Chamber shall reserve it in whole or in part and shall fix the further procedure. If, on the other hand, this question has not been raised under Rule 50, the Chamber may lay down a time limit for the applicant to submit any claims for just satisfaction that he may have.

2. For the purposes of ruling on the application of Article 50 of the Convention, the Chamber shall, as far as possible, be composed of those judges who sat to consider the merits of the case. Those judges who have ceased to be members of the Court shall be recalled in order to deal with the question in accordance with Article 40, paragraph 6 of the Convention; however, in the event of death, inability to sit, withdrawal or exemption from sitting,

the judge concerned shall be replaced in the same manner as was applied for his appointment to the Chamber.

3. When the judgment finding a breach has been delivered under Rule 51 and does not contain a ruling on the application of Article 50 of the Convention, the plenary Court may decide, without prejudice to the provisions of paragraph 1 above, to refer the question back to the Chamber.

4. If the Court is informed that an agreement has been reached between the injured party and the Party liable, it shall verify the equitable nature of such agreement and, where it finds the agreement to be equitable, strike the case out of the list by means of a judgment. Rule 49, paragraph 3 shall apply in such circumstances.

Rule 55

SIGNATURE, DELIVERY AND NOTIFICATION OF THE JUDGMENT

1. The judgment shall be signed by the President and by the Registrar.

2. The judgment shall be read out by the President, or by another judge delegated by him, at a public hearing in one of the two official languages. It shall not be necessary for the other judges to be present. The Agents of the Parties, the Delegates of the Commission and the applicant shall be informed in due time of the date and time of delivery of the judgment.

   However, in respect of a judgment striking a case out of the list or relating to the application of Article 50 of the Convention the President may direct that the notification provided for under paragraph 4 of this Rule shall count as delivery.

3. The judgment shall be transmitted by the President to the Committee of Ministers.

4. The original copy, duly signed and sealed, shall be placed in the archives of the Court. The Registrar shall send certified copies to the Party or Parties, to the Commission, to the applicant, to the Secretary General of the Council of Europe, to the Contracting States and persons referred to in Rule 37, paragraph 2 and to any other person directly concerned.

Rule 56

PUBLICATION OF JUDGMENTS AND OTHER DOCUMENTS

1. [As amended by the Court on January 26, 1989.] The Registrar shall be responsible for the publication of:

- judgments of the Court;
- documents relating to the proceedings, including the report of the Commission but excluding any document which the President considers unnecessary or inadvisable to publish;
- verbatim records of public hearings;
- any document which the President considers useful to publish.

Publication shall take place in the two official languages in the case of judgments, applications or requests instituting proceedings and the Commission's reports; the other documents shall be published in the official language in which they occur in the proceedings.

2. Documents deposited with the Registrar and not published shall be accessible to the public unless otherwise decided by the President either on his own initiative or at the request of a Party, of the Commission, of the applicant or of any other person concerned.

Rule 57

REQUEST FOR INTERPRETATION OF A JUDGMENT

1. A Party or the Commission may request the interpretation of a judgment within a period of three years following the delivery of that judgment.
2. The request shall state precisely the point or points in the operative provisions of the judgment on which interpretation is required. It shall be filed with the registry in forty copies.
3. The Registrar shall communicate the request, as appropriate, to any other Party, to the Commission and to the applicant, and shall invite them to submit any written comments within a time limit laid down by the President of the Chamber. The President of the Chamber shall also fix the date of the hearing should the Chamber decide to hold one.

Written comments shall be filed with the registry; they shall be filed in forty copies when they are submitted by a Party or by the Commission.

4. The request for interpretation shall be considered by the Chamber which gave the judgment and which shall, as far as possible, be composed of the same judges. Those judges who have ceased to be members of the Court shall be recalled in order to deal with the case in accordance with Article 40, paragraph 6 of the Convention; however, in the event of death, inability to sit, withdrawal or exemption from sitting, the judge concerned shall

285

be replaced in the same manner as was applied for his appointment to the Chamber.

5. The Chamber shall decide by means of a judgment.

Rule 58

REQUEST FOR REVISION OF A JUDGMENT

1. A Party or the Commission may, in the event of the discovery o
   a fact which might by its nature have a decisive influence and
   which, when a judgment was delivered, was unknown both to
   the Court and to that Party or the Commission, request the
   Court, within a period of six months after that Party or the
   Commission, as the case may be, acquired knowledge of such
   fact, to revise that judgment.
2. The request shall mention the judgment of which the revision i
   requested and shall contain the information necessary to show
   that the conditions laid down in paragraph 1 have been complied
   with. It shall be accompanied by the original or a copy of al
   supporting documents. The request and supporting document
   shall be filed with the registry in forty copies.
3. The Registrar shall communicate the request, as appropriate, to
   any other Party, to the Commission and to the applicant, and
   shall invite them to submit any written comments within a time
   limit laid down by the President. The President shall also fix the
   date of the hearing should the Chamber decide to hold one.

   Written comments shall be filed with the registry; they shall be
   filed in forty copies if they are submitted by a Party or by the
   Commission.
4. The request for revision shall be considered by a Chamber
   constituted in accordance with Article 43 of the Convention
   which shall decide whether the request is admissible or not under
   paragraph 1 of this Rule. In the affirmative, the Chamber shal
   refer the request to the Chamber which gave the original judg
   ment or, if in the circumstancs that is not reasonably possible, i
   shall retain the request and examine the merits thereof.
5. The Chamber shall decide by means of a judgment.

Appendix 6

OFFICIAL APPLICATION FORM

> Voir Note explicative
> *See Explanatory Note*

COMMISSION EUROPÉENNE DES DROITS DE L'HOMME
EUROPEAN COMMISSION ON HUMAN RIGHTS

Conseil de l'Europe - *Council of Europe*
Strasbourg, France

REQUÊTE
APPLICATION

présentée en application de l'article 25 de la Convention européenne des Droits de l'Homme, ainsi que des articles 43 et 44 du Règlement intérieur de la Commission

under Article 25 of the European Convention on Human Rights and Rules 43 and 44 of the Rules of Procedure of the Commission

IMPORTANT: La présente requête est un document juridique et peut affecter vos droits et obligations.
This application is a formal legal document and may affect your rights and obligations.

287

I - LES PARTIES
THE PARTIES

A.   LE REQUÉRANT
   THE APPLICANT
   (Renseignements à fournir concernant le requérant et son représentant éventuel)
   (Fill in the following details of the applicant and any representative)

1. Nom de famille ....   2. Prénom(s) ....
   Name of applicant   First name(s)

3. Nationalité ....   4. Profession ....
   Nationality   Occupation

5. Date et lieu de naissance ....
   Date and place of birth

6. Domicile ....
   Permanent address

   .... 7. Tel N°. ....

8. Adress actuelle ....
   At present at
   ....
   Le cas échéant, *(if any)*

9. Nom et prénom du représentant* ....
   Name of representative*

10. Profession du représentant ....
    Occupation of representative

11. Address du représentant...
    Adress of representative

    .... 12. Tel N°. ....

B.   LA HAUTE PARTIE CONTRACTANTE
   THE HIGH CONTRACTING PARTY

   (indiquer ci-après le nom de l'Etat contre lequel la requête est dirigée)
   (Fill in the name of the country against which the application is directed)

13.
   ....

---

* Si le requérant est représenté, joindre une procuration signée par le requérant en faveu
  du représentant.
  A form of authority signed by the applicant should be submitted if a representative is appointed

II - EXPOSÉ DES FAITS
STATEMENT OF THE FACTS

(Voir chapitre II de la note explicative)
(See Part II of the Explanatory Note)

14.

III - EXPOSÉ DE LA OU DES VIOLATION(S) DE LA CONVENTION
ALLÉGUÉE(S) PAR LE REQUÉRANT, AINSI QUE DES ARGU-
MENTS A L'APPUI
*STATEMENT OF ALLEGED VIOLATION(S) OF THE CONVEN-
TION AND OF RELEVANT ARGUMENTS*

(Voir chapitre III de la note explicative)
(See Part III of the Explanatory Note)

14.

IV - EXPOSÉ RELATIF AUX PRESCRIPTIONS DE L'ARTICLE 26 DE LA CONVENTION
STATEMENT RELATIVE TO ARTICLE 26 OF THE CONVENTION

(Voir chapitre IV de la note explicative. Donner pour chaque grief, et au besoin sur une feuille séparée, les renseignements demandés sous ch. 16 et 18 ci-après)
(See Part IV of the Explanatory Note. If necessary give the details mentioned below under points 16 to 18 on a separate sheet for each separate complaint)

16.   Décision interne définitive (date et nature de la décision, organe – judiciaire ou autre – l'ayant rendue)
        Final decision (date, court or authority and nature of the decision).

17.   Autres décisions (énumérées dans l'ordre chronologique en indiquant, pour chaque décision, sa date, sa nature et l'organe – judiciaire ou autre – l'ayant rendue)
        Other decisions (list in order, giving date, court or authority and nature of the decision for each one)

18.   Le requérant disposait-il d'un recours qu'il n'a pas exercé? Si oui, lequel et pour quel motif n'a-t-il pas été exercé?
        Is any other appeal or remedy available which you have not used? If so, explain why you have not used it.

Si nécessaire, continuer sur une feuille séparée
Continue on a separate sheet if necessary

291

V - EXPOSÉ DE L'OBJECT DE LA REQUÊTE
STATEMENT OF THE OBJECT OF THE APPLICATION

(Voir chapitre V de la note explicative)
(See Part V of the Explanatory Note)

19.

VI - AUTRES INSTANCES INTERNATIONALES TRAITANT OU AYANT TRAITÉ L'AFFAIRE
STATEMENT CONCERNING OTHER INTERNATIONAL PROCEEDINGS

(Voir chapitre VI de la note explicative)
(See Part VI of the Explanatory Note)

20.   Le requérant a-t-il soumis à une autre instance internationale d'enquête ou de règlements les griefs énoncés dans la présente requête? Si oui, fournir des indications détaillés à ce sujet.
Have you submitted the above complaints to any other procedure of international investigation or settlement? If so, give full details.

VII - PIÈCES ANNEXÉES
LIST OF DOCUMENTS

(Voir chapitre VII de la note explicative. Joindre copie de toutes les décisions mentionnées sous ch. IV et VI ci-avant. Se procurer, au besoin, les copies nécessaries, et, en cas d'impossibilité, expliquer pourquoi celles-ci ne peuvent pas être obtenues)

(See Part VII of the Explanatory Note. Include copies of all decisions referred to in Parts IV and VI above. If you do not have copies, you should obtain them. If you cannot obtain them, explain why not)

21.   a)..

      b)..

      c)..

VIII - LANGUES DE PROCÉDURE SOUHAITÉE
STATEMENT OF PREFERRED LANGUAGE

(Voir chapitre VIII de la note explicative)
(See Part VIII of the Explanatory Note)

22. Je préfère recevoir la décision de la commission en: anglais/français *
     *I prefer to receive the Commission's decision in : English/French *

IX - DÉCLARATION ET SIGNATURE
DECLARATION AND SIGNATURE

(Voir chapitre IX de la note explicative)
(See Part IX of the Explanatory Note)

23. Je déclare en tout conscience et loyauté que les renseignements qui figurent sur la
     présente formule de requête sont exacts et je m'engage à respecter le caractère
     confidentiel de la procédure de la Commission.
     *I hereby declare that, to the best of my knowledge and belief, the information I have given
     in my application is correct and that I will respect the confidentiality of the Commission's
     proceedings.*

24. Je désire/je ne désire pas* garder l'anonymat à l'égard du public.
     *I do/do not object * to my identity being disclosed.*

Lieu/*Place* .... Date/*Date*...................

....
(Signature du requérant ou de son représentant)
(Signature of the applicant or his representative)

---

* Biffer ce qui ne convient pas
Delete as appropriate

EXPLANATORY NOTE TO APPLICATION FORM

Editor's Note

Below is given the text of the Commission's Explanatory Note that accompanies the application form. Additional comments are contained in italics

EXPLANATORY NOTE

for persons completing the Application Form
under Article 25 of the Convention

INTRODUCTION

These notes are intended to assist you in drawing up your application to the Commission. **Please read them carefully before completing the form,** and then refer to them as you complete each section of the form.

The completed form will be your application or 'petition' to the Commission under Article 25 of the Convention. It will be the basis for the Commission's examination of your case. It is therefore important that you **complete it fully and accurately even if this means repeating information you have already given the Secretariat in previous correspondence.**

You will see that there are nine sections to the form. You should complete all of these so that your application contains all the information required under the Commission's Rules of Procedure. Below you will find an explanatory note relating to each section of the form. You will also find at the end of these notes the text of Rules 43 and 44 of the Commission's Rules of Procedure[1].

---

[1] Rules 43 and 44 of the Commission's Rules of Procedure are contained in Appendix 3 at p. 232 *ante*.

NOTES RELATING TO THE APPLICATION FORM

I. THE PARTIES: Rule 44, para. 1(a), (b) and (c)
(1–13)

If there is more than one applicant, you should should give the required information for each one, on a separate sheet if necessary.

An applicant may appoint a lawyer or other person to represent him. Such representative must be resident in a Convention country, unless the Commission decides otherwise. When an applicant is represented by another person, relevant details should be given in this part of the application form, and the Secretariat will correspond only with the representative.

Apart from situations where there is obviously more than one applicant, consideration should be given to the question of indirect victims and the situation of family members in particular, i.e. a complaint by a mother concerning the denial of contact with her daughter is also a possible violation of the daughter's rights.

II. STATEMENT OF THE FACTS: Rule 44, para. 1(e)
(14)

You should give clear and concise details of the facts you are complaining about. Try to describe the events in the order in which they occurred. Give exact dates. If your complaints relate to a number of different matters (for instance different sets of court proceedings) you should deal with each matter separately.

III. STATEMENT OF ALLEGED VIOLATION(S) OF THE CONVENTION AND OF RELEVANT ARGUMENTS: Rule 44, para. 1(e)
(15)

In this section of the form you should explain as precisely as you can what your complaint **under the Convention** is. Say which provisions of the Convention you rely on and explain why you consider that the facts you have set out in Part II of the form involve a violation of these provisions.

You will see that some of the Articles of the Convention permit interferences with the rights they guarantee in certain circumstances (*see* for instance sub-paras. (a)–(f) of Article 5; para. 1 and para. 2 of

Articles 8–11). If you are relying on such an article try to explain why you consider the interference which you are complaining about is not justified.

Every potential article should be 'pleaded' here. This is especially so in respect of those articles where there is an obvious overlap, i.e. Articles 8, 9 and 11. In general detailed consideration should be given to whether Articles 6, 13 and 14 have been violated in addition (if applicable). Where a violation of Article 5 is alleged, a violation of Article 5(5) should be specifically asserted in addition.

IV. STATEMENT RELATIVE TO ARTICLE 26 OF THE CONVENTION: Rule 44, para. 2(a)
(16–18)

In this section you should set out details of the remedies you have pursued before the national authorities. You should fill in each of the three parts of this section and give the same information separately for each separate complaint. In part 18 you should say whether or not any other appeal or remedy is available which could address your complaints and which you have not used. If such a remedy is available, you should say what it is (*e.g.* name the court or authority to which an appeal would lie) and explain why you have not used it.

V. STATEMENT OF THE OBJECT OF THE APPLICATION: Rule 44, para. 1(d)
(19)

Here you should state briefly what you want to achieve through your application to the Commission.

Whilst neither the Commission nor the Court have power to order a change in legislation or a retrial (for instance), if this is in fact what the applicant wishes, then it should be here stated; by so doing the Commission is given a better idea as to the thrust of the injustice alleged. If the applicant is seeking compensation then this should be stated together with an outline of the nature of the losses. One should include in this section a claim for costs (including the costs of any domestic court proceedings if the applicant has had to bear these).

VI. STATEMENT CONCERNING OTHER INTERNATIONAL PROCEEDINGS: Rule 44, para. 2(b)
(20)

Here you should say whether or not you have ever submitted the complaints in your application to any other procedure of international investigation or settlement. If you have, you should give full details, including the name of the body to which you submitted your complaints, dates and details of any proceedings which took place and details of decisions taken. You should also submit copies of relevant decisions and other documents.

VII.   LIST OF DOCUMENTS: Rule 44, para. 1(f)
(21)

Do not forget to enclose with your application and to mention on the list documents of all judgments and decisions referred to in Sections IV and VI, as well as any other documents you wish the Commission to take into consideration as evidence (transcripts, statements of witnesses, etc.). Include any documents giving the reasons for a court or other decision as well as the decision itself. Only submit documents which are relevant to the complaints you are making to the Commission.

VIII.   STATEMENT OF PREFERRED LANGUAGE:
Rule 44, para. 2(c)
(22)

The official languages of the Commission are English and French. Although the Secretariat conducts correspondence in a number of other languages as well, documents such as the Commission's decision will be communicated to you in one of the two official languages. Indicate which you prefer.

IX.   DECLARATION AND SIGNATURE: Rule 44, para. 2(d) and (e)
(23-24)

The declaration includes an undertaking to respect the confidentiality of the Commission's proceedings. Under Article 33 of the Convention the Commission meets *in camera*. This means that the contents of case files, including all pleadings, must be kept confidential. The Commission's decisions on the admissibility of your case may, however, be made available to the public. If you have any objection to your name being made public, you should inform the Secretariat of this.

If the application is signed by the representative of the applicant, it should be accompanied by a form of authority signed by the applicant himself (unless this has already been submitted): Article 43, para. 3.

Appendix 7

EUROPEAN COMMISSION OF HUMAN RIGHTS

AUTHORITY

I   [insert name of applicant]

of   [applicant's address]

Hereby authorise   [representative's name]

of   [representative's address]

to represent me in the proceedings before the European Commission of Human Rights, and in any subsequent proceedings under the European Convention on Human Rights, concerning my application introduced under Article 25 of the Convention against the United Kingdom.

....
[signature]

....
[date]

Appendix 8

LEGAL AID RULES: COMMISSION

Rule 1

The Commission may, either at the request of an applicant lodging an application under Article 25 of the Convention or *proprio motu*, grant free legal aid to that applicant in connection with the representation of the case:

   a. where observations in writing on the admissibility of that application have been received from the High Contracting Party conerned in pursuance of Rule 48, paragraph 2(b), or where the time limit for their submission has expired; or
   b. where the application has been declared admissible.

Rule 2

Free legal aid shall only be granted where the Commission is satisfied:

   a. that it is essential for the proper discharge of the Commission's duties;
   b. that the applicant has not sufficient means to meet all or part of the costs involved.

Rule 3

1. In order to determine whether or not applicants have sufficient means to meet all or part of the costs involved, the Commission shall require them to complete a form of declaration stating their income, capital assets and any financial commitments in respect of dependents, or any other financial obligations. Such declaration shall be certified by the appropriate domestic authority or authorities.

2. Before making a grant of free legal aid, the Commission shall request the High Contracting Party concerned to submit its comments in writing.
3. The Commission shall, after receiving the information mentioned in paragraphs 1 and 2 *above*, decide whether or not to grant free legal aid and shall inform the parties accordingly.
4. The President shall fix the time limits within which the parties shall be requested to supply the information referred to in this rule.

Rule 4

1. Fees shall be payable only to a barrister-at-law, solicitor or professor of law or professionally qualified person of similar status. Fees may, where appropriate, be paid to more than one such lawyer as defined above.
2. Legal aid may be granted to cover not only lawyers' fees but also travelling and subsistence expenses and other necessary out-of-pocket expenses incurred by the applicant or appointed lawyer.

Rule 5

1. On the Commission deciding to grant legal aid, the Secretary shall, by agreement with the appointed lawyer, fix the rate of fees to be paid.
2. The Secretary shall as soon as possible notify the Secretary General of the Council of Europe of the rate of fees so agreed.

Rule 6

The Commission may, at any time, if it finds that the conditions set out in Rule 2 above are no longer satisfied, revoke its grant of free legal aid to an applicant, in whole or in part, and shall at once notify the parties thereof.

Rule 7

In case of urgency when the Commission is not in session, the President or one of the Vice-Presidents may exercise the powers conferred on the Commission by this Addendum. As soon as the Commission is again in session, the President or the Vice-President concerned shall report to it on the action which has been taken.

Appendix 9

LEGAL AID RULES: COURT

The European Court of Human Rights,
Having regard to the Convention for the Protection of Human Rights
and Fundamental Freedoms and the Protocols thereto;
Having regard to the Rules of Court,
Adopts the present addendum to the Rules of Court:

Rule 1

DEFINITIONS

1. For the purposes of the present addendum:
   (a) the term 'applicant' is to be understood as meaning the
   person, non-governmental organisation or group of individuals who, after lodging a complaint with the Commission
   under Article 25 of the Convention, has expressed the desire,
   in accordance with Rule 33 of the Rules of Court, to take part
   in the proceedings before the Court;
   (b) the term 'President' is to be understood as meaning the
   President of the Court until the constitution of the Chamber or
   in the event of relinquishment of jurisdiction under Rule 51 of
   the Rules of Court, and the President of the Chamber in all
   other instances.
2. Subject to the foregoing, the terms used herein shall, unless
   the context otherwise requires, have the same meaning as they
   have in the Rules of Court.

Rule 2

REQUESTS FOR INFORMATION REGARDING LEGAL AID BEFORE THE COMMISSION

1. Unless the information is already available to him, the Registrar

shall enquire whether or not the applicant applied for, and, if so, whether or not he was granted, legal aid in connection with the representation of his case before the Commission pursuant to the addendum to the Rules of Procedure of the Commission.

2. At the same time the Registrar may, on the instructions of the President, ask the Commission to produce to the Court the file relating to the grant or refusal, if any, of legal aid to the applicant.

Rule 3

CONTINUATION IN FORCE OF A GRANT MADE BY THE COMMISSION

1. Subject to the provisions of Rule 5 herein, where the applicant has been granted legal aid in connection with the representation of his case before the Commission, that grant shall continue in force for the purposes of his representation before the Court.
2. The President may, however, instruct the Registrar to obtain from the applicant information evidencing that the conditions laid down in Rule 4, paragraph 2 herein are fulfilled. The Registrar shall bring any information so obtained to the attention of the Agents of the Parties and the Delegates of the Commission, in order to give them the opportunity to verify its correctness.

Rule 4

GRANT OF LEGAL AID BY THE PRESIDENT

1. Where the applicant did not receive a grant of legal aid in connection with the representation of his case before the Commission or had such a grant revoked, the President may at any time, at the request of the applicant, grant free legal aid to the applicant for the purposes of his representation before the Court.
2. Legal aid may be so granted only where the president is satisfied that:
    (a) the applicant lacks sufficient means to meet all or part of the costs involved; and
    (b) such a course is necessary for the proper conduct of the case before the Court.
3. In order to determine whether or not the applicant lacks the sufficient means, the Registrar shall ask him to complete a form of declaration stating his income, capital assets and any financial

commitments in respect of dependants, or any other financial obligations. Such declaration shall be certified by the appropriate domestic authority or authorities. This certified declaration may be replaced by a certificate of indigence delivered by the appropriate domestic authority or authorities as listed in the appendix to this addendum.

4. Before the President makes a grant of legal aid, the Registrar shall request the Agents of the Parties and the Delegates of the Commission to submit their comments in writing.

5. After receiving the information mentioned in paragraphs 3 and 4 and, if appropriate, Rule 2, paragraph 2 *above*, the President shall decide whether or not legal aid is to be granted and to what extent. The Registrar shall notify the applicant, the Agents of the Parties and the Delegates of the Commission accordingly.

6. The Registrar, on the instructions of the President, shall fix the time limits within which the information referred to in this Rule is to be supplied.

Rule 5

REVOCATION OR VARIATION OF A GRANT

The President may, if he is satisfied that the conditions stated in Rule 4, paragraph 2 are no longer fulfilled, at any time revoke or vary, in whole or in part, a grant of legal aid made or continued in force under the present addendum. The Registrar shall at once notify the applicant, the Agents of the Parties and the Delegates of the Commission accordingly.

Rule 6

FEES AND EXPENSES PAYABLE

1. Fees shall be payable only to the advocates or other persons appointed in accordance with Rule 30 of the Rules of Court.

2. Legal aid may be granted to cover not only fees for representation but also travelling and subsistence expenses and other necessary out-of-pocket expenses incurred by the applicants or by their representatives.

3. After consulting the representatives, the Registrar shall, on the instructions of the President, fix the amount of fees to be paid. The Registrar shall also in each case decide what particular

expenses referred to above at paragraph 2 are to be covered by the grant of legal aid.

Rule 7

DEROGATION FROM PROCEDURAL REQUIREMENTS

In case of urgency, the President may sanction a derogation from the procedural requirements of this addendum provided that the derogation in question is essential for the proper conduct of the case before the Court.

Rule 8

ENTRY INTO FORCE AND TRANSITIONAL ARRANGEMENTS

This addendum shall come into force at a date [November 1, 1983] to be fixed by the President of the Court. Pending such entry into force, the grant of legal aid to an applicant in connection with the representation of his case before the Court shall continue to be governed by the addendum to the Rules of Procedure of the Commission.

APPENDIX

NATIONAL AUTHORITIES COMPETENT TO DELIVER A CERTIFICATE OF INDIGENCE

The declaration of means referred to in Rule 4, paragraph 3 of the addendum to the Rules of Court (Rules on legal aid to applicants) may be replaced by a certificate of indigence delivered by the appropriate domestic authority or authorities. The competent domestic authorities are as follows:

AUSTRIA   The mayor of the locality where the applicant has his or her legal or actual residence.

BELGIUM   The direct taxation department of the district in which the applicant lives issues him with a certificate of income or, with his authorisation, express and in writing, issues such to another person or administrative department.

The request, accompanied by such authorisation, may be addressed either to the local direct

	taxation department or to the Administration centrale des contributions directes, 45, rue Belliard, B–1040 Bruxelles.
CYPRUS	The Social Welfare Services, Ministry of Labour and Social Insurance.
DENMARK	The local tax authority.
FINLAND	The social welfare authority in the municipality of the applicant's place of domicile.
FRANCE	The mayor of the municipality in which the applicant lives.
GERMANY	None. The applicant submits a prescribed form, duly completed and with supporting documents, which is forwarded to the Federal Ministry of Justice.
GREECE	(a) A certificate from the mayor or president of the district in which the applicant lives giving details of his family situation, his employment and his assets; and
	(b) a certificate from the tax authority showing that the applicant has made a tax return for the previous three years with the results thereof.
ICELAND	The *Rikisskattstjóri* (Director of Internal Revenue), Skúlagotu 57, IS-Reykjavik.
IRELAND	The Chief Inspector, Department of Social Welfare, 101/104 Marlboro Street, IRL-Dublin 1.
ITALY	(a) Certification, by a responsible section of the tax authorities, of a declaration of means prepared by the applicant; or
	(b) certificate of indigence issued by the mayor of the municipality in which the applicant lives.
LUXEMBOURG	On production of a certificate stating the amount of tax paid the previous year, the College of Mayor and Aldermen of the municipality in which the applicant lives issues a certificate of indigence.
NETHERLANDS	The local government *(gemeentebestuur)* in accordance with Article 11 of the Legal Aid Act *(Wet Rechtsbijstand on- en minvermogenden)*.
NORWAY	The local tax authority *(ligningskontor)* of the district in which the applicant lives.
PORTUGAL	The local government *(junta de frequesia)* for the district in which the applicant lives.
SAN MARINO	The certificate of indigence is issued by the office of the Secretary of State for Internal Affairs following a declaration made by the San Marinese tax office.

SPAIN	The district office of the Finance Minister *(Delegación de Hacienda)* for the district in which the applicant lives.
SWEDEN	The local tax authority *(lokala skattemyndigheten)* certifies the means of persons requesting free legal aid.
SWITZERLAND	The local tax authority for the applicant's place of residence.
TURKEY	*(a)* The mayor of the municipality in which the applicant lives; or *(b)* the elders' council for the village of district in which the applicant lives (Article 468 of the Code of Civil Procedure).
UNITED KINGDOM	*(a) England and Wales* DHSS, Legal Aid Assessment Office, No. 3 The Pavilions, Ashton on Ribble, Preston, PR2 2PA; *(b) Scotland* The Scottish Legal Aid Board, 44 Drumsheugh Gardens, Edinburgh, EH3 7SW.

The relevant information concerning two States—Liechtenstein and Malta—has not yet been communicated to the registry of the Court.

Appendix 10

DECLARATION OF APPLICANT'S MEANS

1. Name of applicant and number of application:
   ....
   ....
   ....

2. Are you married, divorced or single?
   ....
   ....

3. Nature of your employment, name of employer:
   (if not at present employed, give details of your last employment)
   ....
   ....
   ....
   ....

4. Details of net salary and other net incomes (*e.g.* interest from loans and investments, allowances, pensions, insurance benefits, etc.) after deduction of tax:
   ....
   ....
   ....
   ....
   ....

5. List and value of capital assets owned by you:
   (a) Immovable property (*e.g.* land, house, business premises)
   ....
   ....
   ....
   ....
   ....

(b) Movable property and nature thereof (*e.g.* bank balance, savings account, motor-car, valuables)

. . . .
. . . .
. . . .
. . . .

6. List of your financial commitments:
    (a) Rent, mortgage and other charges

    . . . .
    . . . .

    (b) Loans and interest payable thereon

    . . . .
    . . . .

    (c) Maintenance of dependants

    . . . .
    . . . .

    (d) Any other financial obligations

    . . . .
    . . . .

7. What contribution can you make towards your legal representation before the Commission of Human Rights?

    . . . .
    . . . .

8. The name of the person whom you propose to assist you
    (*see* Rule 4 of these Rules of Procedure)

    . . . .

I certify that the above information is correct.

Signed: Dated:

Appendix 11

(*See pages 88–98 above*)

Sunday Times v. *United Kingdom (No. 2)* (2 E.H.R.R. 317; November 6, 1980, Series A, No. 38)

Extract

III The Strasbourg costs

23. According to the Court's case law, costs and expenses will not be awarded under Article 50 unless it is established that they were actually incurred, were necessarily incurred and were also reasonable as to *quantum* (*see, inter alia,* the above-mentioned *Neumeister*[1] judgment, pp. 20–21, 43, and the above-mentioned *König*[2] judgment, pp. 18–19, 24–26).

1. WERE THE COSTS ACTUALLY INCURRED?

24. The applicants did not have the benefit of free legal aid before the Commission and in their relations with the Delegates (*c.f.* the *Luedicke, Belkacem* and *Koç* judgment of March 10, 1980, Series A, No. 36, p. 8, 15, and the *Artico* judgment of May 13, 1980, Series A, No. 37, p. 19, 40). More generally, with one exception, neither the Government nor the Commission suggested that any of the Strasbourg costs had not been actually incurred: in the absence of any evidence to the contrary, the Court sees no need to call for vouchers in respect of the remaining items.
25. The exception referred to is a sum of £7,500 in respect of work done between 1974 and 1979 by Mr Whitaker, as agent for the

---

[1] 1 E.H.R.R. 136; May 7, 1974, Series A, No. 17
[2] 2 E.H.R.R. 469; March 10, 1980, Series A, No. 36

applicants and Legal Manager of Times Newspapers Limited, in settling memorials, preparing for and attending at the hearing before the Commission and instructing counsel for the hearing before the Court. The Commission's Delegates express 'considerable doubts' about this item, questioning whether it was actually incurred since the said activities appeared to belong to the normal functions of a company's legal manager and to be covered by his ordinary remuneration. The Government subsequently agreed that a question of principle was involved but, without accepting that this was necessarily relevant, drew the Court's attention to the fact that under English practice the costs recoverable by a successful litigant would include at least part of those referable to the services of a salaried solicitor.

In the absence of any evidence, the Court must assume that the activities in question were indeed covered by Mr Whitaker's ordinary remuneration. However, if an employee, by devoting his time to particular litigation, does work of a kind which would otherwise be done by independent lawyers, it is in general reasonable to consider the part of his salary that represents a normal reward for that work as an expense of his employer. Although the English practice is not conclusive in the autonomous context of Article 50 (*see* paragraph 15 *above*), it is noteworthy that similar considerations appear to underlie that practice. Neither the Government nor the Commission contested that in the present case Mr Whitaker rendered services which would otherwise have had to be provided by independent lawyers paid by Times Newspapers Limited. The Court therefore concludes that the expense of £7,500 can be regarded as actually incurred.

2. WERE THE COSTS NECESSARILY INCURRED?

26. Both the Government and the Commission have commented on the necessity of incurring certain of the Strasbourg costs. The items will be taken in turn.

(A) COSTS REFERABLE TO UNSUCCESSFUL SUBMISSIONS

27. The Government contended that the applicants should be denied costs incurred in advancing extensive submissions which were rejected by the Commission and the Court, arguing that *ex hypothesi* those costs were not necessary to the establishment of a breach of the Convention. They cited, in particular, the allegations that the applicants were subject to continuing restraints in breach of Article 10, that the restriction on their freedom of expression was not 'prescribed by law' within the meaning of that Article and that there had been discrimination contrary to Article 14 read in conjunction with Article 10 (*see* the Court's judgment of April 26, 1979, pp. 28, 30, 42–43, 46 and 69).

The applicants replied that they had to assert their case to the best of their ability and that evaluation by hindsight was the wrong approach. 28. The Court cannot accept the Government's contention, even on the assumption that there is a satisfactory method of surmounting the difficulties of calculation which it involves. In its *Neumeister*[3] judgment (pp. 2, 4, 19–20, and 42), the Court drew no distinction between costs referable to successful pleas under Article 5(3) and costs referable to unsuccessful pleas under Articles 5(4) and 6(1). Whilst it is in the interests of a proper and expeditious administration of justice that the Convention institutions be not burdened with pleas unrelated or extraneous to the case in hand, the submissions now in question cannot be so described. They all bore on the situation created for the applicants by the injunction ordered by the House of Lords and the kernel of each of them was Article 10. Moreover, a lawyer has a duty to present his client's case as fully and ably as he can and it can never be predicted with certainty what weight a tribunal may attach to this or that plea, provided that it is not manifestly otiose or invalid.

(B) Fees paid to three counsel for services rendered in 1978/79: £12,000

29. The Government claimed that the expense of instructing three counsel was not necessarily incurred, whereas the Delegates had no difficulty in accepting that it was.

30. Whilst it is true that the applicants were not parties to the proceedings before the Court and that the rôle of their counsel was limited to assisting the three Delegates of the Commission, it has to be remembered that the latter does not represent the applicants, its main function being to 'assist' the Court, 'in the capacity of defender of the public interest' (*see* the *Lawless*[4] judgment of November 14, 1960, Series A, No. 1, pp. 11 and 16). The association of the applicants with the proceedings in this way is of evident utility. However, bearing in mind that the Delegates were already assisted by Mr Whitaker and that two of the applicants themselves: Mr Harold Evans and Mr Knightley, were also present at the hearings, the Court takes the view that it was not necessary for more than one counsel, namely Mr Lester as leading counsel, to attend on that occasion. On the other hand, the services in question included not only the appearance before the Court but also the preparation within a relatively short time of a substantial memorial involving much detailed research. Whilst expressing no opinion as to the precise number of counsel necessary for this purpose, the Court does not consider that one would have sufficed. Taking these factors and the circumstances of the case into account, the Court retains a sum of £10,000 under this head.

[3] 1 E.H.R.R. 136; May 7, 1974, Series A, No. 17
[4] 1 E.H.R.R. 1; November 14, 1960, Series A, No. 1

(c) TRAVEL AND HOTEL EXPENSES

(I) DECEMBER 1975 (PROCEEDINGS BEFORE THE COMMISSION): £604.85

31. The Government claimed that it was not necessary for Mr James Evans, as adviser to the applicants, and Mr Page and Mr Knightley, two of the three individual journalist applicants, to attend the Commission hearings. The Court sees no reason to differ from the Commission, which expressed a contrary opinion, on a matter falling essentially with the latter's province. It therefore accepts as necessary the whole of this item which relates to expenses occasioned by the attendance of these three persons and of Mr Whitaker.

(II) APRIL 1978 (HEARINGS BEFORE THE COURT): £1,319.60

32. The Government disputed this item as regards, firstly, the proportion thereof referable to the attendance of three counsel and, secondly, the necessity for the presence at the hearings of Mr Knightley, Mr Harold Evans (the editor of *The Sunday Times*) and Mr James Evans, as solicitor to the applicants. For the Delegates, the second point depended on the Court's standard of necessity.
33. The Court has already dealt with the question of counsel (*see* paragraph 30 *above*) and therefore disallows the sum of £377 referable to the attendance of the two junior counsel accompanying Mr Lester. For similar reasons, bearing in mind that Mr Whitaker was present as well as Mr Lester, it excludes the further sum of £175.40 claimed in respect of Mr James Evans.
  On the other hand, the Court considers that the presence of Mr Knightley and Mr Harold Evans, as applicants, was of value and sees no reason for not following the solution adopted in the *König* judgment (pp. 19 and 26).
  In the result, the Court accepts as necessarily incurred under this head the travel and hotel expenses for Mr Lester, Mr Knightley, Mr Harold Evans and Mr Whitaker, namely £767.20.

(III) APRIL 1979 (DELIVERY OF THE COURT'S JUDGMENT OF APRIL 26): £705

34. The Government questioned the necessity for the presence on this occasion of Mr Harold Evans, Mr Knightley and Ms Potter. The Delegates also had 'considerable doubts' about this item.
35. The Court agrees. Whilst the wish of these three applicants to hear the judgment delivered is only too understandable, it cannot be said, for the purposes of Article 50, that their presence was necessary, bearing particularly in mind that Mr Whitaker was also in the court-

room. The Court therefore retains under this head only the expenses occasioned by the latter's attendance, namely £176.25.

(D) DISBURSEMENTS

(I) OPINIONS ON CONTEMPT LAW FROM EIGHT COUNTRIES: £2,000

36. For the Government, this disbursement was not necessarily incurred; for the Delegates, it depended on the Court's standard of necessity: they stated that the Commission would not normally obtain such opinions from a party but that they might have been necessary for the preparation of the applicant's submissions.

37. The applicants pointed out that the question of the uniqueness of the English law of contempt of court had arisen before the Commission. All the same, the Court was not satisfied that this disbursement was necessary for the determination of the issues arising and it therefore disallowed this item.

(II) COPIES OF THE BOOK THALIDOMIDE: MY FIGHT: £52.60

38. The Delegates were of the view that whether this disbursement should be taken into account depended on the Court's standard of necessity. The Government, in their supplementary memorial, claimed that the expense was not necessary.

39. The book was supplied to the Court by the applicants on their own initiative shortly before the hearings of April 24 and 25, 1978. Although it provided some background information, the Court does not consider that the book was necessary for the presentation of their case and therefore excludes this item.

(E) OTHER EXPENSES

40. Neither the Government nor the Commission contested, and the Court perceives no reason to question, the necessity for the other expenses mentioned in the schedule of the Strasbourg costs. Those expenses, namely the sum of £7,500 in respect of work done by Mr Whitaker (*see* paragraph 25 *above*) and disbursements referable to translation (£26.84), typing (£231.62), air freighting and carriage of documents (£50.02 and £20) and telephone calls (£250), total £8,078.48.

3. WERE THE COSTS REASONABLE AS TO *QUANTUM*?

41. It remains to be ascertained whether the expenses accepted by the Court as actually and necessarily incurred are reasonable as to *quantum*.

The Delegates stated that they did not propose to consider the actual amounts in themselves. The Government made the general observation that the costs claimed, especially counsels' fees, exceeded in *quantum* the sums that would normally be recoverable under the English system of assessment of costs (*see* paragraph 9 *above*). However, the Court does not consider that it has to pursue this point since, in the context of a claim for legal expenses under Article 50, it is not bound by domestic scales or standards (*see* the *König*[5] judgment, pp. 18–19, 22–23 and 25). As regards the amounts themselves, the Court is of the opinion that none of them can be regarded as out of proportion.

42.   By way of a final alternative submission, the Government invited the Court to hold that any costs awarded should in any event not exceed a sum calculated by reference to the current rates payable under the scheme for free legal aid operated by the Commission. They pointed in particular to the fact that the Commission scale was the only single standard available and to the anomalies that would arise if it were not adopted. The Delegates repeated the doubts which they had already expressed in connection with a similar submission by the Government of the Federal Republic of Germany in the *König* case.

In that case, the Court saw no reason for refusing full reimbursement of the costs incurred in so far as they proved reasonable (*see* the *König* judgment, pp. 19 and 24). The Court is not persuaded that it should adopt a different solution in the present instance and accordingly does not accept the Government's submission.

4.   COSTS OF THE ARTICLE 50 PROCEEDINGS

43.   In their observations filed on February 21, 1980, the applicants stated that it was 'reasonable to add a further figure to date of £3,000' in respect of the proceedings under Article 50. Neither the Government nor the Commission suggested that this expense had not been actually or necessarily incurred.

Whilst the applicants have not provided any details concerning this item, it appears to relate to work done by Mr Whitaker and can therefore be regarded as actually incurred for the reasons stated in paragraph 25 *above*. It was described as a figure 'to date' but there is no evidence of any expenditure since February 1980 other than that referable to the preparation of the document which the Court decided not to take into account (*see* paragraph 5 *above*). The Court does not consider that it has to make further enquiries in this respect: it was clearly necessary to incur some expenditure in connection with the Article 50 proceedings and a figure of £3,000 does not prove to be unreasonable.

[5] 2 E.H.R.R. 496; March 10, 1980, Series A, No. 36

5. INTEREST

44.   Neither the Government nor the Delegates commented specifi
cally on the applicants' claim for 'interest at 10 per cent. per annum
from the date of the relevant judgments (*i.e.* April 26, 1979 and
whenever judgment is given on the issue under Article 50) until
payment'.

Since no award was made in the Court's judgment of the April 26
1979, it is only the present judgment that is 'relevant' for this purpose
Moreover, it may be assumed that the United Kingdom will comply
promptly with the obligation incumbent on it under Article 53 of the
Convention. The Court therefore does not find it necessary to accede to
this claim.

45.   The items accepted by the Court in paragraphs 30, 31, 33, 35, 40
and 43 *above* total £22,626.78.

Appendix 12
(See page 67)

COUNCIL OF EUROPE
COMMITTEE OF MINISTERS

Resolution DH (90) 28

HUMAN RIGHTS
APPLICATION No. 11157/84
D. v. *THE FEDERAL REPUBLIC OF GERMANY*
(Adopted by the Committee of Ministers on 16 November, 1990 at the 448th meeting of the Ministers' Deputies)

The Committee of Ministers, under the terms of Article 32 of the Convention for the Protection of Human Rights and Fundamental Freedoms (hereinafter referred to as "the Convention");

Having regard to the report drawn up by the European Commission of Human Rights in accordance with Article 31 of the Convention relating to the application lodged on July 27, 1984 by Mrs D. against the Federal Republic of Germany (Application No. 11157/84);

Whereas on September 1, 1989 the Commission transmitted the said report to the Committee of Ministers and whereas the period of three months provided for in Article 32, paragraph 1, of the Convention elapsed without the case having been brought before the European Court of Human Rights in pursuance of Article 48 of the Convention;

Whereas in her application the applicant complained, *inter alia*, of the excessive length of civil proceedings brought by her against a surgeon;

Whereas the Commission declared the application admissible on December 15, 1988 as regards the above-mentioned complaint and in its report adopted on July 12, 1989 expressed the opinion, by seventeen votes to one, that there had been a violation of Article 6, paragraph of the Convention;

Agreeing with the opinion expressed by the Commission in accordance with Article 31, paragraph 1, of the Convention;

Having examined the proposals made by the Commission concerning just satisfaction for the applicant;

Decides, having voted in accordance with the provisions of Article 32, paragraph 1, of the Convention that there has been a violation of Article 6, paragraph 1, of the Convention in this case;

Recommends, under Rule 5 of the Rules adopted by the Committee of Ministers for the application of Article 32 of the Convention, that the Government of the Federal Republic of Germany pay to the applicant the sum of 9000 DM in respect of non-pecuniary damage and in respect of costs and expenses;

Decides, therefore, that no further action is called for in this case.

Appendix 13

THE RIGHT OF INDIVIDUAL PETITION

Dates of Recognition

STATE	CONVENTION	PROTOCOL No. 1	PROTOCOL No. 4	PROTOCOL No. 6	PROTOCOL No. 7
Austria	03.09.58	03.09.58	18.09.69	01.03.85	01.11.88
Belgium	14.06.55	14.06.55	21.09.70	—	—
Bulgaria	07.09.92	07.09.92	—	—	—
Cyprus	01.01.89	01.01.89	—	—	—
Czech Republic	01.01.93	01.01.93	01.01.93	01.01.93	01.01.93
Denmark	03.09.53	18.05.54	02.05.68	01.03.85	01.11.88
Estonia	—	—	—	—	—
Finland	10.05.90	10.05.90	10.05.90	01.06.90	01.08.90
France	03.05.74	03.05.74	03.05.74	01.03.86	01.11.88
Germany	03.09.53	13.02.57	01.06.68	01.08.89	—
Greece	20.11.85	20.11.85	—	—	—
Hungary	05.11.92	05.11.92	05.11.92	01.12.92	01.02.93
Iceland	03.09.53	18.05.54	02.05.68	01.06.87	01.11.88
Ireland	03.09.53	18.05.54	29.10.68	—	—
Italy	01.08.73	01.08.73	27.05.82	01.01.89	—
Liechtenstein	08.09.82	—	—	01.12.90	—
Lithuania	—	—	—	—	—
Luxembourg	03.09.53	18.05.54	02.05.68	01.03.85	01.07.89
Malta	23.01.67	23.01.67	—	—	—
Netherlands	31.08.54	31.08.54	23.06.82	01.05.86	—
Norway	03.09.53	18.05.54	02.05.68	01.11.88	01.01.89
Poland	01.05.93	—	—	—	—
Portugal	09.11.78	09.11.78	09.11.78	01.11.86	—
San Marino	22.03.89	22.03.89	22.03.89	01.04.89	01.06.89
Slovak Republic	01.01.93	01.01.93	01.01.93	01.01.93	01.01.93
Slovenia	—	—	—	—	—
Spain	01.07.81	27.11.90	—	01.03.85	—
Sweden	03.09.53	18.05.54	02.05.68	01.03.85	01.11.88
Switzerland	28.11.74	—	—	01.11.87	01.11.88
Turkey	28.01.87	28.01.87	—	—	—
United Kingdom	14.01.66	14.01.66	—	—	—

Appendix 14

GENERAL INFORMATION AND KEY ADDRESSES

Key Addresses

European Commission of Human Rights
Secretary to the Commission
CONSEIL DE L'EUROPE
F-67075 Strasbourg Cedex
FRANCE

Tel: (010 33) 88 41 2000
Fax: (010 33) 88 41 2792
Telex: EUR 870 943 F

Foreign and Commonwealth Office
London SW1A 2AH

Tel: 071 270 3852
Fax: 071 270 3884

UNITED NATIONS
Centre for Human Rights
8-14, avenue de la Paix
1211 Geneva 10, Switzerland

Strasbourg

Strasbourg is the capital city of the Alsace, with a population of 400,000. It is the seat of the Council of Europe and one of the seats of the European Parliament. The Council of Europe, Parliament buildings and the Human Rights buildings form a complex which lies some four miles to the north-east of the city centre. To the north and west the complex is bounded by the Bassin de l'Ill, a canal interchange; to the south and east lies the Orangerie, which is the city's largest park.

The city adjoins the Rhine and is encircled by canals; with a large outer ring of waterways for the commercial river traffic. At the centre of the city is an awesome cathedral and the old town—La petite France—which itself lies within a network of ancient canals; with working locks, medieval half-timbered houses and countless cafes, restaurants and 'winstubs' (taverns). The food is dominated by steaks and sauerkraut; Strasbourg itself being famous for its foie gras, tarte flambée and asparagus.

Strasbourg airport is about 30 minutes by bus or taxi from the city centre, lying some seven miles to the south-west. The airport bus runs to and from the centre (the central station) every 30 minutes during peak hours at an approximate cost of £4.50. A taxi ride is only slightly quicker at a cost in the region of £20.00.

INFORMATION

International Telephone Code: 010 33

Tourist information:
Main Office
17, place de la Cathédrale - F 67082 STRASBOURG Cedex

Tel: 88 52 28 28
Fax: 88 52 28 29
Strasbourg airport. Tel: 88 64 67 67

HOTELS

**** Four Star Hotels

Grand, 12 pl. de la Gare. Tel: 88 32 46 90
Hilton, av. Herrenschmidt. Tel: 88 37 10 10
Régent Contades, 8 av. de la Liberté. Tel: 88 36 26 26

*** Three Star Hotels:

Altéa, Pont de l'Europe. Tel: 88 37 10 10
Baumann, 15 pl. de la Cathédrale. Tel: 88 32 42 14
Bristol, 4-5 pl. de la Gare. Tel: 88 32 00 83
Cathédrale, 12 pl. Cathédrale. Tel: 88 22 12 12
Citadines, 50 r. du Jeu-des-Enfants. Tel: 88 75 34 34
de la Dauphine, 30 r. de la 1 Armée. Tel: 88 36 26 61
du Dragon, 2 r. de l'Écarlate. Tel: 88 35 79 80
de France, 20 r. du Jeu-des-Enfants. Tel: 88 32 37 12
Hannong, 15 r. du 22-Novembre. Tel: 88 32 16 22
Holiday Inn, 20 pl. de Bordeaux. Tel: 88 37 80 00

Mercure, 25 r. Thomann. Tel: 88 75 77 88
Monopole-Métropole, 14 r. Kuhn. Tel: 88 32 11 94
Maison Rouge, 4 des Francs-Bourgeois. Tel: 88 32 08 60
Novotel, quai Kléber. Tel: 88 22 10 99
de l'Orangerie, 58 allée de la Robertsau. Tel: 88 35 10 69
des Princes, 33 r. Geiler. Tel: 88 61 55 19
des Rohan, 17 r. du Maroquin. Tel: 88 32 85 11
Royal, 3 r. du Marie-Kuss. Tel: 88 32 28 71
Le Scana, 7 r. de la Chaine. Tel: 88 32 66 60
Sofitel, pl. Saint-Pierre-le-Jeune. Tel: 88 32 99 30
Terminus Plaza, 10 pl. de la Gare. Tel: 88 32 87 00
Villa d'Est, 12 r. Jacques-Kablé. Tel: 88 36 69 02

** Two Star Hotels

Arcade, 7 r. de Molsheim. Tel: 88 22 30 00
Bruxelles, 13 r. Kuhn. Tel: 88 32 45 31
Campanile, r. Charles-Péguy. Tel: 88 29 46 46
Carlton, 15 pl. de la Gare. Tel: 88 32 62 39
Central, 10 pl. Marché-aux-Cochons. Tel: 88 32 03 05
Cerf d'Or, 6 pl. de l'Hôpital. Tel: 88 36 20 05
Climat de France, 59 rte du Rhin. Tel: 88 60 10 52
Continental, 14 r. du Marie-Kuss. Tel: 88 22 28 07
de la Couronne. Tel: 88 32 35 45
Eden, 16 r. d'Obernai. Tel: 88 32 41 99
Esplanade, 1 boul'd Leblois. Tel: 88 61 38 95
de l'Europe, 38 r. du Fossé-des Tanneurs. Tel: 88 32 17 88
Gutenberg, 31 r. des Serruriers. Tel: 88 32 17 15
Hommelet Rouge, 2 q. des Bâteliers. Tel: 88 35 48 92
Ibis, 1 r. Sébastopol. Tel: 88 22 14 99
de l'Ill, 8 r. des Bateliers. Tel: 88 36 20 01
Kléber, 29 pl. Kléber. Tel: 88 32 09 53
Lutétia, 2 bis r. du Général-Rapp. Tel: 88 35 20 45
Moderne, 1 q. de Paris. Tel: 88 32 07 33
National, 13 pl. de la M rsange. Tel: 88 32 15 50
Pax, 24, r. du Faubourg-National. Tel: 88 32 14 54
du Rhin, 7 pl. de la Gare. Tel: 88 32 35 00
Saint-Christophe, 2 pl. de la Gare. Tel: 88 22 30 30
Suisse, 4 r. de la Rape. Tel: 88 35 22 11
Tour Service, 18 r. de la Tour. Tel: 88 29 41 41
Aux Trois Roses, 7 r. de Zurich. Tel: 88 36 56 95
Union Européenne, 8 q. Kellermann. Tel: 88 32 70 41
Urbis, 13 r. du Faubourg-National. Tel: 88n75 10 10
Vendôme, 19 r. Marie-Kuss. Tel: 88 32 45 23
Victoria, 7 r. Marie-Kuss. Tel: 88 32 13 06

Appendix 15

BIBLIOGRAPHY

Berger, V., *Case Law of the European Court of Human Rights*, Vol. I: 1960–87, Vol. II: 1988-90, Roundhall Press, Dublin, 1989 and 1992.
Each court decision is summarised in 3 or 4 pages followed by a short bibliography of relevant articles.

Brett, R., *The Development of the Human Dimension Mechanism of the Conference on Security and Co-operation in Europe*, Human Rights Centre, University of Essex, 1992.

Brownlie, I., *Basic Documents on Human Rights* (third edition), Clarendon Press, Oxford, 1992.
This contains the texts of the major Human Rights Declarations, Conventions and Covenants.

Fawcett, J.E.S. *The Application of the European Convention on Human Rights* (second edition), Clarendon Press, Oxford, 1987.
An academic text by a distinguished former President of the Commission.

Hannum, H., *Guide to International Human Rights Practice* (second edition), University of Pennsylvania Press, 1992.
An overview of international human rights law and practice; the contributors concentrating upon the practical application of the various international mechanisms.

Mathijesen, P. *A Guide to European Community Law* (fifth edition), Sweet & Maxwell, London, 1990.
A general introduction to the law of the European Community.

Sieghart, P. *The International Law of Human Rights*, Clarendon Press, Oxford, 1983.
A comprehensive academic text, comparing the rights and freedoms guaranteed by the various international documents.

Van Dijk, P. and van Hoof, G.H.J *Theory and Practice of the European Convention on Human Rights* (second edition), Kluwer, 1990.
The most up-to-date and comprehensive academic text on the Convention.

INDEX